Praise for
Perform Your Best on the Bar Exam Performanc~~e Test (MPT)~~

"A book like this is long overdue. As far as I can tell, the large commercial bar review courses have yet to fully master how to train students to take the MPT. Mary Campbell Gallagher provides students with a detailed, well-constructed method for succeeding on the MPT and similar exams."

—Louis J. Sirico, Jr., Professor of Law, Director of Legal Writing, Villanova University School of Law, Member, Board of Directors, Legal Writing Institute (former), Member, Editorial Board, *Legal Writing: The Journal of the Legal Writing Institute*

"Mary Campbell Gallagher has set a new standard in bar exam preparation materials. One of the reasons so many people have trouble with bar exams is that they don't want to spend time practicing to take the exam by actually taking practice exams under exam conditions. The tone of the instructions here is calm, straightforward, and authoritative. The effect is to instill confidence in the applicant and persuade the applicant that with practice, success is very much possible. I like the way the instructions are given more than once in different ways. Providing so much hands-on practical information is also helpful, like tips about using subject headings and about exactly what a passing answer should contain and how it should look, including length. The instruction in this book is simply priceless."

—Prince C. Chambliss, Jr., President, Board of Law Examiners, Tennessee (former), Member, Evans Petree, Memphis, Tennessee (former), Author, *Prince of Peace: A Memoir of an African-American Attorney Who Came of Age in Birmingham During the Civil Rights Movement* (2010), Author, "Creating Compelling Defense Arguments and Strategies in Personal Injury Litigation", in *Representing Defendants in Personal Injury Cases: Leading Lawyers on Developing a Defense Strategy, Navigating the Discovery Process, and Litigating Disputes* (2011)

"This book is excellent practice and guidance for the California Performance Test (PT), as well as the MPT."

— Travis Wise, Practicing attorney and California Bar Exam Expert, Author, *The California Bar Exam Primer*

"*Perform Your Best on the Bar Exam Performance Test (MPT)* is the Swiss Army knife of the MPT."

— *Practitioner-reviewer on Amazon.com*

Praise for
Scoring High on Bar Exam Essays

"The bar candidate is actually taught to write analytically. All 1Ls, as well as all 3Ls, should read it...."

— *Law Student Journal*

"This book may be the best money you can spend on bar exam preparation."

— *St. John's University Law School Forum*

"Do not take the bar exam without this book! If you are serious about passing the bar exam, you should stop reading this review immediately and BUY DR. GALLAGHER'S BOOK! Even if you are unable to take her excellent course (which I HIGHLY recommend), you MUST add this book to your list of bar preparation materials. By practicing Dr. Gallagher's simple, effective writing method, and using the sample essays she provides, you will be trained to write any bar exam essay quickly, efficiently, and successfully. Dr. Gallagher helped me to pass the New York Bar Exam on the first try! If you're tired of unsuccessful attempts to pass the bar, or if you're a first-timer who never wants to take that dreaded exam again, GET SCORING HIGH ON BAR EXAM ESSAYS NOW!"

— Joyce Smith, Member, New York bar

"Very informative and detailed. Essays provide great guidance. This book should be a required book for not only the bar, but also law school."

— Dawna Snipes

"Significant jump in performance. I purchased this book during my first year of law school after first semester grades came out. The information and instruction Dr. Gallagher provides is worth more than what you will pay for the book. After reading this book and practicing the prescribed techniques, my law school grades greatly improved. Thanks, Dr. Gallagher, for this very valuable tool. I plan to use it on the bar exams as well!"

— Christopher A. Brock, Member, New York bar

Other Books by Mary Campbell Gallagher, J.D., Ph.D.

Perform Your Best on the Bar Exam Performance Test (MPT): Train to Finish the MPT in 90 Minutes "Like a Sport™", With 12 Actual MPT Tasks, 12 Sample Answers, Point Sheets, and Complete Analyses

Scoring High on Bar Exam Essays: In-Depth Strategies and Essay-Writing Practice That Bar Review Courses Don't Offer, With 80 Actual State Bar Exam Questions and Answers

Teaching Secondary English, Alternative Approaches, with Thomas J. Brown and Rosemary Turner

Write Fast Legal Memos™ Workshops

You can invite Dr. Mary Campbell Gallagher to offer one of her Write Fast Legal Memos™ Workshops in your law firm or law office. Every participant will receive a copy of this book. In addition, every participant will have abundant opportunity to practice the component skills of fast legal writing, with feedback, in a stimulating and collegial setting. At the end of the day, participants will be on the way to building the strong habits that support efficient legal writing.

For information on inviting Dr. Gallagher to provide an on-site workshop, write to: Info@BarWrite.com.

For information on Dr. Gallagher's frequent public CLE programs in New York City, visit: www.BarWrite.com.

WRITE FAST LEGAL MEMOS
"Like a Sport™"

2014 FIRST EDITION

CLE Training for Practicing Lawyers
Using the Unique Systems and Selected MPT Tasks from the Book
Perform Your Best on the Bar Exam Performance Test (MPT)

Mary Campbell Gallagher, J.D., Ph.D.

Founder and President, BarWrite® and BarWrite Press

New York City
BarWrite Press
www.BarWrite.com

BarWrite® Press
Post Office Box 1308
New York, NY 10028-0010   USA
Staff@barwrite.com

www.BarWrite.com and www.PerformYourBestontheBarExamPerformanceTest.com

BarWrite® and BarWrite® Press are registered trademarks
of Mary Campbell Gallagher & Co., Inc.

Dr. Gallagher gratefully acknowledges the assistance of the National Conference of Bar Examiners, the copyright owner, in granting permission to reprint materials from past MPT examinations. Permission to use the NCBE's questions does not constitute an endorsement by NCBE or otherwise signify that NCBE has reviewed or approved any aspect of these materials or the company or individuals who distribute these materials. Materials that have been licensed by the NCBE included Multistate Performance Tests Copyright © 1998, 1999, 2000, 2002, 2003, 2008, 2009 by the National Conference of Bar Examiners. All rights reserved.

Cataloging-in-Publication Data

Gallagher, Mary Campbell.
Write fast legal memos "like a sport" / Mary Campbell Gallagher.
--1st ed.
p. cm.
ISBN 978-0-9706088-4-0

1. Legal composition.   I. Title.

KF250.G35 2012 808.06'634
QBI12-600067
Printed in the United States of America

10 9 8 7 6 5 4 3 2 1

ATTENTION: UNIVERSITIES, LAW SCHOOLS, LAW FIRMS, NON-PROFITS, AND PROFESSIONAL ORGANIZATIONS. Dr. Gallagher offers the Fast Legal Memos™ Workshop for law firms and other groups. Quantity discounts are available on bulk purchases of this book for educational purposes or as gifts. For information on Dr. Gallagher's availability or on bulk purchases, contact: Info@BarWrite.com.

Contents

Acknowledgments..iv

Introduction v

Part I: Learning to Write Legal Memos Efficiently, "Like a Sport™" 1

What This Book Does 2

Six Steps to Using This Book to Write Legal Memos More
Efficiently, "Like a Sport™" 4

The Logical Structure of the Discussion in the Memorandum 11

Time and Organization on the Basic Memorandum...................21

The **Speed Memos**™ System Panoramic Overview 23

Part II: Six Memorandum Tasks....................................**25**

A. Organizing a Legal Memo Where the Work Product
    Requires Statutory Analysis: *In re Lisa Peel*....................28

B. Organizing a Legal Memo Where the Work Product
    Requires Commenting on a Draft Agreement: *In re Velocity Park*..............38

C. Organizing a Legal Memo Where the Work Product Requires
    Analyzing Relationships between Case Law and Codes:
    Phoenix Corporation v. Biogenesis, Inc.......................48

D. Organizing a Legal Memo Where the Work Product Requires
    Evaluating the Constitutionality of a Proposed Code:
    In re Gardenton Board of Education 58

E. Organizing a Legal Memo Where the Work Product Requires
    Statutory Analysis, Second Example: *In re Steven Wallace* 65

F. Organizing a Legal Memo Where the Work Product Requires
    Comparing Two Statutes or Regulations:
    Franklin Asbestos Handling Regulations 72

Sample Answer and Analysis Materials

Materials for Task A: *In re Lisa Peel* 84

Materials for Task B: *In re Velocity Park* 95

Materials for Task C: *Phoenix Corp. v. Biogenesis, Inc* 103

Materials for Task D: *In re Gardenton Board of Education*......................112

Materials for Task E: *In re Steven Wallace* 122

Materials for Task F: *In re Franklin Asbestos Handling Regulations* 131

Conclusion 142

About the Author...143

Acknowledgments

My thanks to the students who have worked through these exercises in the BarWrite® Boot Camps in New York City and at law schools across the country. You proved that lawyers write faster and better when they learn to break tasks down into separate skills. The key to improvement is practicing those separate skills one at a time, the way athletes practice skills one at a time. That's where the title comes from, *Write Fast Legal Memos "Like a sport™."* You showed it can be done. My thanks as well to Elizabeth Dutertre, who generously stepped in to apply her keen eye to the manuscript and saved it from many infelicities.

Mary Campbell Gallagher, J.D., Ph.D.

New York City

Introduction

This book teaches an easy-to-learn, time-saving, system for organizing and writing basic legal memoranda. The aim is to develop junior lawyers' habits so they can write legal memos more efficiently. In other words, to develop the habits they will need to write "speed memos." If writing memos is partly intellectual and partly habitual, this book is chiefly about the habitual part. The idea came to me while I was putting together the last pages of my study guide for performance tests called *Perform Your Best on the Bar Exam Performance Test (MPT): Train to Finish the MPT in 90 Minutes "Like a Sport*™*."* On the MPT, which is a component of the bar examination in 35 jurisdictions, bar candidates must demonstrate their practice-readiness by using simulated law office materials and research sources to research, organize, and produce a work product inside 90 minutes. The California Performance Test (PT) allows three hours. It occurred to me that if the systems I teach, and the habit-building practice I provide, help bar candidates to write memos on the bar exam under tight time constraints, wouldn't the same systems and materials also help junior lawyers? They have tight time constraints, too.

Thus, while the introductory materials in this book are designed expressly for junior lawyers aiming to write more efficient short memos, the six MPT memo tasks, with my answers and analyses, come from *Perform Your Best*. The National Conference of Bar Examiners designs the simulated law office tasks on the Multistate Performance Test (MPT). The design is excellent, and I did not see how I could improve on it. Likewise, the device I teach for analyzing tasks on the MPT, the MPT-Matrix™, is useful not just on the bar exam, but for practicing researching and organizing simple basic law office tasks in law practice. The systems I teach for following the instructions in the "Partner Memo" on the bar exam also work for following the instructions of real supervisors in real law offices. Finally, my analysis of each sample answer here will be as useful to junior lawyers as it is to bar candidates.

BarWrite® offers writing Boot Camps in New York City and around the country. Students' writing improves enormously over a short period of time, and I am delighted to say that the students love the systems. The Boot Camps prove my theory that building habits and competence in legal writing is a lot like building habits and competence in playing basketball. That's how legal writing is "like a sport." Repetition is key. When junior lawyers use the skill-building exercises in this book, they gain habits that make them more independent and more able to write efficient memos without resorting to handbooks or pestering their supervisors with mechanical questions. I hope this book may also free superiors of some of their supervisory duties.

I look forward to hearing from you about how successful this book has been.

Part I

Learning to Write Legal Memos Efficiently, "Like a Sport™"

What This Book Does

This book teaches a time-saving system for organizing and writing basic legal memoranda that is easy to learn. Illustrating its lessons with simulated law-office tasks that have appeared on the Multistate Performance Test (MPT), the book teaches the **Four-Part Speed Memos**™ System, which you can use to produce short memos efficiently. You will use it to discover the main issues in your task and to understand and follow the instructions your supervisor gives you. The **Speed Memos**™ System allows you to stay focused on the instructions from your supervisor, to keep control of your research and your time as you structure your work product, to present your work product so that it looks professional and so that your visual presentation helps the reader understand the logical structure of your work, and to complete your work within the time allowed.

How is learning to write legal memoranda according to this system "like a sport™?" Watch basketball players, and you will see that they practice one skill at a time, whether dribbling or shooting hoops. They perfect each skill separately, developing strong habits. Then they put the skills together when they play a game. That is our model here. Learn to outline quickly, learn to structure a memorandum quickly, learn to separate a "Discussion" section into three parts. Develop strong habits as you practice each skill separately. Then, when you must write a full legal memorandum, you will have strong habits to call on, not just dimly-remembered theoretical generalities about what legal memos should look like.

This book teaches you a sample format for office memoranda. It also teaches you a new rule for structuring legal documents, which I call the Rule of Three™. This rule will help you organize every work product into three parts. Finally, this book teaches you how to find touchstones for structuring your work product within the materials in the task itself. [1]

This book teaches systems for:

    A. Managing time;

    B. Managing research;

    C. Organizing work;

    D. Managing research notes and research threads.

Here in **Part 1: Learning to Write Legal Memoranda Efficiently, "Like a sport™,"** you will find step-by-step instructions for training yourself to write legal memos more efficiently. It teaches the four-part **Speed Memos**™ System, including the time-saving MPT-Matrix™. You will learn to organize your research materials, organize your work product quickly, and complete a competent, well-organized, draft.

In Part 2, Six Legal Memorandum Tasks with Analyses and Sample Answers, you will find six practice Memorandum Tasks, Sample Answers, Notes on Analyzing the Tasks, and MPT-Matrixes™, plus the NCBE Point Sheets.

---

[1] For how to outline a legal essay and structure a legal paragraph, consult the book by the same author called *Scoring High on Bar Exam Essays: In-depth Strategies and Essay-Writing Practice that Bar Review Courses Don't Offer, with 80 Full-Length Sample Essays,* 3rd ed. (2006). It is available from legal bookstores everywhere, and from LegalBooksDistributing.com and Amazon.com.

Part 2 gives you:

A. **Six (6) legal memorandum tasks.** These reflect basic patterns for legal memoranda that are often encountered in the practice of law; [2]

B. **NCBE Point Sheets for each task.** These describe key points of law that could be included;[3]

C. **A Sample MPT-Matrix™ for each memorandum task.** The MPT-Matrix™ is the unique time-saving graphic display on which you will plot your research on easy-to-use map coordinates. The sample MPT-Matrix™ for each task shows you how to use the File and Library materials and how the parts of the MPT task fit together;

D. **A sample answer for each memorandum task.** This shows you what a finished work product might look like;

E. **A note on how to analyze each task.** This analysis explains the memorandum task and tells you how to perform your most important job, which is to understand and outline the instructions your supervisor gives you. It explains how to create your own MPT-Matrix™, as well as how to apply the Rule of Three, so that the structure of your work product will be clear both to you and to your supervisor, and you will write a well-organized memorandum.

Completing the tasks in this book and learning the systems this book teaches will help increase your competence for the masterful practice of law.

---

[2] The sample tasks have been constructed by the National Conference of Bar Examiners and include simulated law office materials in the File and simulated research materials in the Library.

[3] The Point Sheets come from the National Conference of Bar Examiners.

Six Steps to Using This Book to Write Legal Memos More Efficiently: "Like a Sport™"

In this book, you will learn a system for organizing and drafting a legal memo efficiently. This is a system that I have taught, tested, and refined over a period of years in the Bar-Write® Boot Camps.[4] When you learn to use the system this book teaches, you will become more competent in basic lawyering skills, and that will make it easier for you to meet the demands of practicing law. I call it the **Speed Memos™** System.

This book teaches you how to organize and write basic legal memoranda under time pressure. It does not, let us be clear, teach you to achieve the highest level of lawyerly skill. Instead, along with your law school legal writing courses, this book gives you solid training in the most basic skills you will need in practice. Once you master these skills, you will have the confidence that comes from building on a firm foundation.

The system teaches you to keep your research materials for simple memos, including those in this book, on one easy-to-access piece of paper, a time-saving graphic display called the MPT-Matrix™. In this book you will also learn how to decide on a clear and simple structure for your work product and then how to make sure that your underlined headings and your spacing of your paragraphs on every page display the organization of your memo.

You can train yourself to produce a lawyerlike work product "Like a sport™."

With care and commitment, you can use this book to train yourself to produce a lawyer-like legal memo. Exercising a skill is its own reward. As your competence grows, you will increasingly enjoy performing these tasks.

Here is the SIX-STEP approach to training.

1. Study the table of contents and read the first part of this book.

First, study the Table of Contents to survey what this book offers and in what order. Then read the first part of this book to understand how to use the system this book teaches, and how this book is organized.

Every one of the six (6) task chapters in this book includes not only a memorandum-writing task but also my sample answer showing you what an answer might look like, and a note on analyzing the task explaining how to outline and organize that particular MPT task. The time-saving MPT-Matrix™ for each task is a unique feature of the "Like a

---

[4] In the BarWrite® Legal Memo Boot Camps, junior lawyers learn the systems this book teaches for analyzing the key types of tasks, preparing the MPT-Matrix™, and completing tasks efficiently. The Boot Camps provide abundant opportunity for practice and feedback. For information on the classes that BarWrite® offers to help law school graduates either in law firm and non-profit practice or in preparing for the bar exam, visit the BarWrite® web site, at http://www.BarWrite.com, where you can also sign up for free study materials. The BarWrite® Blog provides tips for legal writing as well as for studying for the bar exam. http://www.BarWriteBlog.com.

Sport™" treatment. It displays graphically how the parts of the materials in your law office (the "File") and the research materials (the "Library") fit together for completion of the work product.

For every memorandum task, this book provides both a sample "Like a Sport™" answer and a "Like a Sport™" note on analyzing the task, as well as the "Like a Sport™" MPT-Matrix™. To give you additional information about what your memorandum might contain, this book also features six NCBE (6) Point Sheets.[5] The Point Sheets provide additional points of law. They are neither sample answers nor explanations of how to outline or analyze your memoranda.

2. Read slowly through part 1, learning to write legal memos efficiently, "Like a sport™."

Focus on the basics of the **Speed Memos**™ System. This part teaches you step-by-step how to use the MPT-System™, including the MPT-Matrix™. It also tells you how many minutes to spend on each part of the task. This MPT-System™ is different from the systems you have used in law school or a law office. Learning it takes a little patience, but it saves so much time in the end that the effort is more than worthwhile. When you master this system you will strengthen skills that will enhance your performance in law practice.

3. Do one memo task without concern for time limits.

Pick an MPT task to do. Read the instructions in the Partner Memorandum, go through the File and the Library, create the MPT-Matrix™, and write an answer. Do not concern yourself with time limits. Then look at the **Speed Memos**™ sample answer and the **Speed Memos**™ note on analyzing the task. See what the Point Sheets say. Note how much longer you took than 90 minutes. Ask why that was. Adjust accordingly.

4. Practice within the time limits.

Up until this point, you will have been working without regard to time limits. The reality of developing strong habits for basic memos, however, is that staying within the time limits is essential to success. After you write that first memo without time limits, you must start practicing within the time limits. You must hold yourself to the time limits this book teaches for accomplishing each part of the process, so that you learn how to finish the entire work product in 90 minutes. No fudging.

For example, observing the time limits in the four-part **Speed Memos**™ System, spend 90 minutes reading and completing the memo task called *In re Lisa Peel*, making the MPT-Matrix™, and drafting the work product. Stick strictly to the time limits. Compare your work with the sample answer. Read the Note on Analyzing for the task. Study the MPT-Matrix™. This will train you in using the **Speed Memos**™ System. It will also introduce you to memo-writing, the subject of this book.

Practice with a stopwatch or a kitchen timer. From this point on, always stick to the time limits when you practice. If you do not finish part of your practice task within the time limit suggested for that part of the task in the four-part **Speed Memos**™ System, put down your pen. Look at what you have finished, and compare it with what you ought to have finished. Cut out the unneeded words in your draft and look again. Learn from the experience.

---

[5] The Point Sheets are among the materials the National Conference of Bar Examiners (NCBE) prepares for each simulated task.

5. Use other tasks in this book for additional practice of particular memo skills. You may focus on outlining memo tasks with MPT-Matrixes™ or completing memo tasks under time limits or any other skill.

Depending on the level of skill you have achieved so far, you may choose to outline or draft more or fewer of the other tasks in this book. This book will give you abundant opportunity to use your skills on a variety of types of memoranda, either simply preparing the outlines or else completing the tasks in 90 minutes.

One technique you can use each time you practice drafting a work product is to compare your paragraphs with the paragraphs in the sample work product in this book. Then cut out the extra words in your own paragraphs. Count how many words you have cut. Have you used adjectives or adverbs you did not need? Have you used circumlocutions where American legal writing goes straight to the point? Have you used the passive voice? The passive voice allows for digressions and vagueness. American legal writing prefers the active voice. Change passive to active.

Another technique you can use to train yourself to be concise, even when you are walking around or doing daily tasks, is to speak a sentence of legal prose, and then say the same thing again, but better, in fewer words. Become accustomed to brevity. Learn to prefer it. This will help you in all of your writing.

This book gives you skill-strengthening exercises and analyses. Practice organizing and writing memos using this book, develop your ability to manage the time, and you will be strengthening the skills and habits you need to become a more efficient drafter of legal memos and a more competent lawyer.

Office Memoranda

Piper, Morales & Singh
Attorneys at Law
One Dalton Place
West Keystone, Franklin 33322

MEMORANDUM

To: Junior Lawyer

From: Mary Campbell Gallagher

Re: Basic Memorandum Format

Date: November 1, 2013

INTRODUCTION

The word "Introduction" is centered at the top of the section. You will write two or three sentences, setting out the supervising lawyer's task assignment and briefly stating what you have accomplished and your conclusions.

DISCUSSION

The word "Discussion" is centered at the top of the section. You will divide the Discussion into two or three sections, following the supervising lawyer's directions. Each section will have a powerful topic heading that uses both law and facts: *Because defendant claimed that his product that was actually made of colored water would cure acne, and the plaintiff relied on that claim and was harmed, defendant may be liable for fraud.*

CONCLUSION

The word "Conclusion" is centered at the top of the final section. The Conclusion part of the memorandum summarizes what the task was and what the writer has accomplished. It presents the writer's conclusions. It may also make recommendations.

Note: The word MEMORANDUM is centered at the top of the page, under the law office letterhead, and underlined. The heading is flush left and has "To," "From," "Re," and "Date."

An Objective Office Memorandum Considers Both Sides of the Question

This section teaches you how to write a basic office memorandum. Every time the supervising lawyer asks a junior lawyer for a memorandum for him or herself, that is a request for an office memorandum. An office memorandum will normally be objective, but the supervising lawyer will tell the junior lawyer if it should be persuasive, instead. Every time a supervisor asks for information or for considerations on both sides of the question, rather than for arguments just on one side, the supervisor is asking for an objective memorandum. The supervisor asking for an objective memorandum usually tells the junior lawyer to "evaluate" or to "discuss" or to "analyze." *Write an objective memorandum analyzing whether or not the law applies to our client's case.* Thus, an objective memorandum will normally consider both sides of the question and take an on-the-one-hand/on-the-other-hand approach. To make sure the reader understands what kind of memorandum you are submitting, the Introduction to your objective office memorandum can say, "You have asked me to write an objective memorandum." Important warning: Where the assignment is to write an objective memorandum, the junior lawyer who writes a persuasive argument will be penalized.

That said, although the supervising lawyer wants to hear both sides of the question, an objective memorandum should reach conclusions. After presenting the arguments on both sides, the junior lawyer must also indicate the more likely outcome. The underlined topic heading for each section will argue law, facts, and the conclusion. See pp. 21–22 below.

A Persuasive Memorandum Argues Only One Side of the Question

Where the supervisor tells the junior lawyer to write an office memorandum that presents arguments, rather than just information, he or she is asking for a persuasive office memorandum. For example, the supervisor may ask the junior lawyer to write a memorandum that presents the best arguments in favor of the client's case.

A persuasive memorandum must argue only one side of the case. The lawyer who writes an objective discussion, looking at both sides of the issue, saying on-the-one-hand/on-the-other-hand, will not fulfill the supervisor's assignment. A junior lawyer must make it entirely clear to the reader that the memorandum is either objective or persuasive. The best way, where appropriate, is to state plainly that the memorandum is either objective or persuasive. The Introduction to a persuasive office memorandum can say, "You have asked me to write a persuasive memorandum."

Whether objective or persuasive, office memoranda should have the same format. This book suggests one basic format. That format will serve nicely for the intensive practice that this book provides. In practice, a law office may have its own variation on this format. See below.

Every Office Memorandum Must Display its Own Structure Visually

A lawyer's work product must always look professional. Thus, the task in preparing a law office memorandum is not just to follow the supervisor's instructions; it is to demonstrate lawyering skills while making the fact of following instructions so visually obvious that the supervisor knows just by flipping the pages that the junior lawyer has followed instructions.

Does the supervisor say that the memorandum must have three sections? It is not enough to sit back and think quietly about three different subjects. Rather, the Discussion part of the work product must have three sections that are both intellectually and visually entirely separate from each other. That is, the three separate sections will be clearly distinct on the page. Each section will have its own persuasive topic heading, which is underlined, and each section will have a number at the start: Section 1, Section 2, Section 3. It is so important to display the structure of the work visually that the careful lawyer will always number and letter the parts of the work product, leaving abundant white space in between sections.

Legal writing is a visual exercise, not just an intellectual exercise. And consider this. Not only does labeling the parts make the work product look professional, it also helps the supervisor understand the junior lawyer's reasoning, so it makes the memorandum easier to read.

Using the Most Common Basic Law Office Memorandum Format

This book helps build the habit of using the most common basic law office memorandum format. For the sake of efficiency in teaching you the skills you will need to research, organize, and write legal memos, this book uses this short basic format:

1. Introduction

2. Discussion

3. Conclusion

In all formats, the key sections of the memorandum normally follow the Rule of Three™. That is, with minor variations, the memorandum has at least these three parts: Introduction, Discussion, and Conclusion. In the Introduction to the basic memorandum format this book teaches, the lawyer summarizes the problem to be solved and briefly suggests how the writer has resolved it. *You have asked me to evaluate whether our client has a cause of action in negligence. I have concluded that he probably does, but that further research is necessary.* In the Discussion, the memo takes up three aspects of the problem one after another, in turn. In the Conclusion, the memo again states the problem and, based on the factors considered in the Discussion, it states how the writer comes out. *Having evaluated all of the facts in the file and the applicable law, I have concluded that our client may have a cause of action in negligence, and I have suggested further avenues for research.* Thus, the memo begins and ends with a summary paragraph, the Introduction at the beginning and the Conclusion at the end. In between, in the section called Discussion, the memorandum sets out the arguments from law and fact that lead the writer to the Conclusion. So the entire memorandum has three parts. The Discussion section itself will often have three parts, as well.

Practicing using this structure helps a junior lawyer learn to produce a well-organized work product that also looks good. Once you have established this habit, you can easily vary this format to conform to the format your own law office uses. The format in use in a particular law office may or may not also have a section for Questions Presented and a section for Brief Answers, and it may or may not have a section for Facts.

Law firms may use a format that makes those topics into separate sections:

1. Introduction
2. Questions Presented
3. Brief Answers
4. Facts
5. Applicable Statutes
6. Discussion
7. Conclusion

Notice that the additional parts are in general redundant. In a well-drafted memo, the Introduction can include the Questions Presented and the Brief Answers. The Discussion will include the Facts and will quote the Statutes at appropriate length. Law firms make these sections separate not because they add anything new, but because labeling them as separate sections makes reading the memo faster and easier. Having these separate sections saves the reader the trouble of searching for key information.

With any traditional memo format, whether the basic format this book teaches or a variation used in a law office, a lawyer knows what to write first, second, and third. A junior lawyer would be best advised, even when given flexible instructions, to produce a work product that conforms either to the standard memo format for that law office or to the most common basic law office memorandum format illustrated here. Those traditional memo formats look professional on the page, and appearance is always important. A professional-looking work product can only help the junior lawyer's relationship with the supervisor, and it will, again, make the paper easier to read.

The Logical Structure of the Discussion in the Memorandum

The Structure of the Discussion Part of the Memorandum Must be Clear and Follow the Instructions of the Supervising Lawyer

A lawyer must always choose a structure for the memorandum that responds to the supervising lawyer's instructions. The Partner Memo in the materials in this book will always state clearly what the work product must accomplish. The junior lawyer must organize the content of the work product so that the reasoning of the memorandum makes conformity to the Partner Memo's instructions obvious. This chapter contains suggestions for organizing that content. Which topic should you discuss first? Which second? What is the appropriate order for presenting the material? Note that the tasks in this book will normally include one or more documents that help the junior lawyer to organize the work product or that provide models to follow.

In deciding how to organize the Discussion, the junior lawyer will usually choose from among the following methods of organization:

1. Order according to the conventions of legal analysis, e.g., statutory analysis.

2. If the Partner Memorandum stipulates an order, use the order stipulated.

3. If an Office Memorandum in the File stipulates an order, use that order.

4. If another document in the File requiring a response provides an order, you have the option of following that order.

5. Use the order in the applicable statute or case law.

6. Use logical order: threshold or dispositive issues first; most important issues first; alternative analyses last.

Normally you will choose from among the following patterns.

1. Order according to the conventions of legal analysis.

The supervising lawyer may expect the memo to present the analysis in a conventional order. If the task requires statutory analysis, for example, the memorandum will follow the conventional order for statutory analysis: the writer will take each part of the statute in turn, employ interpretations suggested by applicable cases, use external materials where necessary and permitted, and finally apply the statute to the facts of the case. The task *In re*

Lisa Peel requires interpretation of a statute, the Franklin Reporter Shield Act (FRSA). The Partner Memo makes this request:

> Please draft an objective memorandum for me analyzing whether we can use the Franklin Reporter Shield Act to move to quash Peel's subpoena.

Case law says that the burden of proving that the FRSA applies is on the party seeking its protection. The FRSA protects only reporters, so the first question in the memo must be whether the client, who is a blogger, qualifies as a reporter under the FRSA.

To define "reporter," you will look first to the statute, dividing the first applicable code section into its component parts. Then you will interpret those parts by using the cases and then, where necessary and permitted, by using such external sources as newspaper articles and dictionaries. Finally, you will apply these authorities to the facts of the case. We demonstrate interpretation of a statute using case law and a newspaper article here:

> Under section 901(a) of the FRSA, a reporter is "any person regularly engaged in collecting, writing or editing news for publication through a news medium." In *Bellows*, where the court took up the similar question whether a photographer is a reporter under the FRSA, the court said that the key to whether a person is a reporter is the person's intent at the inception of news-gathering. According to *America Today*, some bloggers have press credentials. *America Today*, July 5, 2007.

In another variation on statutory analysis in the memorandum materials in this book, the File may contain a proposed code, rather than a statute currently in force. The partner's task memo tells the junior lawyer to evaluate each section of the proposed code in turn. The junior lawyer will take one code section at a time, employing other statutes, case law, and external sources. This is the organizing principle in, for example, the MPT task in this book called *In re Gardenton Board of Education*.

2. If the Partner Memo stipulates an order, use the order stipulated.

The Partner Memo may, for example, instruct the junior lawyer to discuss two questions, one of which involves two sub-questions. The junior lawyer must follow the structure the task memo dictates. For *In re Steven Wallace*, for example, the task memo gives two very specific instructions:

> First, analyze the legal and factual bases of the trustee's claim that the painting is an asset of the bankruptcy estate under the Bankruptcy Act and the Franklin Commercial Code (FCC).

> Second, for each of the four defenses under FCC § 2-326(3), discuss how the facts we already know support the defense, identify additional facts that might be helpful to us, state why they would be helpful, and indicate from what sources we might be able to obtain them.

These instructions require the junior lawyer to handle the two main questions that counsel would have to answer, in the order that anyone would have to answer them. First, analyzing law and facts, is the painting an asset of the bankruptcy estate? Second, how could counsel put together a factual argument in support of each of the four statutory defenses?

3. If an Office Memorandum in the File stipulates an order, use that order.

The Partner Memo may tell the junior lawyer to organize the memorandum in accordance with the instructions in an Office Memorandum in the File. That second document will tell the junior lawyer how to organize the work product.

4. If another document in the File requiring response provides an order, the lawyer has the option of following that same order.

A second document in the File may require a response. For example, the task may be to evaluate the arguments in opposing counsel's brief. The junior lawyer has the option of using the structure of that brief to outline the analysis in the work product. For example, in *Phoenix Corporation v. Biogenesis, Inc.*, the task memo states:

> Please prepare a memorandum evaluating the merits of Phoenix's argument for Amberg & Lewis's disqualification, bringing to bear the applicable legal authorities and the relevant facts as described to me by Ms. Ravel.

The junior lawyer must examine Phoenix's brief and will probably decide to follow the same outline Phoenix uses, simply analyzing the arguments against each of the propositions Phoenix asserts. The first topic heading in the Phoenix brief states:

> This Court Should Disqualify Amberg & Lewis from Representing Biogenesis Because It Has Violated an Ethical Obligation Threatening Phoenix with Incurable Prejudice in Its Handling of Phoenix's Attorney-Client Privileged Document.

Thus, the junior lawyer's memorandum will present the contrary arguments, first, that Amberg & Lewis has not violated an ethical obligation and, second, that Amberg has not threatened Phoenix with incurable prejudice.

Note that in this case, the task is to write an analytic memorandum for the partner, not to draft a brief for the court. The subject matter is the arguments in the other side's brief. Drafting a brief would be entirely different. In sophisticated law practice, incidentally, the brief for the appellant does not dictate the structure of the brief for appellee. Counsel in that circumstance will make an independent decision about optimal order for the brief for appellee.

5. Use the order in the applicable statute or case law.

The applicable statute or leading case may provide a list of options and, if so, it usually makes sense to evaluate the options in the order given. The instructions in the Partner Memo may, for example, tell the junior lawyer to evaluate the client's options in light of a customer's anticipatory repudiation of a contract for the sale of goods. Under UCC 2-610, the client may:

(a) for a commercially reasonable time await performance by the repudiating party; or

(b) resort to any remedy for breach (Section 2-703 or Section 2-711), even though he has notified the repudiating party that he would await the latter's performance and has urged retraction; and

(c) in either case suspend his own performance or proceed in accordance with the provisions of this Article on the seller's right to identify goods to the contract notwithstanding breach or to salvage unfinished goods (Section 2-704).

The junior lawyer would normally evaluate the client's options in the order of the subsections of UCC 2-610.

6. Use logical order. Threshold or dispositive issues first; or most important issues first.

Normally, a memo or brief will treat threshold issues or dispositive issues, or most important issues, first, suggesting a conclusion for each issue. The following section may begin by assuming that that first conclusion is correct, and discussing the next most important question. The last section may begin with a contrary hypothesis, roughly as follows: "But if that is not the conclusion, . . ." The organizing principles just listed are commonly used in law practice.

Reminder: The most important single thing you do when you prepare to complete any law office task is to make sure that you understand your assignment. To perform the simulated tasks in this book, you must read the instructions in the Partner Memo with exquisite care.

Time and Organization on the Simplified Memorandum

The Speed Memos™ System Aids Organization and Ends Legal Research Nightmares.

If you have experience doing legal research, you know that you may become entangled in a research nightmare in which you discover increasing numbers of research paths to follow, you want to take notes, and as you do so, the amount of paper on your desk multiplies. Meanwhile, you may forget what problem you are trying to solve. When you remember what problem you are trying to solve, you cannot remember where you wrote down the notes you took on the research materials that you found earlier, notes that might lead you to the solution. You have piles of notes. You have written the same thing in several different places. But how do these pieces of paper fit together to produce a memorandum? Where are the notes you are looking for? When will you find the time to complete the project? The **Speed Memos™** System eliminates these legal research nightmares.

Time is always a challenge for lawyers. In a law office, your time is always limited. Preparation and practice are the keys to confident, accurate, work.

Pilots facing an emergency have seconds to react, but they know exactly what to do because they have practiced all of their emergency procedures so many times.

The **Speed Memos™** System teaches you exactly what to do to produce a lawyerlike work product within the time allowed. This part of the book will teach you key procedures and walk you through specific examples.

If you take the time now to learn to use the **Speed Memos™** System, including the MPT-Matrix™, you will:

- Save an enormous amount of time;
- Understand the issues and be responsive to the instructions in the Partner Memo;
- Create a solid **MPT-Matrix™** that shows you how to organize your legal research materials quickly and confidently;
- Develop your memo-writing skills, "like a sport™."
- Finish the task promptly.

Once you have learned this system, you will be prepared for any short memorandum.

Seeing the Big Picture

Using MPT materials to develop lawyering skills is entirely appropriate, because they simulate tasks in the practice of law. The purpose of the **Speed Memos™** System this book teaches is to help you develop habits and skills to organize your work, use your time efficiently, and write strong and effective memoranda. Accordingly, one key component of the **Speed Memos™** System is the time-saving MPT-Matrix™, which you should use for the tasks in this book and which you also can use for simple memoranda in law practice.

The MPT-Matrix™ is a graphic display that is both a map of your research and a plan for writing your work product. Here we give you a panoramic overview of the whole **Speed Memos**™ System.

The task materials in this book are divided into the File and the Library. Ninety minutes are allowed for completion of each task. I suggest allowing at least 35 minutes for reading and outlining the work product, then allowing 45 minutes for completing your draft, leaving five minutes at the end for checking everything and proofreading.

The File and the Library Concern the Specific Task.

The File is a collection of documents from the fictitious law office. The most important document in the File and, indeed, in the entire packet, is the Partner Memo ("task memo," "supervisor memo"), a memo from a fictitious supervising attorney. It gives you instructions for completing the particular task. Following these instructions meticulously is key to achieving success. The Library is a collection of legal authorities. It may include simulated hornbook materials, statutes, and case law. In sum, the packet always contains: (1) the File, including the Partner Memo, and (2) the Library.

The **Speed Memos**™ System addresses all of the challenges of performing these tasks, including the challenge of organizing research and finishing the work product efficiently. Organizing legal research is rarely easy.

*The **Speed Memos**™ System Meets the Time-Management Challenge.*

Writing these basic memos requires you to demonstrate skills that are important for the practice of law. You must read carefully, follow directions, and organize well. For many junior lawyers, however, the biggest challenge is managing time. Many lawyers have no idea how long it takes them to do their work. They are totally flummoxed by having to finish an entire law office task, including doing the research and producing the work product, start to finish, in 90 minutes, as bar candidates must do on the MPT.

Finishing these memo tasks in 90 minutes is entirely possible, however. The **Speed Memos**™ System assures that you can complete the task in 90 minutes:

1. You know how much time to spend on each part of the task.
2. If the memo is a simple one, you can keep track of all research on one simple one-page MPT-Matrix™. You need not take extensive notes, so there is no risk of losing your research.
3. You need never read anything in the File or Library more than once.
4. You can keep control of your time and complete the job.

In writing an efficient legal memo, clarity of focus and efficiency are everything. Efficiency means that you do not have time for meditating on the case, for searching your memory for similar situations, for writing long introductory sections, or for demonstrating extensive knowledge. The Panoramic Overview below shows you how the time-saving MPT-Matrix™ works.

The **Speed Memos**™ System Panoramic Overview

The MPT-Matrix™ is one central, time-saving, device in the **Speed Memos**™ System. You should use it to save time in producing all six of the work products for the six simple memorandum tasks in this book. In addition, you can use it with simple tasks in law practice. To give a rapid overview of this process using a particular example, let us take a straightforward task, called *Ronald v. Department of Motor Vehicles*. You will first survey the materials in the File and the Library. Next, read the Partner Memo. The Partner Memo is the most important document in every task. You must read the instructions in the Partner Memo with exquisite care, take the instructions apart into their smallest pieces, and respond fully to each one. Your task in *Ronald* is to write a persuasive memorandum for submission to an administrative tribunal.

You will start by drawing a blank MPT-Matrix™. Turn your paper sideways, because you will probably need more columns than rows. Your MPT-Matrix™ will take up the whole page. You must draw the matrix by hand, on paper. The computer will not work.

Sample Blank MPT-Matrix™

	A.	B.	C.	D.	E.
1.					
2.					
3.					
4.					

The Partner Memo instructs you to draft a legal memorandum that will persuade the administrative law judge to vacate the suspension of your client's driver's license. The Partner Memo says that your client has already introduced evidence before the administrative tribunal to show that the DMV has failed to prove that her blood-alcohol level exceeded the permissible level. For many other tasks, you will have to tear the Partner Memo instructions apart into many separate topics. Here, however, the partner gives you only three straightforward instructions for what your memorandum must argue.

Down the lefthand column of the MPT-Matrix™ you will list the three instructions from the Partner Memo, giving each one a short name and a number. The Partner Memo instructs you to argue that:

1. The police officer did not have reasonable suspicion to stop Ms. Ronald;

2. The administrative law judge cannot rely solely on the blood test report to find that Ms. Ronald was driving with a prohibited blood-alcohol concentration; and

3. In light of all the evidence, the DMV has not met its burden of proving by a preponderance of the evidence that Ms. Ronald was driving with a prohibited blood-alcohol concentration.

Insert these three instructions as a numbered list in the left-hand column of your MPT-Matrix™.

	A.	B.	C.	D.	E.	F.	G.	H.
1. Officer had no reasonable suspicion to stop.								
2. DMV cannot rely on lab test report.								
3. DMV has failed to meet its burden of proof.								

Now write the names of the documents across the top of the MPT-Matrix™, using a capital letter for each one.

	A. Franklin Vehicle Code secs. 352, 353	B. Franklin Evidence Code secs. 1278, 1280, Franklin A.P.A. sec. 115, Franklin Code of Regulations sec. 121	C. Transcript of Administrative Hearing 2/23/09	D. Police Incident Report 12/19/08	E. Crime Lab Test Report 12/29/08	F. *Pratt v. DMV* (Franklin Ct. App. 2006)	G. *Schwartz v. DMV* (Franklin Ct. App. 1994)	H. *Rodriguez v. DMV* (Franklin Ct. App. 1994)
1. Officer had no reasonable suspicion to stop.								
2. DMV cannot rely on lab test report.								
3. DMV has failed to meet its burden of proof.								

The most important single thing you do when you prepare to complete any law office task is to make sure that you understand your assignment. To perform the simulated tasks in this book, you must read the instructions in the Partner Memo with exquisite care. Normally you will have to tear apart each instruction in the Partner Memo into small pieces, and possibly take apart a statute, as well. The instructions in *Ronald v. DMV* case are unusually straightforward.

Read the File and the Library, starting with the statutes.

Now you are ready to read the File and the Library. Always read the statutes first. Cases usually interpret statutes, not the other way around. Except for taking the statutes first, you will read through the entire File and Library in the order in which the documents appear, starting with the File. You will read these materials only once.

Index the materials.

As you read along, you will underline each part you are going to use in responding to the instructions in the Partner Memo. Then on the MPT-Matrix™ you will note the page number of that information from the File and Library. You will put the page number of the material you are going to use in the MPT-Matrix™ at the intersection of the row indicating the instruction in the Partner Memo and the column indicating the document in the File or Library where the material appears. I call this action "indexing."

To take one example, information that appears in the statutes on page P-6, and that you will use to argue that the police officer had no reasonable suspicion to stop your client, will go at the intersection of row 1 and column A. That information responds to the instruction in row 1, using the statute at column A. Thus, the page where the information appears is page P-6, and the map coordinates are 1-A. That is, the number of the row, plus the letter of the column.

Accordingly, part of the first section of your MPT-Matrix™ will look like this:

	A. Franklin Vehicle Code
1. Officer had no reasonable suspicion to stop.	**P-6.**

You will need to read through the entire File and Library only once, noting on the time-saving MPT-Matrix™ each place where you will use information to respond to the instructions in the Partner Memo. One of the beauties of the MPT-Matrix™ is that you need never copy the information from the File or Library into a separate note, or take any notes at all.

To illustrate indexing, on the following page is a completed MPT-Matrix™ for *Ronald v. Department of Motor Vehicles*. In what follows, I explain the steps by which you will have noted the page numbers in each line.

	A. Franklin Vehicle Code secs. 352, 353	B. Franklin Evidence Code secs. 1278, 1280, Franklin A.P.A. sec. 115, Franklin Code of Regulations sec. 121	C. Transcript of Administrative Hearing 2/23/09	D. Police Incident Report 12/19/08	E. Crime Lab Test Report 12/29/08	F. Pratt v. DMV (Franklin Ct. App. 2006)	G. Schwartz v. DMV (Franklin Ct. App. 1994)	H. Rodriguez v. DMV (Franklin Ct. App. 1994)
1. Officer had no reasonable suspicion to stop.	P-6		P-2, P-3			P-8, P-9		
2. DMV cannot rely on lab test report.		P-6, P-7	P-2		P-5		P-10, P-11	
3. DMV has failed to meet its burden of proof.	P-6		P-2, P-3	P-4			P-10, P-11	P-13

What the MPT-Matrix™ shows. The first row of the MPT-Matrix™ indicates that as you were reading through the File and the Library, you noted that on page P-6 you found the Franklin statutes governing driving with a prohibited blood-alcohol percentage, related to reasonable suspicion to stop. On pages P-2 and P-3, you found the facts in the transcript of the administrative hearing relevant to whether or not your client drove with a prohibited blood-alcohol percentage. On pages P-8 and P-9, in the case called *Pratt v. DMV* (Franklin Ct.App. 2006), you found reference to *Terry v. Ohio* (U.S. 1968), establishing the standard for reasonable suspicion, which justifies police stops with less than probable cause. *Pratt* spells out the application of the reasonable suspicion standard to cases under Sections 352 and 253 of the Franklin Vehicle Code.

Map Coordinates. When you want to refer to the place on the MPT-Matrix™ where you noted a page number, you can use the map coordinates. That is, the number of the row, plus the letter of the column. The map coordinates for using the statute regarding driving with an impermissible blood-alcohol level to respond to the first instruction in the Partner Memo are 1-A. This is because you will respond to the instruction in row 1 by using information in column A.

Cross-referencing. At the same time that you are reading along, while noting those page numbers in your MPT-Matrix™, however, you are also underlining the sections you intend to use for your work product, right where you find them in the documents in the File and the Library. You do not need to copy anything; you just underline the words you want to use, taking care not to underline too many words. Next to that material, you note the map coordinates in the margin. This is so you can spot the material quickly when you scan that page. I call this "cross-referencing."

To respond to the third instruction in the Partner Memo, for example, you use another section of the Franklin Vehicle Code that you find on page P-6 of the Library. You underline the words you intend to use where you find them in the statute. In the margin next to that code section in the Library, you note the map coordinates for the intersection of the row and the column on the MPT-Matrix™ where you will use the material (3-A).

---

§ 353 Administrative suspension of license by Department of Motor Vehicles for prohibited blood-alcohol level on chemical testing

(a) Upon receipt by the Department of Motor Vehicles of a laboratory test report from any law enforcement agency attesting that a forensic alcohol analysis performed by chemical testing determined that a person's blood had 0.08 percent or more of alcohol while he or she was operating a motor vehicle, the Department of Motor Vehicles shall immediately suspend the license of such person to operate a motor vehicle for a period of one year.

(b) Any person may request an administrative hearing before an administrative law judge on the suspension of his or her license under this section. <u>At the administrative hearing, the Department of Motor Vehicles shall bear the burden of proving by a preponderance of the evidence that the person operated a motor vehicle when the person had 0.08 percent or more of alcohol in his or her blood.</u>   **3-A**

How to use the time-saving MPT-Matrix™ to draft your memorandum.

When you are ready to draft the memorandum the Partner Memo instructed you to prepare, you will first review the instructions in the Partner Memo again to make sure you are doing exactly what the partner told you to do. This is important. It is remarkably easy to get into the research and forget exactly what the issue was. Next, you will refer to each row of your MPT-Matrix™, one row after the other. All your research is right in front of you. You have reduced the voluminous pages of the File and the Library to a single sheet of paper. You are not lost in a sea of copied-out material. To quote or refer to your research sources, you only have to go to the pages in the File or Library that you have noted in the MPT-Matrix™. When you look at each page of the File or Library you have noted, you will find your cross-references. In the margin next to the material you intend to use you will have noted the map coordinates for that material in your MPT-Matrix™.

The map coordinates for using the information in the hearing transcript in *Ronald* are 1-C, because you will be responding to the instruction in row 1 by using information in column C. The map coordinates for using the *Pratt* case are 1-F, because you will respond to the instruction in row 1 by using information in column F.

Persuasive Section Headings.

Your persuasive headings should include both law and facts. You will spend time crafting them.[6] The three persuasive section headings in a memorandum might be as follows. Each part of the memorandum will respond to one of the instructions in the Partner memo.

> I. The totality of the circumstances fails to provide a reasonable suspicion justifying the officer's stop of petitioner's vehicle.

---

[6] See Gerald Lebovitz, "Getting to the Point: Pointers About Point Headings," *New York State Bar Association Journal,* January 2010, at 64.

II. The blood test report does not satisfy the public records exception to the hearsay rule, and it cannot, by itself, support a finding of driving with a prohibited blood-alcohol level.

III. The department of Motor Vehicles has not met its burden of proving by a preponderance of the evidence that petitioner was driving with a prohibited blood-alcohol concentration.

Overview

1. Draw the MPT-Matrix™. Use a whole page.

2. Survey the materials in the File and the Library. Read the Partner Memo and list a short name for each instruction (or sub-topic) down the leftmost column of your MPT-Matrix™, along with instructions from any second document the Partner Memo refers to, giving each instruction or sub-topic a number.

3. List names of the documents in the File and Library across the top of the MPT-Matrix™, and give each one a capital letter.

4. Read the statutes. Then read the File and Library, underlining words you will use, noting map coordinates in the margin. (Cross-referencing)

5. Note page numbers of that material in the MPT-Matrix™, at the intersection of the row for the instruction or topic and the column for the document. (Indexing)

6. Review the instructions in the Partner Memo again. Write your work product, using the MPT-Matrix™ as your outline, taking the rows in order from top to bottom.

7. Review the instructions in the Partner Memo one final time to be sure you have followed the instructions. Make sure the format and tone of your work product are correct, and that you have handled ethical issues.

8. Submit your work product.

Note that in the sample MPT-Matrixes™, this book provides words as well as numbers. Your own MPT-Matrixes™ will not usually contain many words. You will rely primarily on page numbers in your own MPT-Matrixes™. This book presents both page numbers and words so that you can see not only which pages in the File and Library you will use, but also which material you will underline.

Word to the Wise

Format is key for giving yourself a structure and for creating the best professional impression. Make sure that the reader can see the logical structure of your work product just by looking at your pages.

In performing any law office task, give yourself a structure by choosing a standard law office format for your task: memo, brief, and so on. In this book, the format is the law office memo. Your work product will usually have three main parts. Note how many subsections your work product will have. Divide your time available by the number of subsections. Control your time.

After you have written all your paragraphs, at the end, if you have not already done so, go back and insert a short clear persuasive heading for every section. Your section headings should state succinctly your argument for each section, using both law and facts. Incorporate in each section heading the key word or words from your topic outline.

Improper: <u>The facts prove plaintiff's case.</u>

Proper: <u>By moving the books off-site, the library violates the terms of the founding documents.</u>

Underline your heading, leave space above it, and otherwise make it obvious to the reader's eye what your section headings are. The reader must be able to follow your argument visually. Wait! You aren't quite finished yet.

Take five (5) minutes, and re-check everything.

Check that the work product follows the instructions in the Partner Memo. Following instructions to the letter is vital. Check that the format and tone are correct, that you have identified and dealt with all ethical issues, and that each part of the work product has a persuasive heading that is underlined. Proofread. Proofread again.

1. Go back through your work product.
2. Make sure that you have used all of the material in your MPT-Matrix™.
3. Make sure that you have handled every single topic down the left-hand column of your MPT-Matrix™, that is, that you have completely analyzed the instructions in the Partner Memo.
4. Quickly check over the beginning and end of your work product. Is the format correct?
5. Does the Introduction to your memorandum state what the task is?
6. Does the Conclusion state that you have completed your task?
7. Have you used the correct tone for the task?
8. Read the Partner Memo again. Did you do exactly what the partner told you to do? Did you address each topic? Did you answer all of the partner's questions?
9. Proofread. Then proofread again.

Make sure that the format is correct and complete. Make sure that the sections of your document are visually distinct. It is not enough that your work product does what it is supposed to do. Your format must make it visually obvious to the reader that you have done so.

Make sure that your tone is correct for the task. Reread the instructions in the Partner Memo again to make sure that you have done exactly what the partner asked you to do, and that you have hit all the topics. Make sure that you have also stated plainly exactly what you have done. Proofread. Proofread again.

Good work! You have done a good job on your memorandum task, and you have completed it within the 90 minutes allowed!

At-a-Glance:
Summary of the Four-Part *Speed Memos*™ System

I.   Step One. Outline. Five (5) minutes.

Skim the entire File and Library quickly to see what is there. Read the instructions in the Partner Memo and any other key document. List short names for the topics down the leftmost column of your MPT-Matrix™ and number them.

II.   Step Two. Thirty-five (35) minutes.

Complete the MPT-Matrix™. Index and cross-reference. Complete the framework of the **Speed Memos** MPT-Matrix™ by noting the names of the documents in the File and the Library across the tops of the columns in the Matrix and giving each one a capital letter. Then fill in the MPT-Matrix™ by reading straight through the File and Library materials, starting with the statutes, entering page numbers of useful material at the intersection of the appropriate rows and columns in the MPT-Matrix™ (indexing). As you go along, you will also be noting those MPT-Matrix™ map co-ordinates in the margins of the File and Library next to the material you will use (cross-referencing).

III.   Step Three. Forty-five (45) minutes.

Create the work product. Check again to make sure that you are following the directions in the Partner Memo and any other key documents. Then write at least one sentence for each section of your work product. Finally, complete your work product.

IV.   Step Four. Five (5) minutes.

Re-check everything and proofread. Check that the work product follows the instructions in the Partner Memo. Check that the format and tone are correct, that you have dealt with all ethical issues, and that each part of the work product has a persuasive heading that is underlined. Proofread. Proofread again.

Part II:

Six Memorandum Tasks with Sample Answers and Analyses

Introduction

This part contains six memorandum tasks that you can use to strengthen your lawyering skills. As you practice, you will find yourself becoming proficient at reading and outlining the Partner Memo, completing your research, and writing your work product within the time allowed. With sufficient practice, you should be able to complete a simple, basic, work product competently inside 90 minutes. These tasks all come from the Multistate Performance Test (MPT), released by the National Council of Bar Examiners (NCBE).

Each task gives you not merely the task itself and the Point Sheets but also guidance to help you succeed on other law-office tasks. In this section you will find:

(1) The NCBE materials for each MPT task, including the File and the Library and the Point Sheets;

(2) The Speed-Memos System™ MPT-Matrix™;

(3) The Speed-Memos System™ Sample Answer;

(4) The Speed-Memos System™ Note on Analyzing the Task.

An MPT-Matrix™ shows graphically how the materials in the File and the Library work together. Your own MPT-Matrix™ will contain page numbers for the passages you want to use, plus a couple of words. Each MPT-Matrix™ following, however, contains more words, as well as page numbers. This is so that you can see why certain material has been chosen.

Each "Sample Answer" shows you one way to respond to the instructions in the Partner Memo. These sample answers are illustrations, not models. Keep in mind that you need not write long answers or hit all possible points in order to write a good memo. This book gives answers that are sometimes fuller than you can write within the 45 minutes recommended. And the Point Sheets from the NCBE often provide additional legal points. Each Note on Analyzing explains how to read and outline the instructions in the Partner Memo and how to structure your answer.

Recommended steps for self-teaching appear in Part 1. Take this opportunity to strengthen your professional competence. Do not merely glance at a task, jot a few notes, and then look at the sample answer or the Note on Analyzing for that task. Do the work. Then, when you have completed each task, set your MPT-Matrix™ side-by-side with the Speed-Memos System™ MPT-Matrix™. See how you could have found more issues in the instructions in the Partner Memo. Then look at your answer alongside the sample answer. You will learn one way to make a visual presentation. Remember, you want your supervising lawyer to see the logical structure of your work just by looking at the pages.

Read the Note on Analyzing. Did you understand how to read the instructions in the Partner Memo and outline the task? Have you used an appropriate memorandum format? Does your work product have three parts? Do your persuasive headings contain both law and facts? Are they powerful?

Use these memo tasks to gain the habits in legal research, organization, and presentation that you will use in daily practice.

Name of Task	Type of Task	Context	Purpose	Type of Legal Analysis
A. *In re Lisa Peel*	Objective memorandum	Litigation	Evaluate potential of client's case	Statutory interpretation
B. *In re Velocity Park*	Objective memorandum	Contract drafting	Analyze proposed document	Document and case analysis, suggestions for re-drafting
C. *Phoenix Corporation v. Biogenesis, Inc.*	Objective memorandum	Litigation	Evaluate merits of opposing party's arguments	Statutory and case law analysis and application
D. *In re Gardenton Board of Education*	Objective memorandum	Code analysis and drafting	Analyze proposed school district speech code section-by-section and suggest revisions	Statutory and case law analysis and application, with suggestions for deleting, adding or re-drafting sections
E. *In re Steven Wallace*	Objective memorandum	Litigation	Advise client on how to respond to demand from trustee in bankruptcy	Statutory and case law analysis and application, with suggestions for factual investigation
F. *Franklin Asbestos Handling Regulations*	Persuasive and objective memorandum	Litigation	Frame best arguments and evaluate regulations, section-by-section	Statutory interpretation and case law analysis and application

P1

FILE

Task A:
Organizing a Legal Memo Where the
Work Product
Requires Statutory Analysis:

In re Lisa Peel

Black, Fernandez & Hanson LLP
Attorneys at Law
Suite 215
396 West Main Street
Greenville, Franklin 33755

M E M O R A N D U M

To: Applicant
From: Henry Black
Re: Peel subpoena
Date: February 26, 2008

Our client, Lisa Peel, has just been subpoenaed by the local district attorney to testify before a grand jury. The subpoena directs her to bring notes concerning any and all persons interviewed regarding an item she posted on her Web log (blog). These notes will reveal the identities of her sources for the information she posted on her blog. Peel promised to protect the confidentiality of her sources. She seeks our advice on whether she has grounds to resist the subpoena.

I am somewhat familiar with the Franklin Reporter Shield Act (FRSA). However, I do not know if the FRSA applies to Peel and her blog. Please draft an objective memorandum for me analyzing whether we can use the FRSA to move to quash Peel's subpoena.

You need not include a separate statement of facts, but be sure to use the facts in your analysis. Be sure to address both sides of the issue; that is, discuss any facts or law that may prevent Peel from claiming the protection of the FRSA.

Do not concern yourself with any First Amendment issues; another associate is researching those arguments.

TRANSCRIPT OF INTERVIEW WITH LISA PEEL

February 22, 2008

Atty: Lisa, nice to see you. What can I do for you?

Peel: You can make this subpoena go away.

Atty: Tell me more. Why don't you start at the beginning?

Peel: A couple of years ago, I retired from teaching, and my husband and I moved to Greenville here in Montgomery County. To find out more about my new community, I started attending the meetings of several public bodies—the library and school boards, the park district board, and the town council. The more I went, the more I got to know people, and the more I became part of the scene. People got to know and trust me. Soon, I realized that there was a lot going on that the public should know about.

Atty: Did you think about getting the local newspaper involved?

Peel: Most of the towns in this county are too small to support a daily paper. So there is only one daily paper covering all of Montgomery County. The publisher believes the paper should boost the local communities, and he discourages the reporters from doing any stories and investigations that might portray the communities in a bad light.

Atty: So what did you do?

Peel: About a year ago, I started an Internet blog. As you know, often the owner of the blog starts a discussion and others can post comments.

On my blog, I posted the agendas of the Greenville town council, library and school boards, and sometimes the planning commission. After the meetings, I posted the minutes, my summary of the minutes, and my own commentary about how these decisions would affect the town. Within weeks, over 400 people visited the blog, and about a quarter of them commented on what I wrote or added questions that others would respond to. I actually had citizens engaged in learning what their government was doing.

At first I updated the blog only occasionally. Then it generated so much interest that I decided to update it more often.

Atty: How often do you update it?

Peel: I generally post new items on Friday, but sometimes I may not get around to it until later in the weekend. I have movie reviews and gardening tips on the blog and also share news of my family. I post pictures of my pets and places where I've traveled. I'll also post announcements about the library's bake sale and events like that.

Atty: Do your readers pay for access to your blog?

Peel: No, it's free. At first, I kept the blog wide open; anyone could access it and post anything—anonymously if they wanted to. But then I decided that letting anyone post anything might not be wise. So now, anyone can access it at no cost. But if you want to post a comment or a question, you have to register. Registering is also free. In the past two months, I've had over 3,500 registrants in this town of 38,000 people, and people have visited the site more than 15,000 times. I've also picked up a couple of local businesses, which pay me to post their ads on my blog.

Atty: So, tell me about the subpoena.

Peel: One day, I got a call from an individual familiar with the school district administration. This person told me that the Greenville School District was losing the use of $10,000 worth of audiovisual and computer equipment purchased with district funds because the stuff was going to the home of the assistant superintendent. Well, $10,000 isn't a lot of corruption, I concede, but it is public money and it was intended to buy equipment for schoolchildren.

So I investigated and got confirmation from a couple of sources. I wrote a piece about what I found out and posted it on my blog. I brought you a hard copy of the posting. Now the Montgomery County District Attorney wants to know the sources of my information.

Atty: Why not reveal your sources?

Peel: To get to the truth, especially the truth about public corruption, I have to talk to people on the inside. But insiders will never talk to me if they think their names will become public because they're worried about losing their jobs. So I get inside information from confidential sources, let people know about it by getting the word out, and suddenly the government starts investigating or the public starts asking questions.

Atty: Do you get paid for this work?

Peel: Not much. The little income that comes from the sponsors' ads, I use for my expenses: computer upgrades, copy costs, telephone costs, gas for traveling, that sort of thing.

Atty: Do you know why the district attorney subpoenaed you?

Peel: I have a couple of guesses. Now that I've exposed this scandal, he has to investigate. I suspect he is embarrassed to learn about this from my blog. Also, the district attorney is just being lazy. Think about it—how many people are in a position to know about this going on at the school? He just needs to start asking the right people and the information will come out. But, regardless of the reason, I have to protect my sources. I may be retired and this blog may be my hobby, but right now it is the only avenue for real news in this county.

Atty: I'm somewhat familiar with the Franklin Reporter Shield Act—we may have an argument that you are protected by it, but I doubt that "blogs" or "bloggers" are specifically mentioned in the Act. I am also concerned that you've never worked as a reporter before.

Peel: But I work just like a real reporter. I attend public meetings, read agendas, minutes, budgets, etc. I make calls to the officials and other staff members and interview them. I then post the official agendas and minutes, along with my summaries and comments. The amount of time varies, but I usually spend 12–15 hours a week on my blog.

Atty: I see your point. Well, we'll do some research and get back to you soon.

Peel: Thanks. I look forward to hearing from you.

P-5

Subpoena Duces Tecum

IN THE DISTRICT COURT FOR MONTGOMERY COUNTY
STATE OF FRANKLIN

SUBPOENA DUCES TECUM

In re Grand Jury Investigation   Grand Jury Case Number 08-7703

TO:

Lisa Peel
9853 S. Elm Street
Greenville, Franklin 33755

YOU ARE COMMANDED TO APPEAR before the Grand Jury duly empaneled in the above-captioned case at the Montgomery County Courthouse, Room 346, March 10, 2008, at 10:00 a.m. YOU ARE COMMANDED TO PRODUCE all reports, files, notes, and other documentation regarding Greenville School District equipment in the possession of Assistant Superintendent Frank Peterson, including all files, notes, reports, and any other documentation taken of or from any and all persons interviewed for or sources described or quoted in the GREENVILLE CITIZEN BLOG operated by Lisa Peel and dated January 4, 2008.

Subpoena requested by the Montgomery County District Attorney's Office.

DATE ISSUED: February 20, 2008

Elliot Wallace
_____
Elliot Wallace
District Attorney

NOTICE:
FAILURE TO COMPLY WITH THIS SUBPOENA MAY RESULT IN FINES OR
IMPRISONMENT OR BOTH.

P-4

Greenville Citizen Blog Posting

GREENVILLE CITIZEN BLOG—IT'S YOUR GOVERNMENT

$10,000 in School Equipment Diverted from Schools to Home of Assistant Superintendent

January 4, 2008: Greenville, Franklin
by Lisa Peel

The Greenville School District approved the purchase of $70,000 worth of new audiovisual and computer equipment for the schoolchildren of the Greenville School District this year, but not all of the equipment is in the schools. As the equipment arrived at the district offices, selected items were redirected to the home of Assistant Superintendent Frank Peterson, according to several sources closely associated with the school district. Sources estimate that Peterson has school district equipment worth over $10,000 at his home at the present time.

According to sources, who would speak only on the condition of anonymity, Peterson took selected items home "to test them out." But instead of returning these materials to the school, he kept them at his home.

At this time Peterson reportedly has at home two fully equipped desktop personal computers with two color printers, two laptop computers, one high-performance scanner, and a digital camera. He also has a classroom multimedia system in his home. That's $10,000 worth of public school equipment that he's using to create his own multimedia studio!

When asked for a response on Peterson's alleged activities, Greenville School Board President Annette Gross said, "We have policies in place to ensure that the public's dollars are spent according to budget."

Citizens should immediately ask President Gross for a full accounting of the purchases and for an investigation of Assistant Superintendent Peterson.

Article from America Today

AMERICA TODAY

July 5, 2007

BLOGS COMPETING WITH NEWSPAPERS AND NETWORKS

Blogs—slang for Web logs—started out as online personal diaries or journals but have rapidly become part of the everyday Web vernacular and are replacing news websites for many readers.

Blog owners or "bloggers" establish Web pages on which they post news items, commentary, information, and links to other sources for readers. Readers are often invited to respond. For example, the blogger might post a movie review, and ask readers to post their opinions. Or the blogger might comment on the latest appropriations bill before Congress and encourage readers to share their views with their representatives.

According to recent surveys, at least 8 million adults in the United States have created blogs, and 30 percent of Americans read one or more blogs regularly. Blogs cover every topic imaginable—technology, sports, medicine, art, entertainment, business, news, and politics. Of course, many blogs still serve as forums for sharing personal experiences, from weddings to the contents of a blogger's junk drawer.

Journalists and politicians have learned the power of blogs and recognize that they are now a force to be reckoned with. For example, during the 2006 Congressional campaigns, bloggers challenged many of the candidates' statements. Several major

bloggers have received press credentials for political events. Most major news outlets have several staff bloggers.

Blogging software is easy to use and inexpensive. Blogging is said to give a voice to those not given attention in the traditional media. It is just this ease of blogging that makes some professional journalists uncomfortable. "The blogger is the reporter, editor, and publisher. Where is the check on the blogger to ensure the truth?" asked Al Rains, Franklin Newspaper Association director. "Blogging isn't reporting; it's just writing. Any hack can offer half-baked commentary on the news of the day and post it online. How is that different from the millions of people who post items on their MySpace or Facebook pages?"

Other journalists see blogging as just another development in journalism—from newspapers to radio to TV to cable news, talk radio, and YouTube. "More means of sharing the news and inviting commentary is better than fewer means. I trust the public to learn from many sources and decide for themselves," says Tanya Browne, a journalism professor at Franklin University. "With so much media consolidation, there are many voices, especially local ones, that will be heard only through these 'alternative' forms of journalism."

LIBRARY

Franklin Reporter Shield Act

§ 900 Preamble

The primary purpose of this Act is to safeguard the media's ability to gather news. It is intended to promote the free flow of information to the public by prohibiting courts from compelling reporters to disclose unpublished news sources or information received from such sources.

§ 901 Definitions

As used in this Act:

(a) "reporter" means any person regularly engaged in collecting, writing, or editing news for publication through a news medium.

(b) "news medium" means any newspaper, magazine, or other similar medium issued at regular intervals and having a general circulation; a radio station; a television station; a community antenna television service; or any person or corporation engaged in the making of newsreels or other motion picture news for public showing.

(c) "source" means the person from whom or the means through which the information was obtained.

§ 902 Nondisclosure of source of information

No court may compel a reporter to disclose the source of any information or any unpublished material except as provided in this Act.

In re Bellows
Franklin Court of Appeal (2005)

During Terrence Johnson's trial for murder, Johnson served a subpoena *duces tecum* upon respondent Peggy Bellows, a newspaper photographer employed by the *Springfield Review*. The subpoena required Bellows to produce certain photographs that she took during a police search of Johnson's residence prior to his arrest. When Bellows refused to produce the photos, the trial court found her in civil contempt and sentenced her to jail. This appeal followed.

The sole issue on appeal is whether Bellows is a reporter whose unpublished photographs are protected by the Franklin Reporter Shield Act (FRSA). In Franklin, reporters have a statutory, qualified privilege protecting their sources and unpublished material from compelled disclosure. FRSA § 902. It is the burden of the party claiming the privilege to establish his or her right to its protection. *Wehrmann v. Wickesberg* (Fr. Sup. Ct. 2002).

We note at the outset that testimonial privileges, in general, are not favored because they "contravene a fundamental principle of our jurisprudence that the public has a right to every man's evidence." *United States v. Bryan*, 339 U.S. 323 (1950). The preamble to the FRSA, on the other hand, states that the FRSA seeks to promote the free flow of information to and from the media by protecting the media's confidential sources. Hence, competing interests must be addressed in determining the FRSA's scope.

We have found few cases that discuss who, beyond members of the traditional media, has status to claim the journalist's privilege. In 2002, the Franklin Supreme Court rejected using the FRSA to protect the identities of those paying for newspaper ads disguised as journalism. *St. Mary's Hospital v. Zeus Publishing* (Fr. Sup. Ct. 2002). The full-page ads recounted a hospital's alleged illegal labor practices and urged a boycott. Similarly, the Columbia Supreme Court rejected the argument that defamatory messages posted on a sports Internet bulletin board (GolfNet) could be construed as "news" or as being "published at regular intervals," and therefore held that the poster of the messages was not protected by the Columbia Reporter Shield Act. *Hausch v. Vaughan* (Col. Sup. Ct. 1995).

In contrast to these cases, the Franklin Supreme Court did grant FRSA protection to a freelance writer for a magazine, *Kaiser v. Currie* (Fr. Sup. Ct. 2004), and to the author of a medical journal article, *Halliwell v. Anderson* (Fr. Sup. Ct. 2002), holding that neither could be compelled to divulge their sources of information.

What we glean from these cases is that the test does not grant "reporter" status to any person simply because that person has a manuscript, a computer, a Web page, or a film. Rather, it requires an intent at the inception of the newsgathering process to disseminate investigative news to the public. Thus in *Hoey v. Fellenz* (Fr. Ct. App. 1989), the court held that the FRSA did not shield two reporters from having to testify about a crime that they happened to witness on their way home from work—when they witnessed the crime, they had no intent to disseminate news to the public. As we see it, the privilege is available only to persons whose purposes are those traditionally inherent to the press: gathering news for publication.

The FRSA defines a reporter as "any person regularly engaged in *collecting*, writing, or editing news for publication through a

Dictionary Definitions

The American Heritage Dictionary of the English Language (4th ed., 2000)

Blog: *noun* [shortened form of Web log], a website that contains an online personal journal with reflections, comments, and often hyperlinks provided by the writer.

Circulation: *noun*, movement in a circle or circuit, especially the movement of blood through blood vessels; ...free movement or passage; the passing of something, such as money or news, from place to place or person to person; the condition of being passed about and widely known, distribution; dissemination of printed material, especially copies of newspapers or magazines among readers; the number of copies of a publication sold or distributed.

Publication: *noun*, the act or process of publishing printed material; the communication of information to the public.

Publish: *verb*, to prepare and issue material for public disclosure or sale; to bring to public attention; to announce.

Reporter: *noun*, a writer, investigator, or presenter of news stories; a person who is authorized to write and issue official accounts of judicial or legislative proceedings.

Lane v. Tichenor
Franklin Supreme Court (2003)

The sole question on appeal is whether the term "recreational purpose," as used in the Franklin Landowner's Recreational Immunity Act ("the Act"), § 730, includes hayrides. Lane brought this action against Tichenor for damages sustained during a hayride on Tichenor's land. On Tichenor's motion, the trial court dismissed the case and the appellate court affirmed.

The Act provides that landowners owe no duty of care to keep their premises safe for entry or use by any person for recreational purposes. The stated purpose of the Act is to "encourage owners of land to make land and water areas available to the public for recreational purposes by limiting their liability toward persons entering thereon for such purposes." § 730(1). Thus, the Act provides immunity only if the land is entered upon or used for a "recreational purpose."

The Act defines the term "recreational purpose" as follows: "[r]ecreational purpose' includes any of the following, or any combination thereof: hunting, fishing, swimming, boating, snowmobiling, motorcycling, camping, hiking, cave exploring, nature study, water skiing, water sports, bicycling, horseback riding, and viewing or enjoying historical, archaeological, scenic or scientific sites, or other similar activities." § 730(2)(c).

Lane argues that because hayrides are not listed among the items defined in the Act, the legislature meant to exclude them from the definition of "recreational purpose," and therefore the Act does not apply here. Tichenor responds that the term "other similar activities" indicates the legislature's intent to broadly define the term "recreational purpose."

In interpreting a statute, the court is constrained to ascertain and give effect to the intent of the legislature. The statutory language is the best indication of the drafters' intent. Where that language is unambiguous, courts must enforce the law as enacted. Each word in the statute, as well as the punctuation used, is to be examined. Where the statute enumerates various covered activities, such enumeration implies the exclusion of all others.

However, in this case the statutory language is not clear, and the enumeration is neither exclusive nor exhaustive. While the legislature provided a list of activities intended as a definition of "recreational purpose," the question is what the legislature meant by "other similar activities." The question, more precisely, is whether hayrides fit within the phrase "other similar activities."

Where the language of a statute is unclear, the court may avail itself of external aids to interpret the statute. One such aid is the rules of construction of statutes, also called the canons of statutory interpretation. These rules or canons guide the court in ascertaining the intent of the legislature.

One canon, *ejusdem generis*, states that when general words follow particular and specific words in a statute, the general words must be construed to include only things of the same general kind as those indicated by the particular and specific words.

When we examine the items specifically enumerated in the Act, we find that the quality or characteristic common to all of them is the enjoyment of nature. While some may find enjoyment in fishing or hunting, others will find enjoyment in viewing historical or scientific sights, and still others in horseback riding or motorcycling. All of these activities take place outdoors and involve nature: the

news medium." § 901(a) (emphasis added). Johnson claims Bellows is not covered by the FRSA for the simple reason that the Act doesn't mention "photographers." He claims that had the legislature intended to protect photographers, it would have included photographers in the statute.

Franklin law concerning statutory construction is clear. The principal rule of statutory construction is to ascertain and give effect to the legislature's intent. To determine the legislature's intent, courts first look to the statute's language. A court must give the legislative language its plain and ordinary meaning and construe the statute as a whole, giving effect to every word therein. When interpreting a statute, words and phrases must not be viewed in isolation but must be considered in light of other relevant provisions of the statute.

Where the language of the statute is clear and unambiguous, the only legitimate function of the courts is to enforce the law as enacted by the legislature. Courts should not depart from the plain language of the statute by reading into it exceptions, limitations, or conditions which conflict with the intent of the legislature. No rule of statutory construction authorizes the courts to declare that the legislature did not mean what the plain language of the statute says.

The record is clear from testimony of the *Springfield Review* editor that Bellows is employed as a photographer for the newspaper and that her permanent assignment is to "photograph newsworthy events." There is no dispute that the *Springfield Review*, a daily newspaper with a daily circulation of more than 100,000 readers, is a news medium. The record is also clear that, in her capacity as a photographer, Bellows does not write or edit.

The question then is whether she collects news by photographing newsworthy events. Where the legislature has supplied a definition, we are constrained to use only that definition. However, the legislature does not define the term "collecting" in the FRSA. In interpreting "the plain and ordinary meaning" of a word, where the legislature has not defined the term, courts may use a dictionary to assist in determining the plain and ordinary meaning. Turning to Merriam Webster's Collegiate Dictionary 720 (10th ed. 1998), we find that collecting means "to bring together, gather, assemble." Taking photographs of events is one way to gather or assemble news. Bellows, by photographing newsworthy events, is regularly engaged in the gathering or assembling of news, and her activities fall within the statutory meaning of "collecting" news for publication.

Furthermore, extending the protections of the FRSA to photographers is consistent with the purpose of the Act. When it enacted the FRSA in 1948, the legislature stated the purpose of the Act as encouraging the free and unfettered flow of information to the public. The more recent amendments to the FRSA extend the protections to undisclosed materials as well as sources. See FRSA § 900. This provision protects the discretion of journalists to determine when and how to publish their materials.

Accordingly, Bellows meets the statutory definition of a reporter as she is a person regularly engaged in collecting news for publication through a news medium. Bellows is protected by the FRSA.

Reversed.

MPT Test Materials

THE MPT

MULTISTATE PERFORMANCE TEST

In re Lisa Peel

POINT SHEET

The MPT point sheet, grading summary, and grading guidelines describe the factual and legal points encompassed within the lawyering task to be completed. They outline all the possible issues and points that might be addressed by an applicant. They are provided to the user jurisdictions for the sole purpose of assisting graders in grading the examination by identifying the issues and suggesting the resolution of the problem contemplated by the drafters. These are not official grading guides. Applicants can receive a range of passing grades, including excellent grades, without covering all the points discussed in these guides. The model answer is included as an illustration of a thorough and detailed response to the task, one that addresses all the legal and factual issues the drafters intended to raise in the problem. It is intended to serve only as an example. User jurisdictions are free to modify these responses in the same way to receive good grades. Applicants need not present their grading materials, including the suggested weights assigned to particular points. Grading the MPT is the exclusive responsibility of the jurisdiction using the MPT as part of its admissions process.

MPT Test Materials

study of nature, the enjoyment of nature, or even travel through a natural setting.

Applying that quality to the present situation, a hayride is just another form of the enjoyment of nature. It is hard to see how hayrides are significantly different from horseback riding, motorcycling, or bicycling—all of which involve transporting oneself or others across the outdoors for enjoyment. One can imagine a group climbing onto a farm wagon, traveling along in the open, watching the stars, and communing with nature.

Lane further argues that while we should not apply this canon of construction at all, if we do, we must conclude that the quality common to all the enumerated or specific activities is that they occur by day.

In this case, the hayride was conducted at night. However, we note that camping occurs overnight and that some fishing does as well. A starlit night far away from the lights and noise of a city, the crisp night air of an October evening, the snap and crackle of fall leaves accompanied by the sounds of night birds, the moonlight faintly illuminating old trees and fallen leaves, can all be enjoyed on a hayride at night under cover of darkness.

Because we hold that hayrides fall within the term "other similar activities" of the Act, we conclude that the trial court properly dismissed the case.

Affirmed.

In re Lisa Peel

DRAFTERS' POINT SHEET

In this performance test item, applicants are employed by a law firm. Applicants' task is to prepare an objective memorandum evaluating whether there are grounds to quash with respect to a subpoena served on the firm's client, Lisa Peel. Peel operates an Internet Web log or "blog," which functions much as a newspaper, reporting news items and commentary; she is not a professional reporter. She recently posted to her blog a report that Greenville School Assistant Superintendent Frank Peterson was using school district equipment in his home. The report was based on information from anonymous sources. Soon after the story was posted, Peel was served a subpoena duces tecum by the district attorney and ordered to appear before a grand jury and to bring notes and other documents concerning the sources of her information. Peel seeks the law firm's advice on whether there are grounds to resist the subpoena.

Applicants must analyze whether Peel is entitled to claim the protection of the Franklin Reporter Shield Act (FRSA), which provides that a reporter cannot be compelled to reveal his or her sources of information except as provided by the Act. The instructional memo instructs applicants not to address any First Amendment issues. To complete the assigned task, applicants must parse and interpret the statute and, in particular, the definitions of "reporter" and "news medium."

The File consists of the instructional memo from the supervising partner, a transcript of the interview with Peel, a copy of the item posted on the blog, the subpoena, and a news article about blogs. The Library consists of excerpts from the FRSA, several dictionary definitions, and two cases bearing on the subject.

The following discussion covers all of the points the drafters intended to raise in the problem. Applicants need not cover all of them to receive passing or even excellent grades. Grading is entirely within the discretion of the user jurisdictions.

I. Overview

The task is to draft an objective memorandum assessing whether there are grounds to quash the subpoena. The work product should resemble a legal memorandum such as one an associate would prepare for a supervising partner. The key issue is whether Peel qualifies as a "reporter," as defined in the Act; if so, she cannot be compelled to reveal the sources of her report, except as provided in the Act.

This is primarily an exercise in statutory interpretation. Applicants should thus examine the definitions provided in the Act, determine the elements of the definition that must be met if Peel is to be protected by the Act, and reach a conclusion regarding whether Peel's blogging activities meet each element. With respect to the key definitions in the Act, it is expected that applicants will arrive at the following conclusions:

- A "reporter" is any person regularly engaged in collecting, writing, or editing news for publication through a news medium.

- Peel regularly engages or involves herself in collecting, writing, or editing the news, specifically, by attending meetings, analyzing public information, interviewing public officials, and writing summaries of and commentaries on their activities.

- The news written by Peel is published through a news medium.

- A "news medium" is any newspaper, magazine, or other similar medium issued at regular intervals and having a general circulation.

- Peel's blog is a publication issued at regular intervals and with a general circulation. Therefore, it qualifies as a news medium within the meaning of the Act.

II. Relevant Facts

Applicants are instructed that they need not draft a separate statement of facts, but that they are expected to incorporate the relevant facts into their analysis. Some applicants may wish to state the facts at length. Others may wish to state only enough facts to set the scene and import other facts as necessary into their discussion of the issues.

A thorough discussion of whether Peel's blogging activities bring her within the Act's coverage would include the following facts:

- Peel began an Internet blog in which she publishes information about public bodies, including the agendas and minutes of public meetings, summaries of the meetings, and her own comments about the importance of these meetings.

- Peel attends meetings, obtains public documents, prepares summaries of the meetings and documents, and writes commentaries about the business of several public bodies. Peel's activities generally take about 12 to 15 hours per week.

- Peel's blog, the Greenville Citizen Blog, has at least 3,500 persons who are registered as readers. In order to post comments to the blog, readers must register with the blog; registration is free. There are likely many additional readers who are not registered.

- Peel usually posts items to the blog every Friday.

- There is no town newspaper and the only newspaper available is a countywide one that does not publish anything critical of the local communities.

- On January 4, 2008, Peel posted a news item to the blog reporting that Greenville School Assistant Superintendent Frank Peterson was keeping school district audiovisual and computer equipment, worth approximately $10,000, in his home for his personal use.

- The blog posting about Peterson is based on information provided by confidential sources.

- The district attorney has subpoenaed Peel to appear before a grand jury and to bring notes concerning the source of her information about Frank Peterson.

III. Analysis

Applicants are told to analyze applicable legal authority and explain how the facts and law support their conclusions. The instructional memo emphasizes that both sides of the issue should be addressed; that is, applicants should discuss not only those facts that support a motion to quash but also those facts that weigh against the motion's success. Applicants should take care to address each of the elements of the definition of a reporter found in the Act. One format is for each element of the definition to be the subject of a separate heading followed by analysis related to that heading. Alternatively, applicants may organize their work product in other ways. The headings appearing below are exemplars only and are not intended as the only acceptable headings.

Whether Peel engages in the activities of a reporter for the purposes of the FRSA.

- At the outset, applicants should note that the person claiming the privilege under the FRSA has the burden to establish his or her right to its protection. *In re Bellows* (Franklin Ct. App. 2005). Thus, in order to successfully resist the subpoena, the burden is on Peel to demonstrate that her blogging activities come within the ambit of the FRSA.

- The FRSA defines a reporter as "any person regularly engaged in collecting, writing, or editing news for publication through a news medium." FRSA § 901(a). Some of the terms in the statutory definition are further defined by statutes and others are not defined. Each of them must be interpreted.
- In interpreting the FRSA, the court must ascertain and give effect to the intent of the legislature. Ordinarily the best indicator of the legislature's intent is the plain and ordinary meaning of the words used in the statute. Where the language is unambiguous, the court must rely on that language, giving effect to all the words in the statutory provision at issue. Where the legislature has defined terms, the court must use the definitions provided in the Act. *Bellows*.
- NOTE: Applicants who rely on the dictionary definition of the term "reporter" have misconstrued the nature of statutory interpretation as explained in *Bellows*. The court is clear that where the legislature has defined a term, the court must rely on that definition.

Peel collects, writes, and edits news.
- To collect news means to "gather or assemble" it. *Bellows*.
  - Peel gathers and assembles the news by obtaining public documents from public bodies, attending their meetings, and interviewing public officials.
  - Peel writes and edits the news by preparing summaries of minutes and other public documents and commentaries on the activities of several public bodies and posting them to her blog.

- The term "news" is not defined in the Act. The plain and ordinary meaning of the term "news" involves activities of public bodies and the use of public monies.
  - Many of Peel's blog postings involve the activities of public bodies.
  - However, Peel's blog is not entirely devoted to news items. She posts recipes, gardening tips, and items about her family, as well as her vacation and pet photos, presumably none of which would be considered newsworthy.

- The FRSA describes a reporter as someone who "regularly engages" in newsgathering activities. FRSA § 901(a). The term "regular" is not defined. However, common usage of the term would include weekly activities of attending meetings and posting items to the blog.
  - In addition, in *Bellows*, the court emphasized that the protections of the FRSA will be extended only to those individuals and organizations having "an intent at the inception of the newsgathering process to disseminate investigative news to the public."
  - Clearly Peel has the intent when she is attending civic meetings and interviewing officials to disseminate the news to the public via her blog. *Cf. Honey v. Fellenz* (cited in *Bellows*) where two reporters were not entitled to claim the protection of the FRSA when they witnessed the commission of a crime on their way home from work.
  - Nevertheless, Peel has no training as a reporter and she is not employed by the traditional media. By contrast, the person deemed a "reporter" for FRSA purposes in *Bellows* was a professional news photographer.
  - Likewise, *Kaiser v. Currie* and *Halliwell v. Anderson*, two cases cited in *Bellows* as examples of situations in which the Franklin courts have granted FRSA protection, involved persons writing for traditional media: a magazine and a medical journal.

Whether Peel's blog qualifies as a "news medium" under the FRSA.
A reporter collects, writes, or edits news for publication through a news medium. FRSA § 901(a). Thus applicants must determine whether Peel's blog is a "news medium" for purposes of the FRSA.
- The term "news medium" is defined in the FRSA as "any newspaper, magazine, or other similar medium issued at regular intervals and having a general circulation...." FRSA § 901(b).

- Neither the term "Web log" nor "blog" is listed in the statute. Thus applicants must discuss whether an Internet blog like Peel's meets the definition of a "news medium."
  - The examples of news media provided in the statute are not an exhaustive or exclusive listing, because the definition includes the term "other similar medium." *See Lane v. Tichenor* (Franklin Sup. Ct. 2003).
  - Arguably, the use of the term "other similar medium" indicates the intent of the legislature to interpret "news medium" in a broad manner.
  - One canon of statutory construction, *ejusdem generis*, is helpful in interpreting the term "other similar medium." The canon states that when general words follow particular and specific words in a statute, the general words must be construed to include only things of the same general kind as those indicated by the particular and specific words. *Lane*.
    - In this case, one key quality common to the particular and specific words listed (i.e., newspapers and magazines) is that they are publications that occur on a regular basis.
    - However, it is also possible that the court may focus on the fact that newspapers and magazines are primarily print media.
    - Arguably, an indication that the legislature intended that the term "news medium" be interpreted in a broad manner is the long list of various forms of media listed in the statute; these media are not limited to print media, but encompass a broad range of means of communication. FRSA § 901(b).
    - And applicants could note that it is now common for newspapers and magazines to have online versions.

- There is a strong argument that, like the listed forms of news media in § 901(b), Peel's blog is published at regular intervals and has a general circulation.
  - The word "publish" means "to prepare and issue material for public disclosure or sale; to bring to public attention; to announce." *American Heritage Dictionary*.
  - Peel posts items to the blog in order to bring them to the attention of the public. This is analogous to the printing and distribution of a newspaper or magazine.
  - Indeed, she states that, because of her blog, "I actually had citizens engaged in learning what their government was doing." (*Interview*)
  - As a general rule, Peel posts new items to the blog on a regular basis— she tries to post new items every Friday. But sometimes it may be later in the weekend before new posts are on her website.
  - Thus, Peel's blog lacks the reliability of most traditional media (e.g., the morning newspaper or 11:00 p.m. news broadcast).
  - Nonetheless, Peel's blog can be distinguished from the Internet bulletin board in *Hauseb v. Vaughan* (Col. Sup. Ct. 1995). In that case, the Columbia Supreme Court, interpreting the Columbia Reporter Shield Act, held that messages posted to an Internet bulletin board, which were posted intermittently, failed to meet that Act's requirement that to be a news medium, the claimed "news" had to be "published at regular intervals."
    - Peel's blog is updated every week.
    - And, unlike an Internet bulletin board, Peel's blog is not designed to be primarily a forum for readers to post messages for others to read. (In fact, she modified her blog so that only registered users could post comments.) Her blog is intended to inform members of her community about local government activities.
  - The term "circulation" is not defined in the Act, but the dictionary defines "circulation" as "the condition of being passed about and widely known, distribution; ...the number of copies of a publication sold or distributed." *American Heritage Dictionary*.

- In order to post to the blog, a reader must register with the blog. This is an act like subscribing, although there is no cost. The current registration for the blog totals over 3,500, or almost 10 percent of the Greenville population.
- The large number of visitors (15,000) to Peel's blog indicates that, in addition to the more than 3,500 registered readers, there are numerous regular or intermittent readers.
  - This relatively large readership is consistent with the statistics showing that millions of Americans either operate, read, or otherwise participate in blogs. *See America Today* article.
- Additionally, the fact that the legislature used a broad range of means of communication or types of media when defining "news medium" suggests that an Internet blog is a news medium.
  - Words in statutes are not to be viewed in isolation but in light of other relevant provisions of the statute. *Bellows*.
- Other news media included in the Act are radio, television, community antenna television, and newsreels. FRSA § 901(b).
- Including a blog in the definition of "news medium" is consistent with the inclusion of more "modern" forms of communication in the Act.
  - Even though "blogs" and "bloggers" did not exist when the Franklin legislature enacted the FRSA in 1948, they are now, as indicated in the *America Today* article, a journalistic force to be reckoned with.

Whether including Peel's blogging activities within the coverage of the FRSA serves the legislative intent underlying the Act.

- The intent of the legislature in enacting the statute was discussed in *Bellows*.
  - The Franklin legislature, in 1948, stated that the purpose of the Act was to encourage the free flow of information. See FRSA § 900 ("The primary purpose of this Act is to safeguard the media's ability to gather news. It is intended to promote the free flow of information to the public . . . .").
  - The purpose of promoting the free flow of information to the public applies here where Peel's blog is dedicated to that purpose, where the item posted on the blog reported on misconduct by a public official, where there is no town newspaper, and where the only newspaper in the county does not engage in investigative journalism.

IV. Conclusion

- Even though Peel is not a professional reporter employed by traditional media, because she is regularly engaged in collecting, writing, and editing the news for publication on her blog, which is a news medium, being published at regular intervals and having a general circulation, she should be deemed a reporter under the FRSA.
- Because she is a reporter under the FRSA, she cannot be compelled to reveal the identity of the source of the information for the article that appeared in the blog.
- Therefore, it is probable that a motion to quash the subpoena based on the FRSA privilege will be successful.

P-1

FILE

Hall & Gray LLP
Attorneys at Law
730 Amsterdam Ave.
Banford, Franklin 33701

MEMORANDUM

To: Applicant
From: Deanna Hall
Re: Liability waiver for Velocity Park
Date: February 26, 2008

Our client, Zeke Oliver, is about to open his new business venture, "Velocity Park," an outdoor skateboarding park (also referred to as a "skate park"). To reduce his liability to those who may be injured while skateboarding, Zeke has brought in a waiver form that he proposes to use. To help me advise him, please review his proposed waiver and prepare a memorandum:

- analyzing whether the proposed waiver will protect Velocity Park from liability for injuries occurring at the skate park;

- suggesting specific revisions to the proposed waiver, including replacement language as well as any changes in the waiver's design and layout (however, you should not redraft the entire waiver); and

- discussing whether any waiver will be enforceable if signed only by a minor.

Task B:
Organizing a Legal Memo Where the Work Product Requires Commenting on a Draft Agreement:

In re Velocity Park

CLIENT INTERVIEW—ZEKE OLIVER

February 22, 2008

Atty: Zeke, come on in. How are things coming along with your new business?

Zeke: I am totally pumped! The construction is right on schedule, and on April 30, 2008, Velocity Park, Banford's first and only skateboarding park, will be open to the public!

Atty: Great. So what can I help you with today?

Zeke: Well, my brother told me that I should require everyone who uses the skateboard park to sign a liability waiver so if someone gets hurt, they can't sue me. I found an entry form from a triathlon in the state of Columbia that I entered last year. It had some stuff about waiving liability, so I just made some changes and added the Velocity Park logo. I was all set to send it to the printer, but then I thought that I should have you look it over first.

Atty: A liability waiver is an excellent idea. And you're right—waivers aren't necessarily interchangeable from one situation to another. Before we discuss your proposed waiver form, let's talk a bit about who will be using the skateboarding park and what activities they will be able to do there.

Zeke: Okay. According to my market research, I expect that most of Velocity Park's visitors will be teenagers and young adults. There will be a minimum age of 10 for using the park. It will have all the basic stuff skateboarders love: a large concrete bowl, a beginners' area, and jumps, sliding rails, and two half-pipes, so advanced skaters can do ollies, kickflips, grinds, and other stunts. I plan to hold skills clinics and offer private lessons. Also, I've hooked up with a couple of skateboard manufacturers to sponsor some competitions, although I don't have anything definite yet. By the way, I've brought a newspaper article that mentions the park.

Atty: Thanks. Will you charge admission for the park? What about equipment rentals?

Zeke: Admission will be $10 for a three-hour block of skateboarding. I want it to be affordable for teenagers. Right now, I have no plans to rent equipment, but the park will have a shop to sell boards, helmets, T-shirts, and accessories. Of course, there will be a concessions area for soft drinks and snacks.

Atty: I assume that skateboarders get a fair number of bumps and bruises. Do you have any particular concerns about injuries at your park?

Zeke: Injuries are just part of skateboarding. Usually they're nothing more than scrapes, bruises, and the occasional sprained wrist from taking a fall. There will be signs posted stating that skateboarders have to wear helmets while using the park.

Atty: Where will skateboarders fill out your waiver form? I notice that it's two pages—that's a fair amount of reading for a teenager waiting to get into the park.

Zeke: Hey, I thought I was doing well to have only a two-page waiver. If I included everything I wanted to, it would be five pages. Anyway, the waivers will be handed out where skateboarders pay the admission fee, and whoever is staffing the cash register will collect them. I suppose some kids may not read it closely, especially if they're anxious to get in and skateboard, but short of reading the waiver to them, I don't know how to get around that. Also the waiver can be printed off of the park's website.

Atty: Will your staff be trained to deal with medical emergencies?

Zeke: I'm in the process of putting together a first-aid station, but kids won't get much more than a bandage there. For anything more serious, staff will be trained to call the skateboarder's emergency contact or an ambulance. I'm not too worried about serious injuries. In my experience, skateboarders have a good sense of what tricks they can do safely. Besides, it's so much better to have kids skateboarding in a park designed for that purpose than on the streets.

Atty: Where do most skateboarders go now in Banford?

Zeke: It's really sad. As soon as the kids find a good place, like a parking lot or cul-de-sac with a nice incline, they get chased out by the neighbors. The city council doesn't like skateboarders either. It's voted to ban skateboarding downtown. That's why I'm opening the park. Unless kids can get to another town in the area with a skateboard park, there's no place to skateboard, apart from streets and driveways in the outlying neighborhoods. Eventually, if Velocity Park succeeds, I'd like to partner with the city of Banford to operate the park and make it free, but until then, I've got my work cut out for me just to make Velocity Park recoup its costs.

Atty: With your business experience, I'm sure it will turn a profit in no time. I'll review this liability waiver and see if it meets your needs. Then we'll meet next week to discuss it.

Zeke: Thanks. I appreciate it. I really need to have this taken care of before the park opens.

DRAFT LIABILITY WAIVER

VELOCITY PARK
SKATEBOARDING
FOR A 21st CENTURY WORLD

1500 North Street
Banford, Franklin 33712
(555)555-1805

Welcome to Velocity Park! Before you hop on your skateboard and start work on your grinds, kickflips, and ollies, be sure to read and complete this form.

Admission Fees
$10 per skateboarder for a three-hour session in the park. $20 gets you an all-day pass. Unlimited monthly passes available for $75.

Hours of Operation
Monday–Friday, noon–8 p.m.
Saturday–Sunday, 10 a.m.–8 p.m.
Hours of operation subject to change without notice. Unanticipated closures will be posted at www.velocityparkskate.com.

Park Rules
➤ Must be 10 years of age or older to enter the skate park.
➤ Only skateboards and in-line skates may be used in the skate park.
➤ To enter and remain inside the skate park, you must wear a helmet.
➤ Inspect your equipment to make sure it is in good working order.
➤ Be considerate of fellow skateboarders, especially those who are younger and/or less skilled.
➤ No food, drink, or smoking allowed inside the skate park except in designated areas. No alcohol or drugs allowed.
➤ Skate park visitors must abide by staff instruction at all times.
➤ Velocity Park is not responsible for lost or stolen items.
➤ Failure to abide by these rules may result in expulsion from Velocity Park.

1. I understand and appreciate that participation in a sport carries a risk to me of serious injury and/or death. I voluntarily and knowingly recognize, accept, and assume this risk and hereby forever release, acquit, covenant not to sue, and discharge Velocity Park, its employees, event sponsors, and any third

parties from any and all legal liability, including but not limited to all causes of action, claims, damages in law, or remedies in equity of whatever kind I have or which hereafter accrue to me, whether such injuries and/or claims arise from equipment failure, conditions in the park, or any actions of Velocity Park, its employees, third parties, or other skateboarders. Velocity Park is not responsible for any incidental or consequential damages, including, but not limited to, any claims for personal injury, property damage, or emotional distress. This release is binding with respect to my heirs, executors, administrators, and assigns, as well as myself.

2. I have been informed of Velocity Park Rules and agree to abide by them.

3. In connection with any injury I may sustain, or illness or other medical condition I may experience during my participation in skateboarding or attendance at Velocity Park, I authorize any emergency first aid, medication, medical treatment, or surgery deemed necessary by attending medical personnel if I am not able to act on my own behalf.

4. In consideration of permission to use the skate park facility, I agree that Velocity Park, its agents, and its employees may use my appearance, name, and likeness in connection with my use of the facility in any Velocity Park publication, including news releases. I further agree that I am not entitled to any compensation for such use of my appearance, name, or likeness.

Name (please print): _____ Sex: _____ Age: _____

(Signed): _____ Date: _____

Emergency Contact Information

Name: _____ Phone No.: _____

Address: _____

How did you hear about Velocity Park?

Would you like e-mail updates about Velocity Park events?   Yes   No

If yes, e-mail address: _____

LIBRARY

Franklin Statutes—Civil Actions

§ 41 Contracts involving minors; limitations on authority of minor.

This section is intended to protect minors and to help parents and legal guardians exercise reasonable care, supervision, protection, and control over minor children.

(a)   A minor cannot make a contract relating to real property or any interest therein.

* * * *

(b)(1)   The contract of a minor may be disaffirmed by the minor himself, either before his majority or within a reasonable time afterwards, unless the contract at issue is one for necessaries, such as food or medical care.

(b)(2)   Where a minor enters into a contract, whether one for necessaries or not, said contract may be enforced against that individual if, upon reaching the age of majority, the individual expressly or implicitly ratifies the contract.

(b)(3)   Subsections (b)(1) and (b)(2) shall not apply to contracts made on behalf of a minor by the minor's parent or guardian.

ARTICLE FROM THE BANFORD COURIER

The Banford Courier   February 2, 2008

SKATEBOARDING: OLD AND NEW INJURIES ON THE RISE

Each year in Franklin, skateboarding results in about 500 visits to hospital emergency rooms, with some 50 skateboarders (usually children and adolescents) requiring hospitalization, usually because of head injuries. Nationally, in 2007, some 15,000 emergency room treatments were skate-board-related. Wrist injuries are the most common, either sprains or fractures. Although rare, deaths from falls and collisions with motor vehicles can occur.

Protective gear, such as helmets, slip-resistant closed-toe shoes, and wrist guards can greatly limit the number and severity of injuries. However, according to J.P. Clyde, a professional skateboarder, injuries could be further reduced if skateboarders paid more attention to the surfaces they ride on. "Studies by the U.S. Consumer Product Safety Commission found that 35 percent of all skateboarding-related injuries could have been avoided if skateboarders really paid attention to the skating environment," he said. "One-third of injuries happen because there's a flaw in the riding surface, whether it's a street, a parking lot, or a skate park. Innocuous objects like pebbles, twigs, bottle tops, or other debris can cause a skateboarder to take a spill. Cracks, potholes, and ruts also pose hazards to the unwary skateboarder."

Dr. Sanford Takei, a sports medicine specialist, agrees. "Beginning skate-boarders—those who have been riding for less than a week—account for one-third of skateboarding injuries overall," he said.

"Obviously, beginners fall more often and may not know how to fall correctly. When experienced riders are injured, it is usually from falls caused by rocks and other irregularities in the riding surface."

But what really has parents in Banford up in arms is a new trend in skateboarding-related injuries: injuries that occur when teenagers mix alcohol or marijuana and skateboards. There has been a rise in reports of teenagers gathering in the Library Mall, drinking alcohol and then skateboarding on home-made ramps and trying risky stunts. Maggie Alden, a student at Banford High School, said that she quit skateboarding in the Mall after seeing a rider fall and break his nose after colliding with another skateboarder. "Those guys are clueless about where they're going," Alden said. "Someone is always trying to start a fight or take someone else's skateboard," she added.

For his part, Zeke Oliver, owner of Velocity Park, which will be Banford's first skate park when it opens in April, appeared relaxed about the risks of skateboarding injuries and aggressive skateboarders. "Look, skateboarding is only going to grow in popularity," he said. "It's a great way for kids to get outside, blow off some steam, and get some exercise."

Lund v. Swim World, Inc.

Franklin Supreme Court (2005)

Tim Lund sued Swim World, Inc., for the wrongful death of his mother, Annie Lund, who suffered a fatal head injury at its facility. The trial court granted summary judgment to Swim World, ruling that the waiver signed by Lund released Swim World from liability. The court of appeal affirmed. For the reasons set forth below, we reverse.

Swim World is a swimming facility with a lap pool open to members and visitors. On May 3, 2001, Lund visited Swim World as part of a physical therapy program. Because Lund was not a Swim World member, she had to fill out a guest registration card and pay a fee before swimming.

The guest registration, a five-inch-square preprinted card, also contained a "Waiver Release Statement," which appeared below the "Guest Registration" section, requesting the visitor's name, address, phone number, reason for visit, and interest in membership. The entire card was printed in capital letters of the same size, font, and color. The waiver language read as follows:

WAIVER RELEASE STATEMENT. I AGREE TO ASSUME ALL LIABILITY FOR MYSELF, WITHOUT REGARD TO FAULT, WHILE AT SWIM WORLD. I FURTHER AGREE TO HOLD HARMLESS SWIM WORLD, AND ITS EMPLOYEES, FOR ANY CONDITIONS OR INJURY THAT MAY RESULT TO ME WHILE AT SWIM WORLD. I HAVE READ THE FOREGOING AND UNDERSTAND ITS CONTENTS.

The card had just one signature and date line. Lund completed the "Guest Registration" portion and signed at the bottom of the "Waiver Release Statement" without asking any questions.

After swimming, Lund used the sauna in the women's locker room. The bench she was lying on collapsed beneath her, causing her to strike her head against the heater and lose consciousness. Lund was rushed to the hospital but died the next day as the result of complications from her head injury.

The complaint alleged that Swim World was negligent in the maintenance of its facilities and that its negligence caused Lund's death.

Summary judgment is granted when there is no genuine issue of material fact and the movant is entitled to judgment as a matter of law. *Samuels v. David* (Franklin Sup. Ct. 1991). The case at bar turns on the interpretation of Swim World's waiver form and whether it relieves Swim World of liability for harm caused by its negligence.

Waivers of liability, also known as exculpatory contracts,[1] are permitted under Franklin law except when prohibited by statute or public policy. As no statute bars the contract at issue, we proceed to a public policy analysis of the exculpatory clause.

Public policy can restrict freedom of contract for the good of the community. Thus, claims that an exculpatory contract violates public policy create a tension between the right to contract freely without government interference and the concern that allowing a tortfeasor to contract away responsibility for negligent acts may encourage conduct below a socially acceptable standard of care.

We examine the particular facts and circumstances of the case when determining whether an exculpatory contract is void and unenforceable as contrary to public policy.

[1] The words "release," "waiver," and "exculpatory agreement" have been used interchangeably by the courts to refer to written documents in which one party agrees to release another from potential tort liability for future conduct covered in the agreement.

Exculpatory contracts are generally construed against the party seeking to shield itself from liability. In *Schmidt v. Tyrol Mountain* (Franklin Sup. Ct. 1996), we set forth two requirements for an enforceable exculpatory clause: "First, the language of the waiver cannot be overbroad but must clearly, unambiguously, and unmistakably inform the signer of what is being waived. Second, the waiver form itself, viewed in its entirety, must alert the signer to the nature and significance of what is being signed." *Id.* We also noted that a relevant consideration in the enforceability of such a clause is whether there is a substantial disparity in bargaining power between the parties.

Thus, a release having language that is so broad as to be interpreted to shift liability for a tortfeasor's conduct under all possible circumstances, including reckless and intentional conduct, and for all possible injuries, will not be upheld. Likewise, release forms that serve two purposes and those that are not conspicuously labeled as waivers have been held to be insufficient to alert the signer that he is waiving liability for other parties' negligence as well as his own.

In *Schmidt*, an action on behalf of a woman who fatally collided with the base of a chair-lift tower while skiing, the plaintiff alleged that the defendant ski resort negligently failed to pad the lift tower. The resort moved for summary judgment, relying on the exculpatory clause in the ski pass signed by the skier. The waiver read, in part: "There are certain inherent risks in skiing and I agree to hold Tyrol Mountain harmless for any injury to me on the premises."

The court in *Schmidt* held that the release was void as against public policy. First, the release was not clear; it failed to include language expressly indicating the plaintiff's intent to release Tyrol Mountain from its own negligence. Without any mention in the release of the word "negligence," and the ambiguity of the phrase "inherent risks in skiing," the court held that the skier had not been adequately informed of the rights she was waiving.

As to the second factor, the form, in its entirety, did not fully communicate its nature and significance because it served the dual purposes of an application for a ski pass and a release of liability. Furthermore, the waiver was not conspicuous, in that it was one of five paragraphs on the form and did not require a separate signature. In addition, we noted that there was a substantial disparity in bargaining power between the parties.

Following *Schmidt*, we hold that Swim World's exculpatory clause violates public policy. First, the waiver is overly broad and all-inclusive. The waiver begins: "I AGREE TO ASSUME ALL LIABILITY FOR MYSELF, WITHOUT REGARD TO FAULT...." Here, it is unclear what type of acts the word "fault" encompasses; it could potentially bar any claim arising under any scenario.[2] We reject Swim World's claim that negligence is synonymous with fault and conclude that the word "fault" is broad enough to cover a reckless or an intentional act. A waiver of liability for an intentional act would clearly violate public policy. *See* Restatement (Second) of Contracts § 195(1) (term exempting party from tort liability for harm caused intentionally or recklessly is unenforceable on grounds of public policy).

Exculpatory agreements that, like this one, are broad and general will bar only those claims that the parties contemplated when they executed the contract. Here, we must determine whether the collapse of a sauna bench was a risk the parties contemplated when the exculpatory contract was executed. If not, the contract is not enforceable.

[2] While including the word "negligence" in exculpatory clauses is not required, we have stated that "it would be helpful for such contracts to set forth in clear terms that the party signing it is releasing others for their negligent acts." *Schmidt*.

Here, given the broadness of the exculpatory language, it is difficult to ascertain exactly what was within Lund's or Swim World's contemplation. Nevertheless, it appears unlikely that Lund, when she signed the guest registration and waiver form, would have contemplated receiving a severe head injury from the collapse of a sauna bench.

Further, Swim World's guest registration and waiver form failed to provide adequate notice of the waiver's nature and significance. Like the contract in *Schmidt*, the form served two purposes: it was both a "Guest Registration" application and a "Waiver Release Statement." The exculpatory language appeared to be part of, or a requirement for, a larger registration form. The waiver could have been a separate document, giving Lund more notice of what she was signing. Also, a separate signature line could have been provided, but was not. Clearly identifying and distinguishing those two contractual arrangements could have provided important protection against a signatory's inadvertent agreement to the release.

Another problem with the form is that the paragraph containing the "Waiver Release Statement" was not conspicuous. The entire form was printed on one card, with the same letter size, font, and color. It is irrelevant that the release language is in capital letters; *all of* the words on the form were in capital letters. Further, the only place to sign the form was at the very end. This supports the conclusion that the waiver was not distinguishable

enough such that a reviewing court can say with certainty that the signer was fully aware of its nature and significance.

Finally, we consider the bargaining positions of the parties. This factor looks to the facts surrounding the execution of the waiver. We hasten to add that the presence of this factor, by itself, will not automatically render an exculpatory clause void under public policy.

Here, the record suggests that there was an unequal bargaining position between the parties. Lund had no opportunity to negotiate regarding the standard exculpatory language in the form. In his deposition, Swim World's desk attendant testified that Lund was simply told to complete and sign the form; the waiver portion was not pointed out, nor were its terms explained to her. No one discussed the risks of injury purportedly covered by the form. The desk attendant further testified that Lund did not ask any questions about the form but that there was pressure to sign it because other patrons were behind Lund waiting to sign in. These facts undeniably generate, at a minimum, a genuine dispute of material fact regarding the parties' disparity in bargaining power.

For these reasons we conclude that the exculpatory clause in Swim World's form violates public policy, and, therefore, is unenforceable.

Reversed.

Holum v. Bruges Soccer Club, Inc.

Columbia Supreme Court (1999)

Pamela Holum registered her seven-year-old son, Bryan, for soccer with Bruges Soccer Club, Inc. (the Club), a nonprofit organization that provides local children with the opportunity to learn and play soccer. Its members are parents and other volunteers. As part of the registration process, Mrs. Holum signed a release form whereby she agreed to release "the Club from liability for physical injuries arising as a result of [Bryan's] participation in the soccer club."

Bryan was injured when, after a soccer practice, he jumped on the goal and swung on it. The goal ripped backward and fell on Bryan's chest, breaking three ribs. Bryan's parents, Phil and Pamela Holum, sued the Club, alleging negligence on their own behalf and on behalf of Bryan. The trial court granted summary judgment to the Club, holding that the release signed by Bryan's mother barred the Holums' action against the Club.

The court of appeal affirmed in part and reversed in part. It held that the release barred Mr. and Mrs. Holum's claims. However, it went on to hold that the release did not bar Bryan's claim. Thus, while the parents' claims were barred, Bryan still had a cause of action against the Club, which a guardian could bring on his behalf, or which he could assert upon reaching the age of majority.

We agree with the court of appeal that therelease applies to the injuries at issue. As to whether the release executed by Mrs. Holum on behalf of her minor son released the Club from liability for Bryan's claim and his parents' claims as a matter of law, we conclude that the release is valid as to all claims. Accordingly, we reverse that portion of the court of appeal decision holding that the release would not prevent Bryan from asserting a claim for his injuries.

We first consider whether the release is valid. In Columbia, with respect to adults, the general rule is that releases from liability for

injuries caused by negligent acts arising during recreational activities are enforceable, whether the negligence is on the part of the participant in the recreational activity or the provider of the activity, in this case, the Club. This approach recognizes the importance of individual autonomy and freedom of contract.

For that reason, the release agreement is valid as to the parents' negligence claim. Mrs. Holum acknowledged that she read the agreement and did not ask any questions. Mr. Holum did not sign the release, but he accepted and enjoyed the benefits of the contract. In fact, when the injury occurred, he was at the practice field, thereby indicating his intention to enjoy the benefits of his wife's agreement and be bound by it. It is well settled that parents may release their own claims arising out of injury to their minor children. Accordingly, we find that Bryan's parents are barred from recovery as to their claims.

Here, however, the release was executed by a parent on behalf of the minor child. The Holums contend that the release is invalid on public policy grounds, citing the general principle that contracts entered into by a minor, unless for "necessaries," are voidable by the minor before the age of majority is reached. The Club, however, argues that the public interest justifies the enforcement of this agreement with respect to both the parents' and the child's claims.

Organized recreational activities provide children the opportunity to develop athletic ability as well as to learn valuable life skills such as teamwork and cooperation. The assistance of volunteers allows nonprofit organizations to offer these activities at minimal cost. In fact, the Club pays only 19 of its 400 staff members. Without volunteers, such nonprofit organizations could not exist and many children would lose

THE MPT

MULTISTATE PERFORMANCE TEST

In re Velocity Park

POINT SHEET

The MPT point sheet, grading summary, and grading guidelines describe the factual and legal points encompassed within the lawyering task to be completed. They outline all the possible issues and points that might be addressed by an applicant. They are provided to the user jurisdictions for the sole purpose of assisting graders in grading the examination by identifying the issues and suggesting the resolution of the problem contemplated by the drafters. These are not official grading guides. Applicants can receive a range of passing grades, including excellent grades, without covering all the points discussed in these guides. The model answer is included as an illustration of a thorough and detailed response to the task, one that addresses all the legal and factual issues the drafters intended to raise in the problem. It is intended to serve only as an example. Applicants need not present their responses in the same way to receive good grades. User jurisdictions are free to modify these grading materials, including the suggested weights assigned to particular points. Grading the MPT is the exclusive responsibility of the jurisdiction using the MPT as part of its admissions process.

the benefit of organized sports. Yet, the threat of liability deters many individuals from volunteering. Even if the organization has insurance, individual volunteers could find themselves liable for an injury.

Faced with the threat of lawsuits, and the potential for substantial damage awards, nonprofit organizations and their volunteers could very well decide that the risks are not worth the effort. Hence, invalidation of exculpatory agreements would reduce the number of activities made possible by the services of volunteers and their sponsoring organizations.

Therefore, although when his mother signed the release Bryan gave up his right to sue for the negligent acts of others, the public as a whole received the benefit of these exculpatory agreements. Because of this agreement, the Club can offer affordable recreation without the risks and overwhelming costs of litigation. Bryan's parents agreed to shoulder the risk. Accordingly, we believe that it is in the public interest that parents have authority to enter into these types of binding agreements on behalf of their minor children. We also believe that the enforcement of these agreements may promote more active involvement by participants and their families, which, in turn, promotes the overall quality and safety of these activities.

A related concern is the importance of parental authority. Parents have a fundamental liberty interest in the care, custody, and management of their offspring.

Parental authority extends to the ability to make decisions regarding the child's school, religion, medical care, and discipline. Invalidating the release as to the minor's claim is inconsistent with parents' authority to make important life choices for their children.

Mrs. Holum signed the release because she wanted Bryan to play soccer. In making this family decision, she assumed the risk of physical injury on behalf of Bryan and the financial risk on behalf of the family as a whole. Apparently, she determined that the benefits to her child outweighed the risk of physical injury. The situation is comparable to Columbia Stat. § 2317, which gives parents the authority to consent to medical procedures on a child's behalf. In both cases, the parent weighs the risks of physical injury to the child and its attendant costs against the benefits of a particular activity.

Therefore, we hold that parents have the authority to bind their minor children to exculpatory agreements in favor of volunteers and sponsors of nonprofit sport activities where the cause of action sounds in negligence. These agreements may not be disaffirmed by the child on whose behalf they were executed. We need not decide here whether there are other circumstances, beyond the realm of nonprofit organizations, which will support a parent's waiver of a child's claims.

Accordingly, we hold that the release is valid as to the claims of both the parents and the minor child.

Affirmed in part and reversed in part.

In re Velocity Park

Drafters' Point Sheet

This performance test requires applicants, as associates at a law firm, to analyze the provisions of a liability waiver for a recreational activity. The client, Zeke Oliver, owns Velocity Park, set to be the first skateboarding park in Banford, Franklin, when it opens in April. Zeke has asked the law firm for advice regarding an appropriate liability waiver that users of the skate park will be required to sign in order to use the park.

In analyzing whether the waiver that Zeke provided is enforceable under Franklin law, applicants are expected to address both the waiver's language and its format. Applicants also must grapple with the issue of whether liability waivers signed only by minors will be enforced to bar actions for negligence arising from the minor's skateboarding injuries.

The File contains the task memorandum from the supervising partner, a client interview transcript, a liability waiver Zeke assembled by taking language from a triathlon entry form/liability waiver, and a newspaper article about the risks of skateboarding. The Library includes a Franklin statute regarding civil actions, a Franklin case, and a case from Columbia.

The following discussion covers all of the points the drafters intended to raise in the problem. Applicants need not cover them all to receive passing or even excellent grades. Grading is entirely within the discretion of the user jurisdictions.

I. Format and Overview

Applicants' work product should resemble a legal memorandum such as an associate would write to a supervising partner. Applicants should analyze the waiver Zeke has proposed, identifying problems with its content and design that may preclude it from being found enforceable by a court. Applicants are told not to rewrite the entire waiver. However, if certain language is overbroad or ambiguous, applicants should suggest replacement language that better conforms to the standards set forth in the cases and explain why the changes are necessary for an enforceable waiver. Further, applicants should recognize that the reach of a waiver is tied to the characteristics of the activity (and potential injuries) at issue. Thus they should incorporate the relevant facts from the client interview and the news article in their analysis of the issues. The task memorandum does not require applicants to organize their answers in any particular order, but the order presented below is a logical manner in which to address the issues.

Applicants should conclude that (1) Zeke's proposed waiver contains significant content and format defects, and (2) while the precise issue has not been addressed by Franklin courts, it is unlikely that a court will enforce an exculpatory contract executed by a minor in this situation.

II. Discussion

In Franklin, a party may use an exculpatory contract to limit its liability exposure, but a court may refuse to enforce such a contract on the grounds that its terms violate public policy. A court considers two factors when determining whether an exculpatory contract is enforceable: whether the waiver of liability language is overly broad and ambiguous and whether the exculpatory clause is conspicuous such that it notifies the signer of the nature and significance of what is being waived. Courts will also consider a third, nondispositive factor: whether there exists a substantial disparity in bargaining power between the parties. *Lund v. Swim World, Inc.* (Franklin Sup. Ct. 2005).

A. Whether the Velocity Park Waiver Is Overly Broad and Ambiguous

Franklin courts construe the language of an exculpatory contract against the party seeking to enforce the contract. *Lund*. To survive a public policy challenge, the exculpatory contract must include a description that "clearly, unambiguously, and unmistakably inform[s] the signer of what is being waived." *Id.* (quoting *Schmidt v. Tyrol Mountain* (Franklin Sup. Ct. 1996)). In *Lund*, the deceased swimmer had signed a waiver in which she agreed "to assume all liability for myself, without regard to fault." The Franklin Supreme Court concluded that, by using only the word "fault," the exculpatory clause was overly broad because it could be construed as waiving any and all claims, even those for the defendant's intentional or reckless acts and omissions.

The key to determining whether the exculpatory language is overly broad is whether the risks that the parties contemplated at the time the waiver was executed can be ascertained. In *Lund*, the court held that the waiver's broad language prevented it from concluding that, at the time Lund signed the waiver, she anticipated the risk of a severe head injury when a sauna bench collapsed under her. Not only did the Swim World waiver refer generally to "fault," it failed to spell out any particular risks for which Lund was waiving the right to sue Swim World.

Here, the Velocity Park waiver fails to satisfy *Lund*'s requirement that exculpatory contracts "clearly, unambiguously, and unmistakably inform the signer of [the rights he or she is waiving]." The relevant paragraphs of the proposed waiver read as follows:

1. I understand and appreciate that participation in a sport carries a risk to me of serious injury and/or death. I voluntarily and knowingly recognize, accept, and assume this risk and hereby forever release, acquit, covenant not to sue, and discharge Velocity Park, its employees, event sponsors, and any third parties from any and all legal liability, including but not limited to all causes of action, claims, damages in law, or remedies in equity of whatever kind I have or which hereafter accrue to me, whether such injuries and/or claims arise from equipment failure, conditions in the park, or any actions of Velocity Park, its employees, third parties, or other skateboarders. Velocity Park is not responsible for any incidental or consequential damages, including, but not limited to, any claims for personal injury, property damage, or emotional distress. This release is binding with respect to my heirs, executors, administrators, and assigns, as well as myself.

2. I have been informed of Velocity Park Rules and agree to abide by them.

1. **The language of the waiver is overbroad.**

   a. Exculpatory clauses are strictly construed against the party seeking to shield itself from liability. *Lund*.

   b. The waiver at issue ostensibly releases Velocity Park from liability "from any and all legal liability, including but not limited to all causes of action, claims, damages in law, or remedies in equity of whatever kind...."

   c. The phrase "any and all legal liability" would presumably cover injuries resulting from intentional and reckless acts, as well as from negligence. As stated in *Lund*, a release that is "so broad as to be interpreted to shift liability for a tortfeasor's conduct under all possible circumstances, including reckless and intentional conduct, and for all possible injuries, will not be upheld."

   - Waivers are not effective to bar liability for intentional acts. *See Lund* (citing Restatement (Second) § 195(1)).

   - The word "negligence" need not appear in a waiver for it to be enforceable, but the better practice is to clearly state that by signing the waiver, the party is releasing others from negligence claims. *Lund*, fn.2.

In re Velocity Park

Drafters' Point Sheet

This performance test requires applicants, as associates at a law firm, to analyze the provisions of a liability waiver for a recreational activity. The client, Zeke Oliver, owns Velocity Park, set to be the first skateboarding park in Banford, Franklin, when it opens in April. Zeke has asked the law firm for advice regarding an appropriate liability waiver that users of the skate park will be required to sign in order to use the park.

In analyzing whether the waiver that Zeke provided is enforceable under Franklin law, applicants are expected to address both the waiver's language and its format. Applicants also must grapple with the issue of whether liability waivers signed only by minors will be enforced to bar actions for negligence arising from the minor's skateboarding injuries.

The File contains the task memorandum from the supervising partner, a client interview transcript, a liability waiver Zeke assembled by taking language from a triathlon entry form/liability waiver, and a newspaper article about the risks of skateboarding. The Library includes a Franklin statute regarding civil actions, a Franklin case, and a case from Columbia.

The following discussion covers all of the points the drafters intended to raise in the problem. Applicants need not cover them all to receive passing or even excellent grades. Grading is entirely within the discretion of the user jurisdictions.

I. Format and Overview

Applicants' work product should resemble a legal memorandum such as an associate would write to a supervising partner. Applicants should analyze the waiver Zeke has proposed, identifying problems with its content and design that may preclude it from being found enforceable by a court. Applicants are told not to rewrite the entire waiver. However, if certain language is overbroad or ambiguous, applicants should suggest replacement language that better conforms to the standards set forth in the cases and explain why the changes are necessary for an enforceable waiver. Further, applicants should recognize that the reach of a waiver is tied to the characteristics of the activity (and potential injuries) at issue. Thus they should incorporate the relevant facts from the client interview and the news article in their analysis of the issues. The task memorandum does not require applicants to organize their answers in any particular order, but the order presented below is a logical manner in which to address the issues.

Applicants should conclude that (1) Zeke's proposed waiver contains significant content and format defects, and (2) while the precise issue has not been addressed by Franklin courts, it is unlikely that a court will enforce an exculpatory contract executed by a minor in this situation.

II. Discussion

In Franklin, a party may use an exculpatory contract to limit its liability exposure, but a court may refuse to enforce such a contract on the grounds that its terms violate public policy. A court considers two factors when determining whether an exculpatory contract is enforceable: whether the waiver of liability language is overly broad and ambiguous and whether the exculpatory clause is conspicuous such that it notifies the signer of the nature and significance of what is being waived. Courts will also consider a third, nondispositive factor: whether there exists a substantial disparity in bargaining power between the parties. *Lund v. Swim World, Inc.* (Franklin Sup. Ct. 2005).

A. Whether the Velocity Park Waiver Is Overly Broad and Ambiguous

Franklin courts construe the language of an exculpatory contract against the party seeking to enforce the contract. *Lund.* To survive a public policy challenge, the exculpatory contract must include a description that "clearly, unambiguously, and unmistakably inform[s] the signer of what is being waived." *Id.* (quoting *Schmidt v. Tyrol Mountain* (Franklin Sup. Ct. 1996)). In *Lund,* the deceased swimmer had signed a waiver in which she agreed "to assume all liability for myself, without regard to fault." The Franklin Supreme Court concluded that, by using only the word "fault," the exculpatory clause was overly broad because it could be construed as waiving any and all claims, even those for the defendant's intentional or reckless acts and omissions.

The key to determining whether the exculpatory language is overly broad is whether the risks that the parties contemplated at the time the waiver was executed can be ascertained. In *Lund,* the court held that the waiver's broad language prevented it from concluding that, at the time Lund signed the waiver, she anticipated the risk of a severe head injury when a sauna bench collapsed under her. Nor only did the Swim World waiver refer generally to "fault," it failed to spell out any particular risks for which Lund was waiving the right to sue Swim World.

Here, the Velocity Park waiver fails to satisfy *Lund's* requirement that exculpatory contracts "clearly, unambiguously, and unmistakably inform the signer of [the rights he or she is waiving]." The relevant paragraphs of the proposed waiver read as follows:

1. I understand and appreciate that participation in a sport carries a risk to me of serious injury and/or death. I voluntarily and knowingly recognize, accept, and assume this risk and hereby forever release, acquit, covenant not to sue, and discharge Velocity Park, its employees, event sponsors, and any third parties from any and all legal liability, including but not limited to all causes of action, claims, damages in law, or remedies in equity of whatever kind I have or which hereafter accrue to me, whether such injuries and/or claims arise from equipment failure, conditions in the park, or any actions of Velocity Park, its employees, third parties, or other skateboarders. Velocity Park is not responsible for any incidental or consequential damages, including, but not limited to, any claims for personal injury, property damage, or emotional distress. This release is binding with respect to my heirs, executors, administrators, and assigns, as well as myself.

2. I have been informed of Velocity Park Rules and agree to abide by them.

1. **The language of the waiver is overbroad.**

   a. Exculpatory clauses are strictly construed against the party seeking to shield itself from liability. *Lund.*

   b. The waiver at issue ostensibly releases Velocity Park from liability "from any and all legal liability, including but not limited to all causes of action, claims, damages in law, or remedies in equity of whatever kind...."

   c. The phrase "any and all legal liability" would presumably cover injuries resulting from intentional and reckless acts, as well as from negligence. As stated in *Lund,* a release that is "so broad as to be interpreted to shift liability for a tortfeasor's conduct under all possible circumstances, including reckless and intentional conduct, and for all possible injuries, will not be upheld."

   • Waivers are not effective to bar liability for intentional acts. *See Lund* (citing Restatement of Contracts (Second) § 195(1)).

   • The word "negligence" need not appear in a waiver for it to be enforceable, but the better practice is to clearly state that by signing the waiver, the party is releasing others from negligence claims. *Lund,* fn.2.

d. Thus, *Zeke's* waiver is too broad to inform a skateboarder of the precise rights waived.

e. Further, the waiver attempts to be a release of claims against not only Velocity Park and its employees, but also against "any third parties."

- This attempt to extend the waiver to unknown third parties is most likely unenforceable under *Lund.*

f. The exculpatory clause also contains repetitive and confusing language (e.g., "[I] hereby forever release, acquit, covenant not to sue, and discharge Velocity Park…"), making it more likely that the average skateboarder at the park—according to Zeke, most Velocity Park visitors will be teenagers and young adults—will not carefully read or understand the agreement before signing it.

2. **The waiver fails to alert the signer to the risks involved in skateboarding.**

a. Overbroad and general exculpatory agreements will be construed to bar only those claims that the parties contemplated when they executed the contract. *Lund.* A waiver that only vaguely refers to the activity at issue will not be deemed sufficient to inform the signer of the risks of the activity and the rights being waived. In *Schmidt v. Tyrol Mountain,* cited in *Lund,* a waiver's reference to the "inherent risks in skiing" was insufficient to inform the skier of the risks she was assuming.

b. The Velocity Park waiver states that the signer "understand[s] and appreciate[s] that participation in a sport carries a risk to me of serious injury and/or death."

- This language is even more vague than the language in *Schmidt* ("the inherent risks in skiing"); it gives no information to the signer about particular risks associated with skateboarding.

c. Thus the waiver should be revised to include language expressly informing the signer of specific skateboarding injury risks and possible causes.

- *The Banford Courier* article states that the most common skateboarding injuries are wrist sprains and fractures, but serious head injuries may also occur.

d. Applicants could redraft the Velocity Park waiver as follows: "I understand and appreciate that skateboarding carries a risk to me of injury from falls or collisions with objects or other skateboarders, including but not limited to bruises, abrasions, sprains and fractures (especially to the wrist), and head injuries, and that these injuries could be severe or even result in substantial disability or death."

- A revised waiver could also mention something to the effect that using the half-pipes, jumps, etc., increases the risk of harm to the skateboarder.
- A thorough waiver might also state that falls are likely due to debris on or irregularities in the riding surface (thus insulating Velocity Park for claims based on a skater falling because he or she ran over a piece of trash).

e. The waiver also should clearly and expressly convey the risks of skateboarding in a park with other skateboarders.

f. Applicants might note that many park users will be teenagers, so the language of the waiver should use terms understandable to someone of a relatively young age, even if the form will have to be signed by parents (*see* discussion *infra* II.D.).

g. Moreover, given the rise in injuries associated with aggressive behavior in skateboarders (e.g., risky stunts, fights), the waiver should include language denying liability for injuries caused by Velocity Park's negligent failure to supervise skateboarders.

h. Applicants could also note that there are other injuries that even a well-drafted waiver may not cover because they were not within the parties' contemplation when the waiver was executed. (For example, a skateboarder gets food poisoning from a hot dog sold by the Velocity Park concession stand.)

B. Whether the Velocity Park Waiver Is Conspicuous

Second, a liability waiver must "alert the signer to the nature and significance of what is being signed." *Lund.* The exculpatory clause must be conspicuous to the signer; its format must visually communicate that the waiver language is important.[3] In *Lund,* the court noted that documents that serve two purposes generally are not sufficiently conspicuous, especially when there is only a single signature line, because the importance of the exculpatory clause may not be clearly distinguishable from the rest of the document. Further, the exculpatory clause in *Lund* was not conspicuous because it was in the same size, font, and color as the rest of the form.

1. *Lund* provides specific examples of how a dual-purpose document may be improved.
   a. The waiver could be a separate document.
   b. There could be a separate signature line for the exculpatory clause.

2. *Zeke's* form serves many purposes and the exculpatory clause is not conspicuous.
   a. The form contains information on park hours, prices, and rules. It also has paragraphs whereby the skateboarder agrees to waive liability, consents to the use of his or her likeness, authorizes medical treatment, provides emergency contact information, and agrees to receive park e-mails.
   b. There are headings for the sections regarding fees, hours, and park rules, but there is no heading for the exculpatory clause or the medical care and use of likeness paragraphs (although these paragraphs are numbered).
   c. The exculpatory clause is in a *smaller* font than is the first part of the form.
   d. There is only one signature line; arguably, the exculpatory clause, consent to medical treatment, and use of likeness parts warrant separate signatures.
   e. The clause does not have any language to the effect of "I have read this form and understand that by signing it I am waiving important rights." (Even the waiver in *Lund* contains the sentence "I have read the foregoing and understand its contents.") Adding such language would emphasize to the skateboarder the nature and significance of the waiver.

C. Whether There Is a Disparity in Bargaining Power Between the Parties

The third public policy factor addressed in *Lund* is the question of whether there is a substantial disparity in bargaining power between the parties. In making this determination, the court will consider "the facts surrounding the execution of the waiver," including whether the signer has an opportunity to negotiate its terms. *Lund.*

1. In *Lund,* there was no opportunity to negotiate the waiver's terms; Lund either signed or didn't swim.
2. The Swim World employee did not alert Lund that the entrance form included a liability waiver, let alone explain its terms to her.
3. The court also noted that there was not enough time to read Swim World's form and make a reasoned decision about the consequences of signing it, because there were other Swim World patrons waiting in line to check in.
4. The court concluded that, at a minimum, there was a genuine dispute of material fact regarding the parties' disparity in bargaining power.

---

[3] Applicants are not expected to redraft the entire waiver or attempt to recreate it in a better format in their answer books (e.g., by redrafting the waiver language using a larger font). However, as directed by the task memo, they should suggest changes that should be incorporated into the waiver's design and layout.

Task C:

Organizing a Legal Memo Where the Work Product Requires Analyzing Relationships between Case Law and Codes:

Phoenix Corporation

v.

Biogenesis, Inc.

FILE

FORBES, BURDICK & WASHINGTON LLP
777 Fifth Avenue
Lakewood City, Franklin 33905

<u>MEMORANDUM</u>

To:	Applicant
From:	Ann Buckner
Date:	February 24, 2009
Subject:	*Phoenix Corporation v. Biogenesis, Inc.*

Yesterday, we were retained by the law firm of Amberg & Lewis LLP to consult on a motion for disqualification filed against it.

Amberg & Lewis represents Biogenesis, Inc., in a breach-of-contract action brought by Phoenix Corporation seeking $80 million in damages. The lawsuit has been winding its way through state court for almost six years. Phoenix is represented by the Collins Law Firm. There have been extensive discovery, motion practice, and several interlocutory appeals over the years, but the matter is now set for jury trial in a month and is expected to last six weeks. Two weeks ago, however, Phoenix filed a disqualification motion after Amberg & Lewis obtained one of Phoenix's attorney–client privileged documents—a letter from Phoenix's former president to one of its attorneys. Yesterday, I interviewed Carole Ravel, an Amberg & Lewis partner. During the interview, I learned some background facts; I also obtained a copy of the letter and Phoenix's brief in support of its disqualification motion.

Please prepare a memorandum evaluating the merits of Phoenix's argument for Amberg & Lewis's disqualification, bringing to bear the applicable legal authorities and the relevant facts as described to me by Ms. Ravel. Do not draft a separate statement of facts, but instead use the facts as appropriate in conducting your evaluation.

TRANSCRIPT OF CLIENT INTERVIEW
February 23, 2009

Buckner: Good to see you, Carole.

Ravel: Good to see you too, Ann. Thanks for seeing me on such short notice.

Buckner: My pleasure. What's the problem?

Ravel: The problem is a motion for disqualification. Here's the supporting brief.

Buckner: Thanks. Let me take a quick look. I'm unacquainted with the science, but the law is familiar. How can I help?

Ravel: To be candid, we've made a few mistakes, and I thought it would be prudent to consult with someone like you with substantial experience in representing lawyers in professional liability and ethics matters.

Buckner: Tell me what happened.

Ravel: Sure. Six years ago, Phoenix Corporation sued Biogenesis for breach of contract in state court, seeking about $80 million in damages. Phoenix is a medical research company; Biogenesis is one of the largest biotechnology companies in the world. Phoenix claims that Biogenesis breached a contract they entered into in 1978. There's a lot about this case that's enormously complicated and technical—all that science that you said you're unacquainted with—but the dispute is fairly simple. Under the agreement, Phoenix granted a license to Biogenesis to use a process that Phoenix invented for genetically engineering human proteins. In exchange, Biogenesis was obliged to pay Phoenix royalties on sales of certain categories of pharmaceuticals that were made using the licensed engineering process. Here is the dispute: While Biogenesis has taken the position that its royalty obligation is limited to the categories of pharmaceuticals specified, Phoenix claims that it extends to other categories of pharmaceuticals as well. If the jury agrees with Biogenesis, it owes nothing more. If the jury agrees with Phoenix, Biogenesis owes about $80 million beyond what it has already paid in royalties.

Ravel: Right. The factual background and procedural history set out in the brief are accurate—but of course we disagree with Phoenix's argument about Biogenesis's royalty obligation.

Buckner: Fine. But what about this Phoenix letter that's allegedly protected by the attorney-client privilege?

Ravel: Here it is, a letter to Peter Horvitz, a Collins partner, from Gordon Schetina, who was then Phoenix's president.

Buckner: Thanks. It certainly looks privileged.

Ravel: It is. I can't deny it. But it's important. Let me go back to the 1978 agreement. Discovery in Phoenix's breach-of-contract action has established to our satisfaction that, by their conduct from 1978 to 1998, Biogenesis and Phoenix revealed that they understood that Biogenesis's royalty obligation was limited to the categories of pharmaceuticals specified in the agreement. During that period, Biogenesis made a lot of money and paid Phoenix a great deal in royalties. It was only in 1998 that Phoenix began to claim that Biogenesis's royalty obligation extended to other categories of pharmaceuticals—when it saw how much more in royalties it could obtain and became greedy to get them.

Buckner: And the Schetina letter...

Ravel: And the Schetina letter amounts to an admission by Phoenix that Biogenesis was correct in its understanding of its limited royalty obligation.

Buckner: So how did you get it?

Ravel: Phoenix's lawyers assume that the Schetina letter was disclosed to us inadvertently during discovery, but they're wrong. The letter arrived on February 2, 2009, by itself, in an envelope with the Collins Law Firm's return address. My assistant opened the envelope and discovered the letter all by itself, with a note reading "From a 'friend' at the Collins Law Firm."

Buckner: Do you know who the "friend" was?

Ravel: No. But it's not hard to guess. Collins is in the process of laying off staff in an effort to increase profits. The letter was obviously sent by a disgruntled employee.

Buckner: That makes sense. But what happened next?

Ravel: When the letter arrived, my team and I were in full trial-preparation mode. Of course, I recognized that the letter appeared privileged on its face; it's a classic confidential communication from a client to an attorney. In our eyes, the letter was a smoking gun. It made our case and we wanted to use it.

Buckner: So what happened?

Ravel: We were pretty sure that we were within the ethical rules. But that same day, two of the associates on my team went out for lunch. As they were discussing the impact of the Schetina letter in what turned out to be too much detail, a man at a neighboring table asked whether they knew who he was. They said no, and the man said he was Peter Horvitz and stormed out. Horvitz called me within minutes, and he was furious. He demanded return of the letter and I refused. A few days later, he filed the disqualification motion.

Buckner: I see. And precisely what is it you'd like us to do for you?

Ravel: Ann, I'd like you to evaluate the merits of Phoenix's argument that we should be disqualified. Trial is only a month away, and Biogenesis would have to incur tremendous costs if it were forced to substitute new attorneys if we were disqualified. And let's be candid, we've been charged with a violation of an ethical obligation and might face some exposure as a consequence.

Buckner: I understand, Carole. Let me do some research, and I'll get back to you.

Ravel: Thanks so much.

IN THE DISTRICT COURT OF THE STATE OF FRANKLIN
FOR THE COUNTY OF LANCASTER

PHOENIX CORPORATION,)	No. Civ. 041033
Plaintiff,)	
)	PLAINTIFF'S BRIEF IN SUPPORT OF
v.)	MOTION TO DISQUALIFY COUNSEL
)	FOR DEFENDANT
BIOGENESIS, INC.,)	
Defendant.)	

I. Introduction

The rule governing this motion is plain: A trial court may—and, indeed, must—disqualify an attorney who has violated an ethical obligation by his or her handling of an opposing party's attorney-client privileged material and has thereby threatened that party with incurable prejudice. Just as plain is the result that the rule compels here: Defendant's attorneys obtained one of plaintiff's attorney-client privileged documents evidently by inadvertent disclosure. In violation of their ethical obligation, they chose to examine the document, failed to notify plaintiff's attorneys, and then refused to return the document at the latter's demand. By acting as they did, they have threatened plaintiff with incurable prejudice. Since this Court cannot otherwise prevent this prejudice, it must disqualify them to guarantee plaintiff a fair trial.

II. Factual Background and Procedural History

In 1977, Phoenix Corporation, a medical research company, invented a process for genetically engineering human proteins—a process essential to the development of entirely new categories of pharmaceuticals capable of managing or curing the most serious conditions and diseases afflicting human beings, including diabetes and cancer.

In 1978, Phoenix entered into an agreement with Biogenesis, Inc., one of the pioneers in the field of biotechnology: Phoenix licensed its invention to Biogenesis, and Biogenesis obligated itself to pay Phoenix royalties on its sales of various categories of pharmaceuticals.

Between 1979 and 1997, Biogenesis produced dozens of pharmaceuticals and generated billions of dollars in revenue as a result of their sale. To be sure, Biogenesis paid Phoenix substantial royalties—but, as it turns out, far less than it was obligated to.

In 1998, Phoenix learned that Biogenesis had not been paying royalties on its sales of all the categories of pharmaceuticals in question, but only categories specified in the 1978 agreement. For the first time, Biogenesis stated its position that the agreement so limited its obligation. Phoenix rejected any such limitation.

Between 1999 and 2002, Phoenix attempted to resolve its dispute with Biogenesis. Each and every one of its efforts, however, proved unsuccessful.

In 2003, Phoenix brought this action against Biogenesis for breach of the 1978 agreement, seeking $80 million in damages for royalties Biogenesis owed but failed to pay. Between 2003 and 2009, Phoenix and Biogenesis have been engaged in extensive discovery and motion practice and in several interlocutory appeals as they have prepared for a jury trial, set to begin on March 30, 2009, and expected to last six weeks.

PHOENIX CORPORATION
1500 Rosa Road
Lakewood City, Franklin 33905

January 2, 1998

CONFIDENTIAL

Peter Horvitz, Esq.
Collins Law Firm
9700 Laurel Boulevard
Lakewood City, Franklin 33905

Dear Peter:

I am writing with some questions I'd like you to consider before our meeting next Tuesday so that I can get your legal advice on a matter I think is important. I have always understood our agreement with Biogenesis to require it to pay royalties on specified categories of pharmaceuticals. I learned recently how much money Biogenesis is making from other categories of pharmaceuticals. Why can't we get a share of that? Can't we interpret the agreement to require Biogenesis to pay royalties on other categories, not only the specified ones? Let me know your thoughts when we meet.

Very truly yours,

Gordon Schetina

Gordon Schetina
President

On February 2, 2009, Phoenix learned, fortuitously, that Biogenesis's attorneys, Amberg & Lewis LLP, had obtained a document evidently through inadvertent disclosure by Phoenix's attorneys, the Collins Law Firm, in the course of discovery.

On its face, the document showed itself to be protected by the attorney-client privilege, reflecting a confidential communication from Phoenix, by its then president Gordon Schetina, to one of its attorneys, Peter Horvitz, seeking legal advice, and clearly the document was not intended for the Amberg firm. Nevertheless, the Amberg firm failed to notify Collins about its receipt of the Schetina letter. As soon as it learned what had transpired, Collins instructed the Amberg firm to return the letter, but the Amberg firm refused.

III. Argument

A. This Court Should Disqualify Amberg & Lewis from Representing Biogenesis Because It Has Violated an Ethical Obligation Threatening Phoenix with Incurable Prejudice in Its Handling of Phoenix's Attorney-Client Privileged Document.

The law applicable to Phoenix's motion to disqualify Amberg & Lewis from representing Biogenesis in this action is clear.

A trial court may, in the exercise of its inherent power, disqualify an attorney in the interests of justice. *Indigo v. Luna Motors Corp.* (Fr. Ct. App. 1998). The court may—and, indeed, must—disqualify an attorney who has violated an ethical obligation by his or her handling of an opposing party's attorney-client privileged material and has thereby threatened that party with incurable prejudice. *Id.* Although the party represented by the disqualified attorney may be said to enjoy an "important right" to representation by an attorney of its own choosing, any such "right" "must yield to ethical considerations that affect the fundamental principles of our judicial process." *Id.* As the court said, "The paramount concern, however, must be to preserve public trust in the scrupulous administration of justice and the integrity of the bar." *Id.*

As will be demonstrated, the law compels the disqualification of Amberg & Lewis.

1. Phoenix's Document Is Protected by the Attorney-Client Privilege.

To begin with, the Schetina letter is protected by the attorney-client privilege. Under Franklin Evidence Code § 954, the "client...has a privilege to refuse to disclose, and to prevent another from disclosing, a confidential communication between client and attorney...." On its face, the Schetina letter reflects a confidential communication from Phoenix's then president, Schetina, to one of its attorneys, Horvitz, seeking legal advice.

2. Amberg & Lewis Has Violated an Ethical Obligation.

Next, Amberg & Lewis has violated an ethical obligation by handling the Schetina letter as it did. In the face of the inadvertent disclosure of attorney-client privileged material, such as evidently occurred in this case, the ethical obligation is plain under Franklin Rule of Professional Conduct 4.4: "An attorney who receives a document relating to the representation of the attorney's client and knows or reasonably should know that the document was inadvertently sent shall promptly notify the sender."

Because on its face the Schetina letter reflects a confidential communication from Phoenix's then president, Schetina, to its attorney, Horvitz, seeking legal advice, and is therefore protected by the attorney-client privilege, Amberg & Lewis should surely have known that the letter was not intended for it. The Amberg firm was at the very least obligated to notify Collins that it had received the letter. It should also have refrained from examining the letter, and should have abided by our instructions. On each point, the Amberg firm acted to the contrary, choosing to examine the letter, failing to notify Collins, and then refusing to return it at Collins's demand.

Even if it should turn out that Amberg & Lewis obtained the Schetina letter as a result of unauthorized disclosure as opposed to inadvertent disclosure, the outcome would be the same. In *Mead v. Conley Machinery Co.* (Fr. Ct. App. 1999) the Court of Appeal imposed an ethical obligation similar to that of Rule 4.4 to govern cases of unauthorized disclosure. It follows that the misconduct of the Amberg firm, as described above, would amount to an ethical violation if the letter's disclosure were unauthorized and not inadvertent.

3. Amberg & Lewis Has Threatened Phoenix with Incurable Prejudice.

Finally, by its unethical actions, Amberg & Lewis has threatened Phoenix with incurable prejudice. The Schetina letter could well prejudice the jury in the midst of a long and complex trial, especially if it were cleverly exploited by Biogenesis. Whether or not any *direct* harm could be prevented by the exclusion of the letter from evidence—which Phoenix intends to seek in the coming days—the *indirect* harm that might arise from its use in trial preparation cannot be dealt with so simply: The bell has been rung, and can hardly be unrung, except by disqualification of Amberg & Lewis—an action that is necessary in order to guarantee Phoenix a fair trial.

Even if it should turn out that Amberg & Lewis obtained the Schetina letter by *unauthorized* disclosure as opposed to *inadvertent* disclosure, the result would not change. It is true that in *Mead v. Conley Machinery Co.*, the Court of Appeal suggested in a footnote that, in cases of unauthorized disclosure, the "threat of 'incurable prejudice'...is neither a necessary nor a sufficient condition for disqualification." But that suggestion is mere dictum, inasmuch as *Mead* did not involve the threat of *any* prejudice, incurable or otherwise.

IV. Conclusion

For the reasons stated above, this Court should grant Phoenix's motion and disqualify Amberg & Lewis from representing Biogenesis in this action.

Respectfully submitted,

Kimberly Block

Kimberly Block
COLLINS LAW FIRM LLP
Attorneys for Plaintiff Phoenix Corporation

Date: February 9, 2009

LIBRARY

Rule 4.4 of the Franklin Rules of Professional Conduct

Rule 4.4. Inadvertent disclosure of attorney-client document

An attorney who receives a document relating to the representation of the attorney's client and knows or reasonably should know that the document was inadvertently sent shall promptly notify the sender.

HISTORY

Adopted by the Franklin Supreme Court, effective July 1, 2002.

COMMENT

[1] Rule 4.4, which was adopted by the Franklin Supreme Court in 2002 in response to *Indigo v. Luna Motors Corp.* (Fr. Ct. App. 1998), recognizes that attorneys sometimes receive documents that were mistakenly sent or produced by opposing parties or their attorneys. If an attorney knows or reasonably should know that such a document was sent inadvertently, then this rule requires the attorney, whether or not the document is protected by the attorney-client privilege, to promptly notify the sender in order to permit that person to take protective measures.

[2] Rule 4.4 provides that if an attorney receives a document the attorney should know was sent inadvertently, he or she must promptly notify the sender, but need do no more. *Indigo v. Luna Motors Corp.*, which predated this rule, concluded that the receiving attorney not only had to notify the sender (as this rule would later require), albeit only as to a document protected by the attorney-client privilege, but also had to resist the temptation to examine the document, and had to await the sender's instructions about what to do. In so concluding, *Indigo v. Luna Motors Corp.* conflicted with this rule and, ultimately, with the intent of the Franklin Supreme Court in adopting it.

[3] Rule 4.4 does not address an attorney's receipt of a document sent without authorization, as was the case in *Mead v. Conley Machinery Co.* (Fr. Ct. App. 1999). Neither does any other rule. *Mead v. Conley Machinery Co.*, which also predated this rule, concluded that the receiving attorney should review the document—there, an attorney-client privileged document—only to the extent necessary to determine how to proceed, notify the opposing attorney, and either abide by the opposing attorney's instructions or refrain from using the document until a court disposed of the matter. The Franklin Supreme Court, however, has declined to adopt a rule imposing any ethical obligation in cases of unauthorized disclosure.

Indigo v. Luna Motors Corp.

Franklin Court of Appeal (1998)

The issue in this permissible interlocutory appeal is whether the trial court abused its discretion by disqualifying plaintiff's attorney for improper use of attorney-client privileged documents disclosed to her inadvertently. We hold that it did not. Accordingly, we affirm.

I

Plaintiff Ferdinand Indigo sued Luna Motors Corporation for damages after he sustained serious injuries when his Luna sport utility vehicle rolled over as he was driving.

In the course of routine document production, Luna's attorney's paralegal inadvertently gave Joyce Corrigan, Indigo's attorney, a document drafted by Luna's attorney and memorializing a conference between the attorney and a high-ranking Luna executive, Raymond Fogel, stamped "attorney-client privileged," in which they discussed the strengths and weaknesses of Luna's technical evidence. As soon as Corrigan received the document, which is referred to as the "technical evidence document," she examined it closely; as a result, she knew that it had been given to her inadvertently. Notwithstanding her knowledge, she failed to notify Luna's attorney. She subsequently used the document for impeachment purposes during Fogel's deposition, eliciting damaging admissions. Luna's attorney objected to Corrigan's use of the document, accused her of invading the attorney-client privilege, and demanded the document's return, but Corrigan refused.

In response, Luna filed a motion to disqualify Corrigan. After a hearing, the trial court granted the motion. The court determined that the technical evidence document was protected by the attorney-client privilege, that Corrigan violated her ethical obligation by handling it as she did, and that disqualification was the appropriate remedy. Indigo appealed.

II

It has long been settled in Franklin that a trial court may, in the exercise of its inherent power, disqualify an attorney in the interests of justice. *See, e.g., In re Klem* (Fr. Ct. App. 1947). Ultimately, disqualification involves a conflict between a client's right to an attorney of his or her choice and the need to maintain ethical standards of professional responsibility. The paramount concern, however, must be to preserve public trust in the scrupulous administration of justice and the integrity of the bar. The important right to an attorney of one's choice must yield to ethical considerations that affect the fundamental principles of our judicial process.

Appellate courts review a trial court's ruling on disqualification for abuse of discretion. A court abuses its discretion when it acts arbitrarily or without reason. As will appear, we discern no arbitrary or unreasonable action here.

A

Indigo's first claim is that the trial court erred in determining that Corrigan violated an ethical obligation by handling the technical evidence document as she did.

From the Franklin Rules of Professional Conduct and related case law, we derive the following, albeit implicit, standard: An attorney who receives materials that on their face appear to be subject to the attorney-client privilege, under circumstances in which it is clear they were not intended for the receiving attorney, should refrain from examining the materials, notify the sending attorney, and await the instructions of the attorney who sent them.

Mead v. Conley Machinery Co.

Franklin Court of Appeal (1999)

The issue in this permissible interlocutory appeal is whether the trial court abused its discretion by disqualifying plaintiff's attorney on the ground that the attorney improperly used attorney-client privileged documents disclosed to him without authorization. *Cf. Indigo v. Luna Motors Corp.* (Fr. Ct. App. 1998) (inadvertent disclosure). We hold that it did and reverse.

I

Dolores Mead, a former financial consultant for Conley Machinery Company, sued Conley for breach of contract. Without authorization, she obtained attorney-client privileged documents belonging to Conley and gave them to her attorney, William Masterson, who used them in deposing Conley's president over Conley's objection.

Conley immediately moved to disqualify Masterson. After an evidentiary hearing, the trial court granted the motion. Mead appealed.

II

In determining whether the trial court abused its discretion by disqualifying Masterson, we ask whether it acted arbitrarily or without reason. *Indigo.*

III

At the threshold, Mead argues that the trial court had no authority to disqualify Masterson because he did not violate any specific rule among the Franklin Rules of Professional Conduct. It is true that Masterson did not violate any specific rule—but it is *not* true that the court was without authority to disqualify him. With or without a violation of a specific rule, a court may, in the exercise of its inherent power, disqualify an attorney in the interests of justice, including where necessary to guarantee a fair trial. *Indigo.*

IV

Without doubt, there are situations in which an attorney who has been privy to his or her adversary's privileged documents without authorization must be disqualified, even though the attorney was not involved in obtaining the documents. By protecting attorney-client communications, the attorney-client privilege encourages parties to fully develop cases for trial, increasing the chances of an informed and correct resolution.

To safeguard the attorney-client privilege and the litigation process itself, we believe that the following standard must govern: An attorney who receives, on an unauthorized basis, materials of an adverse party that he or she knows to be attorney-client privileged should, upon recognizing the privileged nature of the materials, either refrain from reviewing such materials or review them only to the extent required to determine how to proceed; he or she should notify the adversary's attorney that he or she has such materials and should either follow instructions from the adversary's attorney with respect to the disposition of the materials or refrain from using the materials until a definitive resolution of the proper disposition of the materials is obtained from a court.

Violation of this standard, however, amounts to only one of the facts and circumstances that a trial court must consider in deciding whether to order disqualification. The court must also consider all of the other relevant facts and circumstances to determine whether the interests of justice require disqualification. Specifically, in the exercise of its discretion, a trial court should consider these factors: (1) the attorney's actual or constructive knowledge of the material's attorney-client privileged status; (2) the promptness with which the attorney notified the opposing side

Under this standard, Corrigan plainly violated an ethical obligation. She received the technical evidence document; the document appeared on its face to be subject to the attorney-client privilege, as it was stamped "attorney-client privileged"; the circumstances were clear that the document was not intended for her; nevertheless, she examined the document, failed to notify Luna's attorney, and refused to return it at the latter's demand.

B

Indigo's second claim is that the trial court erred in determining that disqualification of Corrigan was the appropriate remedy in light of her violation of her ethical obligation.

The trial court concluded that disqualification was necessary to ensure a fair trial. It did not abuse its discretion in doing so.

The trial court predicated Corrigan's disqualification on the threat of incurable prejudice to Luna. Such a threat has long been recognized as a sufficient basis for disqualification. *See, e.g., In re Klein.* We find it more than sufficient here. Corrigan used the technical evidence document during the deposition of Luna executive Fogel, eliciting damaging admissions. Even if Corrigan were prohibited from using the document at trial, she could not effectively be prevented from capitalizing on its contents in preparing for trial and perhaps obtaining evidence of similar force and effect.

III

Indigo's second claim is that the trial court erred in determining that disqualification of Corrigan was the appropriate remedy in light of her violation of her ethical obligation.

The trial court concluded that disqualification was necessary to ensure a fair trial. It did not abuse its discretion in doing so.

Affirmed.

THE MPT

MULTISTATE PERFORMANCE TEST

Phoenix Corporation
v.
Biogenesis, Inc.

POINT SHEET

The MPT point sheet, grading summary, and grading guidelines describe the factual and legal points encompassed within the lawyering task to be completed. They outline all the possible issues and points that might be addressed by an applicant. They are provided to the user jurisdictions for the sole purpose of assisting graders in grading the examination by identifying the issues and suggesting the resolution of the problem contemplated by the drafters. These are not official grading guides. Applicants can receive a range of passing grades, including excellent grades, without covering all the points discussed in these guides. The model answer is included as an illustration of a thorough and detailed response to the task, one that addresses all the legal and factual issues the drafters intended to raise in the problem. It is intended to serve only as an example. Applicants need not present their responses in the same way to receive good grades. User jurisdictions are free to modify these grading materials, including the suggested weights assigned to particular points. Grading the MPT is the exclusive responsibility of the jurisdiction using the MPT as part of its admissions process.

that he or she had received such material; (3) the extent to which the attorney reviewed the material; (4) the significance of the material, i.e., the extent to which its disclosure may prejudice the party moving for disqualification, and the extent to which its return or other measure may prevent or cure that prejudice; (5) the extent to which the party moving for disqualification may be at fault for the unauthorized disclosure; and (6) the extent to which the party opposing disqualification would suffer prejudice from the disqualification of his or her attorney.[1]

Some of these factors weigh in favor of Masterson's disqualification. For example, Masterson should have known after the most cursory review that the documents in question were protected by the attorney-client privilege. Nevertheless, he did not notify Conley upon receiving them. Also, it appears that he thoroughly reviewed them, as he directly referenced specific portions in his response to Conley's disqualification motion. Finally, Conley was not at fault, since Mead copied them covertly.

Other factors, however, weigh against Masterson's disqualification. The information in the documents in question would not significantly prejudice Conley, reflecting little more than a paraphrase of a handful of Mead's allegations. The court may exclude the documents from evidence and thereby prevent any prejudice to Conley—all without disqualifying Masterson. Exclusion would prevent ringing for the jury any bell that could not be unrung. To be sure, it would not erase the documents from Masterson's mind, but any harm arising from their presence in Masterson's memory would be minimal and, indeed, speculative. In contrast, Mead would suffer serious hardship if Masterson were disqualified at this time, after he has determined trial strategy, worked extensively on trial preparation, and readied the matter for trial. In these circumstances, disqualification may confer an enormous, and unmerited, strategic advantage upon Conley.

In conclusion, because the factors against Masterson's disqualification substantially outweigh those in its favor, the trial court abused its discretion in disqualifying him.

Reversed.

[1] In *Indigo v. Luna Motors Corp.*, we recently considered the issue of disqualification in the context of *inadvertent* disclosure of a document protected by the attorney-client privilege as opposed to *unauthorized* disclosure. The analysis set out in the text above renders explicit what was implicit in *Indigo*, and is generally applicable to disqualification for inadvertent disclosure as well as unauthorized disclosure. Although we found the threat of "incurable prejudice" decisive in *Indigo*, it is neither a necessary nor a sufficient condition for disqualification.

P-14

Phoenix Corporation v. Biogenesis, Inc.

Drafters' Point Sheet

About six years ago, Phoenix Corporation, a medical research company represented by the Collins Law Firm, brought a breach-of-contract action in state court seeking about $80 million in damages against Biogenesis, Inc., a biotechnology company represented by Amberg & Lewis LLP. A jury trial is set to begin in a month and is expected to last six weeks. Two weeks ago, however, Phoenix filed a motion to disqualify Amberg & Lewis as Biogenesis's attorneys. Phoenix claims that Amberg & Lewis violated an ethical obligation threatening incurable prejudice through its handling of one of Phoenix's attorney-client privileged documents, which Phoenix assumes was disclosed inadvertently.

Amberg & Lewis has retained applicants' law firm to consult on the motion for disqualification. Applicants' task is to prepare an objective memorandum evaluating the merits of Phoenix's argument to disqualify.

The File contains the following materials: a memorandum from the supervising attorney describing the assignment (task memo), the transcript of the client interview, the document that is the subject of the disqualification motion, and Phoenix's brief in support of its motion for disqualification. The Library contains Rule 4.4 of the Franklin Rules of Professional Conduct and two cases bearing on the subject.

The following discussion covers all of the points the drafters intended to raise in the problem. Applicants need not cover them all to receive passing or even excellent grades. Grading is left entirely to the discretion of the user jurisdictions.

I. Overview

Applicants are given a general call: "Please prepare a memorandum evaluating the merits of Phoenix's argument for Amberg & Lewis's disqualification...." To complete the assignment, applicants should identify and discuss two key issues: (1) whether Amberg & Lewis has violated the rules of professional conduct, and (2) whether disqualification is indeed the appropriate remedy on the facts as given.

There is no specific format for the assigned task. Applicants' work product should resemble a legal memorandum such as one an associate would draft for a supervising partner. Applicants may choose to follow the lead of Phoenix's motion to disqualify and organize their answer in response to each of the issues raised in Phoenix's supporting brief. However, it should be an objective memorandum; applicants who draft a memorandum that is persuasive in tone have not followed instructions (jurisdictions may want to consider whether points should be deducted from such papers). The task memorandum instructs applicants not to draft a statement of facts but to be sure to incorporate the relevant facts into their discussions.

Applicants should conclude that even if Amberg & Lewis has violated an ethical obligation (and it is not at all clear that it has), disqualification is not the appropriate remedy in this case.

II. Detailed Analysis

These are the key points that applicants should discuss, taking care to incorporate the relevant facts and explain and/or distinguish the applicable case law, in an objective memorandum evaluating the merits of Phoenix's argument to disqualify Amberg & Lewis:

P-15

As a preliminary matter, applicants should set forth the basis for why the Schetina letter may trigger disqualification under the Franklin Rules of Professional Conduct.

- Franklin Evidence Code § 954 provides that a client has a privilege to refuse to disclose, and to prevent another from disclosing, a confidential communication between client and attorney.
- It appears undisputed that the Schetina letter is protected by the attorney-client privilege under § 954.
  - It is a communication, labeled "CONFIDENTIAL," from Phoenix's then president, Schetina, to one of its attorneys, Horvitz.
  - Amberg & Lewis concedes that the letter is privileged.
  - Even if the Schetina letter were not privileged, it relates "to the representation of the attorney's client," which is the standard used in Rule 4.4. In other words, a document does not have to be attorney-client privileged for its handling by opposing counsel to constitute a violation of the Rule.
- In *Indigo v. Luna Motors Corp.* (Fr. Ct. App. 1998), the court affirmed the granting of a motion for disqualification in a case where an attorney inadvertently received privileged materials and did not return them forthwith to opposing counsel.

A. Whether Amberg & Lewis violated its ethical obligation by its handling of the Schetina letter

Applicants should incorporate into their discussion of this issue the following facts surrounding Amberg & Lewis's receipt of the Schetina letter:

- On February 2, 2009, Amberg & Lewis obtained the Schetina letter as a result of the letter's unauthorized disclosure by some unidentified person at the Collins Law Firm, which represents Phoenix. (The letter arrived in an envelope bearing Collins's return address and was accompanied by a note reading "From a 'friend' at the Collins Law Firm.") The letter is dated January 2, 1998, and is labeled "CONFIDENTIAL."[2]
- Amberg & Lewis did not notify Collins of its receipt of the letter.
- Indeed, Amberg & Lewis would like to use the letter in its case against Phoenix—Schetina's statement is essentially an admission that Biogenesis's interpretation of the royalty agreement is the correct one.
- Also on February 2, 2009, Phoenix learned, by chance, that Amberg & Lewis had obtained the Schetina letter, but assumed, incorrectly, that it had done so as a result of inadvertent disclosure by Collins in the course of discovery. Collins instructed Amberg & Lewis to return the letter, but Amberg & Lewis refused.
- In response, Phoenix filed the present motion to disqualify Amberg & Lewis.

Phoenix's argument regarding Amberg & Lewis's handling of the Schetina letter

- In its brief, Phoenix's first argument assumes that the Schetina letter's disclosure was inadvertent and cites Rule 4.4 in support of its position that, at a minimum, Amberg & Lewis was required to "promptly notify the sender" (i.e., the Collins Law Firm) after it received the Schetina letter.

---

[2] The letter states in its entirety: "I am writing with some questions I'd like you to consider before our meeting next Tuesday so that I can get your legal advice on a matter I think is important. I have always understood our agreement with Biogenesis to require it to pay royalties on specified categories of pharmaceuticals. I learned recently how much money Biogenesis is making from other categories of pharmaceuticals. Why can't we get a share of that? Can't we interpret the agreement to require Biogenesis to pay royalties on other categories, not only the specified ones? Let me know your thoughts when we meet."

- If the letter's disclosure was unauthorized, Phoenix contends that *Mead v. Conley Machinery Co.* (Fr. Ct. App. 1999) "imposed an ethical obligation similar to that of Rule 4.4 to govern cases of unauthorized disclosure."
  - Contrary to both Rule 4.4 and *Indigo*, Amberg & Lewis chose to examine the Schetina letter, failed to notify Collins of its receipt, and then refused to return it at Collins's demand.
  - So, either way, whether the disclosure was inadvertent or unauthorized, Phoenix argues that Amberg & Lewis has committed an ethical violation.

Application of Rule 4.4 and relevant case law

Applicants should realize that Phoenix's argument overstates its position and that it is not so clear that Amberg & Lewis has violated the Franklin Rules of Professional Conduct.

- Rule 4.4 provides in its entirety that "[a]n attorney who receives a document relating to the representation of the attorney's client and knows or reasonably should know that the document was inadvertently sent shall promptly notify the sender."
- Thus, under Rule 4.4, an attorney receiving a document disclosed inadvertently need do no more than notify the sender.
- On its face, the text of the rule pertains only to situations involving *inadvertent* disclosure. The comments to Rule 4.4 are very clear on this point. In short, Rule 4.4 does not address the ethical implications for cases of *unauthorized* disclosure of privileged communications.
- Accordingly, Amberg & Lewis's conduct is not forbidden by the plain language of Rule 4.4.

1. *Indigo v. Luna Motors Corp.* is not dispositive.

- In *Indigo*, the plaintiff's attorney received an attorney-client privileged document during document production as a result of inadvertent disclosure. The attorney closely examined the document, which discussed the opposing side's technical evidence, and then used the document at deposition to obtain damaging admissions from the opposing party. Plaintiff's attorney refused opposing counsel's demands to return the document. The court held that this conduct by plaintiff's attorney constituted a violation of an ethical obligation and was grounds for disqualification.
- The *Indigo* court then articulated the following standard for how attorneys should proceed in such situations:
  - An attorney who receives materials that on their face appear to be subject to the attorney-client privilege, under circumstances in which it is clear they were not intended for the receiving attorney, should refrain from examining the materials, notify the sending attorney, and await the instructions of the attorney who sent them.
- The facts of the present case distinguish it from *Indigo*. Here, an unknown Collins employee intentionally sent the Schetina letter to Amberg & Lewis. (Phoenix could not know this, because it is unaware of how Amberg & Lewis came into possession of the Schetina letter.)
  - Presumably, someone at Amberg & Lewis kept the envelope and note that came with the Schetina letter ("From a 'friend' at the Collins Law Firm") and so it can easily prove that the disclosure was unauthorized, as opposed to inadvertent.
- More to the point, in adopting Rule 4.4, the Franklin Supreme Court expressly pulled back from the holding in *Indigo*. *See* Rule 4.4, Comment 2. The Comment explains that when there is an inadvertent disclosure, the attorney "must promptly notify the sender, but need do no more.... *Indigo v. Luna Motors Corp.* conflicted with this rule and, ultimately, with the intent of the Franklin Supreme Court in adopting it."
- Thus, to the extent that it concluded otherwise, *Indigo* conflicts with Rule 4.4 and, ultimately, with the intent of the Franklin Supreme Court in adopting it. Rule 4.4 does not apply to unauthorized disclosure. Notwithstanding *Mead* (discussed below), the Franklin Supreme Court has declined to adopt a rule imposing any ethical obligation in such cases.

2. Application of *Mead*

- In *Mead*, the Franklin Court of Appeal held that an attorney who received privileged documents belonging to an adverse party through an unauthorized disclosure should do the following: "upon recognizing the privileged nature of the materials, either refrain from reviewing such materials or review them only to the extent required to determine how to proceed; he or she should notify the adversary's attorney that he or she has such materials and should either follow instructions from the adversary's attorney with respect to the disposition of the materials, or refrain from using the materials until a definitive resolution of the proper disposition of the materials is obtained from a court."
- But the court goes on to state that violation of this standard, standing alone, does not warrant disqualification.
- So, while *Mead* appears to require Amberg & Lewis to notify the Collins firm that it received the Schetina letter, following the offended law firm's instructions on what to do with the letter is optional—instead, Amberg & Lewis can wait for the court to weigh in on the issue.
  - But, under *Mead*, Amberg & Lewis must still refrain from using the materials until such court resolution is obtained.
- In addition, astute applicants will point out that, while Amberg & Lewis wanted to use the Schetina letter in its case against Phoenix, Phoenix found out that Amberg & Lewis had the Schetina letter the *same day* that Amberg & Lewis received it (when Peter Horvitz, Phoenix's attorney, overheard the associates talking about the letter at lunch). Arguably, Amberg & Lewis could have notified the Collins firm that it had received the letter, if not for the fact that Horvitz found out about it before Amberg & Lewis had a chance to tell him.
- Again, applicants should note that *Mead* was decided in 1999, before the Franklin Supreme Court enacted Rule 4.4 in 2002. It could be implied that, had the court intended that there be an ethical rule regarding the use of privileged documents that were disclosed without authorization, it could have created one.
  - In fact, Comment 3 to Rule 4.4 mentions the *Mead* case and then notes that "[t]he Franklin Supreme Court...has declined to adopt a rule imposing any ethical obligation in cases of unauthorized disclosure."
- As a consequence, *Mead* may lack continuing vitality on the ground that it is inconsistent with the Franklin Supreme Court's presumed intent not to impose any ethical obligation.
  - That being said, it is also arguable that Amberg & Lewis did indeed violate an ethical obligation. Although the Franklin Supreme Court declined to adopt a rule imposing any ethical obligation in cases of unauthorized disclosure, it may have done so because it was satisfied with *Mead*, which had already imposed such an ethical obligation.

3. Even if there was no ethical violation, a violation of a rule is not necessary for disqualification.

- Language in both *Indigo* and *Mead* suggests that a motion for disqualification may be granted by a court even if there has been no rule violation. "It has long been settled in Franklin that a trial court may, in the exercise of its inherent power, disqualify an attorney in the interests of justice." *Indigo*, citing *In re Klein* (Fr. Ct. App. 1947). *See also Mead* ("[w]ith or without a violation of a specific rule, a court may...disqualify an attorney...where necessary to guarantee a fair trial") citing *Indigo*.

4. Conclusion of Issue A

- Phoenix's argument that Amberg & Lewis violated an ethical obligation by its handling of the Schetina letter fails insofar as it incorrectly assumes that Amberg & Lewis obtained the letter as a result of inadvertent, rather than unauthorized, disclosure.

- It appears that Amberg & Lewis would *not* have violated the ethical obligation imposed by Rule 4.4 and, ultimately, with the intent of the Franklin Supreme Court in adopting it, and therefore lacks continuing vitality.

- By contrast, Phoenix's argument that Amberg & Lewis violated an ethical obligation may succeed insofar as it assumes in the alternative that Amberg & Lewis obtained the letter as a result of unauthorized disclosure, depending, as indicated above, on whether *Mead* is still good law in light of the comments to Rule 4.4.

- Accordingly, there is a strong argument to be made that Amberg & Lewis has not violated the letter of the Professional Rules. Nevertheless, because the import of the *Mead* decision is uncertain, that does not end the inquiry and the court will still, most likely, go on to consider whether disqualification is required in the interests of justice.

B. Whether disqualification of Amberg & Lewis is the appropriate remedy

A trial court may, in the exercise of its inherent power, disqualify an attorney in the interests of justice. It must exercise that power, however, in light of the important right enjoyed by a party to representation by an attorney of its own choosing. Such a right must nevertheless yield to ethical considerations that affect the fundamental principles of the judicial process. *Indigo.*

- Phoenix contends that Amberg & Lewis has threatened it with incurable prejudice and therefore disqualification must follow. In Phoenix's view, whether or not any *direct* harm could be prevented by exclusion of the Schetina letter from evidence, the *indirect* harm that might arise from its use in trial preparation cannot be dealt with so simply, inasmuch as "[t]he bell has been rung, and can hardly be unrung." (Pltf's br.)

- It is true that in *Mead* the court suggested in a footnote that, in cases of unauthorized disclosure, the "threat of 'incurable prejudice' . . . is neither a necessary nor a sufficient condition for disqualification." But that suggestion is mere dictum, inasmuch as *Mead* did not involve the threat of *any* prejudice, incurable or otherwise (in *Mead*, the court described the document at issue as "little more than a paraphrase of a handful of [the plaintiff's] allegations").

- Applicants should conclude that disqualification is not mandated in this case.

- Even if Amberg & Lewis violated an ethical obligation, it should not be disqualified.

- Under *Mead*, disqualification in all cases of disclosure, whether inadvertent or unauthorized, depends on a balancing of six factors: (1) the receiving attorney's actual or constructive knowledge of the material's attorney-client privileged status; (2) the promptness with which the receiving attorney notified the opposing side of receipt; (3) the extent to which the receiving attorney reviewed the material; (4) the material's significance, i.e., the extent to which its disclosure may prejudice the party moving for disqualification, and the extent to which its return or other measure may cure that prejudice; (5) the extent to which the party moving for disqualification may be at fault for the unauthorized disclosure; and (6) the extent to which the party opposing disqualification would suffer prejudice from disqualification.

- Contrary to any implication in *Indigo*, the threat of incurable prejudice is neither a necessary nor a sufficient condition for disqualification.

- The balance weighs *against* disqualification here.

- As in the *Mead* case, where the documents were covertly copied, Phoenix is not at fault (Factor 5)—the Schetina letter was passed on to Amberg & Lewis by a disgruntled Collins employee. This favors disqualification.

- Furthermore, Amberg & Lewis knew or should have known of the letter's attorney-client privileged status (Factor 1), did not notify Collins of its receipt (Factor 2), and reviewed it thoroughly—in part because of its brevity (Factor 3). Concededly, these factors favor disqualification.

- But that being said, the Schetina letter nonetheless proves to be of dubious significance (Factor 4). True, it amounts to an admission by Phoenix that Biogenesis was correct in its understanding of its royalty obligation under the 1978 agreement. But its exclusion from evidence would prevent any prejudice to Phoenix. (Contrary to the situations in *Indigo* and *Mead*, where the attorneys in each case made use of the disclosed materials at depositions, here Amberg & Lewis has not yet made any use of the letter.) Moreover, any harm arising from any conceivable non-evidentiary use of the letter would be at best speculative.

- By contrast, Biogenesis would suffer substantial prejudice from Amberg & Lewis's disqualification, inasmuch as it would have to incur appreciable costs if it were forced to attempt to substitute new attorneys for a trial set to begin in a month after six years of preparation. These factors (Factors 4 and 6) disfavor disqualification—and they appear to predominate.

  - Biogenesis enjoys an "important right" to representation by Amberg & Lewis as its chosen attorneys. *Indigo.*

  - And there appear to be no "ethical considerations" so affecting the "fundamental principles of our judicial process" as to require that "right" to "yield." *Id.*

- In sum, disqualification of Amberg & Lewis does not appear necessary to guarantee Phoenix a fair trial.

- Contrary to Phoenix's argument, which relies on language that appears in *Indigo*,[3] disqualification of Amberg & Lewis does not depend solely on the threat of incurable prejudice. Although Phoenix attempts to dismiss the court's analysis in *Mead* as mere dictum, the *Mead* court intended its analysis at least to clarify, and at most to supersede, its earlier language in *Indigo* in order to make plain that disqualification depends on a balancing of factors not reducible to the threat of incurable prejudice alone. In any event, there is no threat of incurable prejudice here. As stated, the exclusion of the Schetina letter from evidence would avoid any prejudice, and any harm arising from its presence in the memory of Amberg & Lewis attorneys would be at best speculative.

---

[3] In *Indigo*, the court relied on the opinion in *In re Klein*, which held that the threat of incurable prejudice "has long been recognized as a sufficient basis for disqualification." *Indigo*, citing *In re Klein*.

FILE

ALLEN, EISNER & THOMAS
Attorneys at Law
1427 Marsden Place
Gardenton, Franklin 33301
(434) 277-8901

MEMORANDUM

TO: Applicant
FROM: Frank Eisner
DATE: February 24, 1998
SUBJECT: Gardenton Board of Education—Proposed Communications Code
for Gardenton High School

Dr. Edwina Kantor, the President of the Gardenton Board of Education, came to see me a few days ago about a new code to regulate the content of student communications at our public high school, Gardenton High. At its next meeting, the Board wants to present for public comment the most restrictive communications code permissible, one that gives the school the greatest flexibility to prevent the publication of offensive material. Dr. Kantor wants me to meet with and advise the Board in advance of that meeting and to be prepared to respond to comments from members of the public who have signed up to speak pro and con about the code.

Over the last few months, parents and civic groups have objected to what they consider to be intemperate, irresponsible reporting, profanity, and sexually charged material of questionable taste appearing in the various student media.

I've included in the file a transcript of my conversation with Dr. Kantor so you can get a better idea of what the issues are and how she'd like to have this matter resolved.

Please prepare a memorandum in which you evaluate the preamble and each of the guideline provisions in the draft of the communications code that Dr. Kantor left with me. Identify the legal issues that can give rise to constitutional challenges to each of the provisions and analyze whether each such provision is likely to be found legally permissible. Make suggestions for deleting, modifying, or adding any items in order to help the Board achieve its goal. Be sure to state your reasons for concluding that each guideline provision is legally permissible or impermissible, as well as the reasons for any suggestions you make. Support your reasons with appropriate discussion of the facts and law.

Task D:

Organizing a Legal Memo Where the Work Product Requires Evaluating the Constitutionality of a Proposed Code:

In re Gardenton Board of Education

TRANSCRIPT OF DISCUSSION WITH DR. EDWINA KANTOR

Lawyer: Thanks for allowing me to record this discussion, Dr. Kantor. It'll make it easier to reconstruct it later on.

Kantor: That's fine. This problem is becoming a real headache.

Lawyer: Tell me what the situation is.

Kantor: With increasing frequency, we've been getting complaints from local residents, some city leaders, parents, and various church and civic groups about the degenerating quality of the subject matter being reported in The Weekly Cougar and the language being used by students in their student theatrical and video productions. In fact, we've come pretty close to being sued for defamation by a number of really irate citizens who've read or seen things published about themselves or their families.

Lawyer: The Weekly Cougar—that's the student newspaper, right?

Kantor: That's right. It's published by the students in the senior journalism class. Students in drama and theatrical arts classes also publish plays. The performances are produced a couple of times a year. Sometimes there are live performances and sometimes the plays are filmed or videotaped by the students in the cinematography department and then shown in the auditorium or in classrooms in lieu of live plays.

Lawyer: Is the Cougar circulated beyond the student body? Who is invited to attend the student theatrical productions?

Kantor: Well, we don't consciously circulate the Cougar off campus. It's intended to be an educational vehicle for training students, but there's nothing to prevent anyone who's interested from getting copies. In order to finance the costs, the students solicit advertisements from local merchants and business operators. But it's not a newspaper of general circulation. As far as the theatrical productions are concerned, the regular annual live performances are advertised around town and admission is charged. The targeted audiences are made up mostly of students and their friends and relatives. Some of the smaller productions—I mean videos and films—are just for student consumption. We've never tried to open either the live plays or the smaller productions to the public at large.

Lawyer: What's the problem?

Kantor: Well, the student reporters for the Cougar have reported stories about individuals, relying on rumor and innuendo, without verifying the facts, without exercising mature judgment, and generally exceeding the boundaries of responsible journalism. They have used some profanity in their stories. They just don't have the experience to know better. As a result, there have been some pretty defamatory and tasteless things published. The plays and theatrical productions have sometimes bordered on being obscene. They frequently deal with sexually charged and morally questionable subject matter that parents, community leaders, and civic groups have found offensive. And, I've got to tell you that I agree with them.

Lawyer: Haven't the school administrators and classroom teachers been able to control the contents sufficiently to avoid these problems?

K Kantor: Not really. It's not that they don't want to. It's just that they haven't had any guidelines, and they've been unsure how far they can go to squelch what some people say is free speech The Board has worked up some guidelines as part of a communications code that we'd like to implement. I'll just leave this copy with you.

Lawyer: All right. Where would you like to end up with this thing?

Kantor: Well, in the best of worlds, we'd like to be able to implement each and every one of the controls we've listed in the draft. It was supposed to be a working draft and was supposed to be kept secret until we were ready to go public with it. Somehow it got out, and the next thing we know the opposition groups are coming out of the woodwork, and we're being threatened with litigation from both sides. The Union for Freedom of Speech is threatening to sue us if we promulgate any code at all, and the Gardenton Civic League is threatening to sue us if we don't. We really want to go as far as the law will allow us in controlling what the kids can publish and in giving the school district and the high school administration something they can enforce without being tied up in litigation. We have to satisfy the parents and the community that we're doing something to curb the problem and, at the same time, convince the students and free speech activists that what we're doing is within the law.

Lawyer: What, specifically, can I do to help?

Kantor: The next public meeting of the Board is scheduled for a week from Friday. The public session begins at 8:00 p.m. We already know from the sign-up list that there are going to be a lot of speakers on both sides of the issue. We are particularly concerned about the Union for Freedom of Speech, which we believe is champing at the bit to sue us. They've told us they'll sue to enjoin us. I think they believe that publication of any code would be a violation of the students' constitutional right of free speech. We'd like you to meet with us before the meeting to advise us on whether or not the draft of the guidelines is something we can lawfully implement. If not, tell us why not, and tell us what we can do. We're not wedded to all the items in the draft. The main thing is that we be able to censor unacceptable language and morally questionable subject matter that runs counter to our educational goals, especially things that open us up to suits for libel and slander and invasion of privacy.

Lawyer: What about procedures for implementing the guidelines?

Kantor: One step at a time. First, let's get agreement on these substantive guidelines at the Board meeting. Then we can turn our attention to the procedures for applying them. Later on, we'll draft some procedures and ask you to look at them.

Lawyer: OK, Dr. Kantor. Let me get to work. I'll see you at the Board meeting at 6:00 p.m. 4 April 26, 2001

STUDENT COMMUNICATIONS CODE FOR GARDENTON HIGH SCHOOL

Preamble:

This Communications Code shall apply to all student publications and media representations produced either as a result of course work or intramural extracurricular activities that are published, distributed, or otherwise disseminated on or off campus. This code shall apply to school newspapers, yearbooks, plays and other literary publications, films, movies, videos, signs, posters, and other photographic productions and graphic displays.

Guidelines for Student Publications and Productions:

1. All student publications and productions shall maintain professional standards of English language and journalistic style.

2. All student publications and productions shall avoid language and depictions that are not in good taste, having regard for the age, experience, and maturity of the general student population.

3. No stories or reports of events shall be published unless the accuracy of the facts and any quotations from individuals have first been verified to the satisfaction of the teacher supervising the publication.

4. No person shall be quoted or photographically depicted in any student publication or production without that person's prior permission and, in the case of a minor, the permission of the minor's parent or guardian, except that persons posing for group photographs shall be deemed to have given their implied consent.

5. No publication, literary piece, play, film, video, or other student production shall include material that:

   a. is libelous or slanderous or violates any person's right of privacy;

   b. contains profanity, which means language that would not customarily be used in local newspapers, to wit: The Gardenton Times or The Morning Herald;

   c. criticizes or demeans any public official, including officials, administrators, and teachers of the school; or

   d. is deemed by the principal not to be in the school's best interest.

6. Material must receive the prior approval of the principal before it is published, distributed or otherwise disseminated.

Procedures for Implementation: [to come later.]

LIBRARY

The Constitution of the United States: Amendment 1

Congress shall make no law respecting an establishment of religion, or prohibiting the free exercise thereof; or abridging the freedom of speech, or of the press; or the right of the people peaceably to assemble, and to petition the Government for a redress of grievances.

Constitution of the State of Franklin: Article I

Section 2. Every person may freely speak, write, or publish his or her sentiments on all subjects, being responsible for the abuse of this right. A law may not restrain or abridge liberty of speech or press.

Franklin Education Act: Section 48. Student Exercise of Freedom of Speech or Press

Students of public schools shall have the right to exercise freedom of speech and of the press including, but not limited to, the use of bulletin boards, the distribution of printed materials or petitions, the wearing of buttons, badges, and other insignia, and the right of expression in official publications, whether or not such publications or other means of expression are supported financially by the school or by use of school facilities, except that expression is prohibited which is obscene, libelous, or slanderous. Also prohibited shall be material which so incites students as to create a clear and present danger of the commission of unlawful acts on school premises or the violation of lawful school regulations, or the substantial disruption of the orderly operation of the school.

Student editors of official school publications shall be responsible for assigning and editing the news, editorial, and feature content of their publications subject to the limitations of this section. However, it shall be the responsibility of journalism advisers or advisers of student publications within each school to supervise the production of the student staff, to maintain professional standards of English and journalism, and to maintain the provisions of this section.

"Official school publications" refers to material produced by students in the journalism, newspaper, yearbook, or writing classes and distributed to the student body either free or for a fee.

emotional maturity of the intended audience. Sensitive topics *might* range from the existence of Santa Claus in an elementary school setting to the particulars of teenage sexual activity in a high school setting. A school must also retain the authority to refuse to associate the school with any position other than neutrality on matters of political controversy. It is only when the decision to censor a school-sponsored publication, theatrical production, or other vehicle of student expression has no valid educational purpose that the First Amendment is so directly and sharply implicated as to require judicial intervention to protect students' constitutional rights.

We cannot reject as unreasonable Principal Reynolds' conclusion that the students who wrote these articles had not sufficiently mastered those portions of the Journalism II curriculum that pertained to the treatment of controversial issues and personal attacks, the need to protect the privacy of individuals whose most intimate concerns are to be revealed in the newspaper, and the legal, moral, and ethical restrictions imposed upon journalists within a school community that includes adolescent subjects and readers. Accordingly, no violation of the First Amendment occurred.

students, parents, and members of the public might reasonably perceive to bear the imprimatur of the school. These activities may fairly be characterized as part of the school curriculum so long as they are supervised by faculty members and designed to impart particular knowledge or skills to student participants and audiences.

Educators are entitled to exercise greater control over this form of student expression to assure that participants learn whatever lessons the activity is designed to teach, that readers or listeners are not exposed to material that may be inappropriate for their level of maturity, and that the views of the individual speaker are not erroneously attributed to the school. Hence, a school may in its capacity as publisher of a school newspaper or producer of a school play disassociate itself not only from speech that would substantially interfere with its work or impinge upon the rights of other students, but also from speech that is, for example, ungrammatical, poorly written, inadequately researched, biased or prejudiced, vulgar or profane, or unsuitable for immature audiences. A school must be able to set standards that may be higher than those demanded in the "real" world.

In addition, on potentially sensitive topics, a school must be able to take into account the

---

Hazelwood School District v. Kuhlmeier

United States Supreme Court (1988)

Respondents contend that school district officials violated their First Amendment rights by deleting two pages of articles from the May 13, 1983 issue of *Spectrum*, the Hazelwood High School student newspaper. Written and edited by the Journalism II class at Hazelwood High, the newspaper was distributed to students, school personnel, and members of the community.

The practice at Hazelwood was for the journalism teacher, Robert Mackinac, to submit each *Spectrum* issue to Eugene Reynolds, the school principal, for his review prior to publication. On May 10, Reynolds objected to two of the articles scheduled to appear in the May 13 edition. One of the stories described three Hazelwood students' experiences with pregnancy; the other discussed the impact of divorce on students at the school, quoting a student's remarks about the cause of her parents' divorce. Reynolds directed Mackinac to withhold the two stories from publication.

The district court found that Principal Reynolds' concern that the pregnant students' anonymity would be lost and their privacy invaded was "legitimate and reasonable," given "the small number of pregnant students at Hazelwood and several identifying characteristics that were disclosed in the article." The deletion of the article on divorce was seen by the court as a reasonable response to the invasion of privacy concerns raised by the named student's remarks. Because the student's parents had not been offered an opportunity to respond, there was cause for "serious doubt that the article complied with the rules of fairness which are standard in the field of journalism and were covered in the textbook used in the Journalism II class."

The Court of Appeals for the Eighth Circuit reversed. We granted certiorari, and we now reverse the decision of the Eighth Circuit and affirm the district court.

The First Amendment rights of students in the public schools are not automatically

coextensive with the rights of adults in other settings and must be applied in the special circumstances of the school environment. A school need not tolerate student speech that is inconsistent with its basic educational mission, even though the government could not censor similar speech outside the school.

Accordingly, we have held that a school could discipline a student for having delivered a speech that was "sexually explicit" but not legally obscene at an official school assembly, because the school was entitled to disassociate itself from the speech in a manner that would demonstrate to others that such vulgarity is wholly inconsistent with the fundamental values of public school education. The determination of what manner of speech in the classroom or in school assembly is inappropriate properly rests with the school board, rather than with the federal courts. It is in this context that respondents' First Amendment claims must be considered.

We deal first with the question of whether *Spectrum* may appropriately be characterized as a forum for public expression. The public schools do not possess all the attributes of streets, parks, and other traditional forums that have been used for purposes of assembly and discussion of public questions. Hence, school facilities may be deemed to be public forums only if school authorities have by policy or practice opened those facilities for indiscriminate use by the general public or by some segment of the public, such as student organizations. The government does not create a public forum by inaction or by permitting limited discourse, but only by intentionally opening a nontraditional forum for public discourse.

Educators have authority over school-sponsored publications, theatrical prod-uctions, and other expressive activities that

Lopez v. Union High School District

Franklin Supreme Court (1994)

The issue presented is whether a school district is precluded by Section 48 of the Franklin Education Act and Article I, Section 2, of the Franklin Constitution from requiring, on the ground of educational suitability, that a film arts class instructor have his students delete the profanity in a student-produced film. We hold that school authorities may restrain such expression because it violates the "professional standards of English and journalism" provision of Section 48.

Plaintiffs, students at Union High School, wrote and produced a film entitled *Melancholianne* in a film arts class. The film addresses the problems faced by teenaged parents. The film dialogue contains profanity and references to sexual activity that the students believed made the film characters more realistic and "real world." The school principal, upon review of the draft of the script, found the language highly offensive and educationally unsuitable. After public hearings, the school board held that "sound educational policy" as well as a district administrative regulation required that the profanity be deleted.[1] Plaintiffs sued for declaratory and injunctive relief challenging the censorship of the videotape script.[2]

We need not decide whether the legislature intended to include the profanity at issue within the term "obscene expression." Legislative history demonstrates the legislature intended to preclude the students' use of "four-letter words" under the auspices of the "professional standards of English and journalism" provision of Section 48. The words of the statute permit prior restraint of material prepared for official school publications when the material "violates" the statute. Further, the legislative history of Section 48 indicates the legislature did not intend to protect student expression that constitutes profanity, especially when the expression is aimed at minors rather than adults. The school authorities have a substantial interest in protecting the student audience from expression that could be embarrassing or detrimental to their stage of development. Censorship of "four-letter words" does not unduly hinder the students' ability to express their ideas or opinions on any subject. It enjoins only the indecent manner in which an idea is expressed.

Having concluded that Section 48 permits prior restraint of profane student expression in official student publications, we must consider whether such restraint is constitutional under the federal or state constitutions. The question is easily answered under the First Amendment. Teaching students to avoid vulgar and profane language is obviously a legitimate pedagogical concern and proper under the First Amendment. *Hazelwood School District v. Kuhlmeier* (U.S. Supreme Court, 1988).

The answer is the same under the Franklin Constitution. This court has adopted a forum analysis to determine when the government's interest in limiting the use of

---

[1] The administrative regulation in question is a "Student Publications Code" that, among other things, confers upon school authorities the power to require that school-sponsored publications maintain "professional standards of English grammar and journalistic writing style" and to prohibit the publication of "obscene" or "profane" material, defining those terms to mean language that would not ordinarily be used in certain specified local newspapers of general circulation.

[2] The parties have not raised or briefed the issue of whether the video is an "official school publication" within the meaning of Section 48. Nevertheless, we see no policy reason for distinguishing between student expression in school-sponsored activities solely on the basis of the medium by which the expression is conveyed.

its property to its intended purpose outweighs the interest of those wishing to use the property for other purposes. We have divided public property into three categories: public, nonpublic, and limited.

A public forum is the traditional soapbox in a town square; no one can be denied access, and prior restraints are rarely permissible. A nonpublic forum is public property that is not a public forum by tradition or design, such as a military base or a jail or a "house organ" school bulletin for dissemination of educational or administrative information to students or faculty, over which school officials retain full power to regulate access and content.

The so-called limited forum is property the state has opened for expressive activity by part or all of the public. "Official school publications" in Franklin fall into the limited forum category. *Melancholianne* is conceptually no different from a school yearbook or newspaper produced in a journalism class. While the primary purpose for producing the videotape is to teach the students writing and film-making skills, the film also serves as an avenue of student expression. Thus, *Melancholianne* is a limited public forum.

When a school publication is deemed to be a limited public forum, school officials must demonstrate that the particular regulation of student expression advances a compelling state interest. Here, the compelling state interests advanced by the board are to maintain an environment where the educational process may occur without disruption, to teach students the boundaries of socially appropriate behavior, to promote "moral improvement," and to teach students to refrain from the use of profane and vulgar language.

School officials must also show that the speech regulations are narrowly drawn to achieve the compelling interest and sufficiently precise to avoid a challenge on grounds that they are void for vagueness. The board has done so here. The board has not censored the students' expression of ideas; rather, the board has prohibited their expression of those ideas by the use of profane language. The board's directive cannot be construed as the type of censorship we have deemed unconstitutional—censorship based on a disagreement with the views presented or censorship designed to avoid discussion of controversial issues. Rather, the board's directive was content neutral and served a valid pedagogical purpose.

Accordingly, the judgment is affirmed.

THE MPT

MULTISTATE PERFORMANCE TEST

In re Gardenton Board of Education

POINT SHEET

The MPT point sheet, grading summary, and grading guidelines describe the factual and legal points encompassed within the lawyering task to be completed. They outline all the possible issues and points that might be addressed by an applicant. They are provided to the user jurisdictions for the sole purpose of assisting graders in grading the examination by identifying the issues and suggesting the resolution of the problem contemplated by the drafters. These are not official grading guides. Applicants can receive a range of passing grades, including excellent grades, without covering all the points discussed in these guides. The model answer is included as an illustration of a thorough and detailed response to the task, one that addresses all the legal and factual issues the drafters intended to raise in the problem. It is intended to serve only as an example. Applicants need not present their responses in the same way to receive good grades. User jurisdictions are free to modify these grading materials, including the suggested weights assigned to particular points. Grading the MPT is the exclusive responsibility of the jurisdiction using the MPT as part of its admissions process.

Leeb v. DeLong

Franklin Court of Appeal (1999)

David Leeb was the student editor of the Rancho High School newspaper. On March 29, 1994, Leeb submitted for the school principal's approval, as required by the school district's communication code, the April Fool's edition. An article appeared under the headline "Nude Photos: Girls of Rancho." According to the article, the July issue of *Playboy* magazine would carry nude photographs of Rancho students, and those interested in posing should sign up at the school darkroom. The article was accompanied by a photograph of five fully clothed female students standing in line with their school books, purportedly with applications in hand. Principal DeLong recognized each of them.

Mr. DeLong formed the opinion that "the article and photograph taken together are damaging to the reputation of each of the girls in the photograph." He was also of the view that the reputation of the school and the school district would be injured by the publication of the material. On March 30, he prohibited distribution of the newspaper. Leeb sued for declaratory and injunctive relief, and the court below granted summary judgment in favor of the school district.

Section 48 of the Education Act and Franklin decisional authority clearly confer editorial control of official student publications on the student editors alone, with very limited exceptions. The broad power to censor in school-sponsored publications for pedagogical purposes recognized by the U.S. Supreme Court in *Hazelwood School District v. Kuhlmeier*

(1988) is not available to this state's educators. Student free speech rights under Section 48 are broader than rights arising under the First Amendment.

Under Education Act Section 48, a school district may constitutionally censor expression from official school publications which it reasonably believes to contain an actionable defamation. A school district may not, however, censor defamatory material that is not actionable because it is privileged or deals with a public figure without malice. *New York Times v. Sullivan* (U.S. Supreme Court, 1964). For example, an article suggesting that a public official is wrong, illogical, or was a poor choice for office could never lead to a recovery in tort, and could for that reason not be suppressed. But the girls in the photograph in this case are not public figures, and the principal's concerns were justifiable. The censorship in this case was not, therefore, precluded either by the federal or state constitutions or by Section 48.

To the extent that the school district's communication code suggests that an article such as one mentioned above about a public official could be censored, the code should be amended. The code should also be amended to require that any decision to delete an item thought to be defamatory should, insofar as it is possible, be limited to the offending material itself.

Judgment affirmed.

In re Gardenton Board of Education

DRAFTERS' POINT SHEET

This performance test deals principally with constitutional law and prior restraints, i.e., the First Amendment rights of high school students in the context of school-sponsored publications. It requires applicants to prepare a factual and legal analysis of a proposed Communications Code (the "Code") in light of state and federal constitutional provisions as modified by statutes and case law. The task for the applicants is to prepare a memorandum to a partner of the law firm telling the partner how the proposed Code complies with or departs from the law and to make suggestions for improvement of the Code. The memorandum should be written as if it were a communication between lawyers, as opposed to a communication to a layperson. Thus, one should expect to see the use of legal terms and citations to statutes and case law. We expect the applicants to follow the directions contained in the file memo from the partner:

• Explore the law in the library, draw conclusions as to how far the school board can push the envelope, and give reasons for those conclusions; and

• Go through each item in the draft Code, state whether it is legally permissible, if need be suggest changes to make it legally permissible, and give reasons for the suggested changes.

Following are the points that emerge from the problem and that should be recognized by the applicants:

1. Legal Analysis:
• There is a tension between the free speech rights that arise under the state and federal constitutions on the one hand, and Section 48 on the other. Section 48 confers upon the students' broader free speech rights than do the constitutional provisions as interpreted by the cases in the library. It also purports to give them editorial control, with certain specified exceptions.
• The "professional standards of English and journalistic style" provision of Section 48 is the board's best argument why it has the power to "clean up" the student publications. Using that as the rationale avoids disputes over whether something is obscene or actionable.

• Ostensibly, Section 48 allows prior restraints only in cases of actionable libel and slander, obscenity, clear and present danger, and situations that would result in violation of the statute. There is language in the case law that suggests that the "professional standards" provisions of the statute allow prior restraint in other circumstances as well. Applicants should be able to reconcile these apparent differences.

• The level of court scrutiny will be determined by whether and to what extent the school-sponsored student publications are "public forums." The case law suggests that a student newspaper is a "limited public forum" and that, therefore, a high level of scrutiny is warranted. The facts suggest that perhaps the public performances of school plays might be "public forums" and subject to yet a higher level of scrutiny. Perceptive applicants will pick up on this nuance.

• There is an issue, resolved by the case law, of whether plays, videos, films, etc. are even covered by the statute or whether it only applies to the "print media" and the publications specifically mentioned in Section 48.

• To what extent do the educational goals of the school and its obligation to inculcate values in the students expand its power to exercise prior restraint? There is language in the cases that deals with this point and with which applicants must deal.

• There are references in the Code to "good taste," "having regard for age, experience, and maturity of the general student population," and the like. Applicants should raise questions about whether

such terms are too vague to withstand legal scrutiny.

• To the extent that the Code (in the Preamble) purports to regulate off-campus speech, it is probably too broad, although there is language in the cases to suggest that if the speaker attempts to link it to school-sponsored activity, the school has the right to disassociate itself by taking action to demonstrate to the community that the school does not approve. Is that justification for off-campus regulation? Probably not.

• Overall, the promulgation of a Code is permissible, but the proposed Code needs to be modified in several respects. *Leeb v. DeLong* is a source for ideas about such modifications.

2. Evaluation of the Proposed Code:
• The scope of the Code as stated in the Preamble (i.e., applying to "all student publications and media representations") is all right. The case law supports a broad interpretation of the statute on this point. Restricting the off-campus distribution of unapproved materials is problematic. The argument in favor of it is that the school has a right to "disassociate" itself, and any case would have to be dealt with sui generis. In *Leeb*, however, the court notes that the broad powers which *Hazelwood* ascribes under the First Amendment are not available here because Section 48 confers upon the students broader speech rights than does the First Amendment. Applicants should recognize this point and might suggest that the off-campus provision should be stricken and troublesome situations handled ad hoc.

• Item 1: Measuring the "professional standards" against local newspapers is the statutory standard (see Section 48) and has the apparent approval of the courts.

• Item 2: The "good taste" language used here is probably too vague to be enforceable and should be modified to be measured against something like local newspapers. The "age, experience, and maturity" provision has received case law approval.

• Item 3: The requirement that facts and quotations be checked for accuracy before publication is probably all right. The case law and the statute suggest that it is part of teaching a high school course in journalism to encourage accurate reporting. Applicants should note, however, that this conflicts to some degree with the provision of Section 48, which confers editorial control on the students, and that it might, nevertheless, be an impermissible prior restraint.

• Item 4: The requirement for obtaining prior permission for quotes and photographs is probably all right. It is supported both by Section 48 and the cases.

• Item 5a: Prohibiting libel, slander, and invasion of privacy by prior restraint is all right, both under the Education Act and the case law.

• Item 5b: Measuring "profanity" against local newspapers is approved by the case law, and regulating profanity by prior restraint is all right. Nevertheless, any publication using local newspapers as the standard of measurement is susceptible of a "void for vagueness" argument.

• Item 5c: The prohibition against criticizing public officials is patently unlawful. Because of *New York Times v. Sullivan*, it is highly unlikely that any such criticism would be actionable defamation. This item should probably be stricken.

• Item 5d: The power to determine what is "not in the school's best interest" is probably too broad and vague to withstand scrutiny. Unless some very restrictive limitations are imposed, this provision should be stricken.

• Item 6: There is nothing wrong in principle with requiring prior approval from the principal. It appears to be supported by the case law.

Task E:

Organizing a Legal Memo Where the Work Product Requires

Statutory Analysis; Second Example:

In re Steven Wallace

FILE

Piper, Morales & Singh

Attorneys at Law

One Dalton Place

West Keystone, Franklin 33322

MEMORANDUM

To: Applicant
From: Eva Morales
Date: July 27, 1999
Subject: Steven Wallace—Painting Titled "Hare Castle"

Steven Wallace, a long-time friend of mine, recently retired as Chair of the English Department at the University of Franklin to pursue full time what has until now been his avocation as an artist. He came in yesterday to get my advice and brought the documents I've included in the file. On reviewing the file, I can see that there are other facts we need in order to advise him properly.

About a year ago, Steven left one of his paintings, a canvas he had titled "Hare Castle," with Lottie Zelinka, an art dealer friend of his, with the understanding that she would try to sell it for him. Ms. Zelinka is the owner of Artists' Exchange, an art gallery here in West Keystone. Ten days or so ago, Ms. Zelinka returned the painting to Steven. A few days ago, he received a letter from Martin Feldner, a bankruptcy practitioner here in town. Mr. Feldner represents Charles Sims, the court-appointed Trustee in Bankruptcy. The letter advises Steven that Ms. Zelinka has filed for bankruptcy and demands that Steven turn "Hare Castle" over to the Trustee in Bankruptcy. Naturally, Steven is upset by this turn of events and wants to know how to respond.

Please draft for me a two-part memorandum:

- First, analyze the legal and factual bases of the trustee's claim that the painting is an asset of the bankruptcy estate under the Bankruptcy Act and the Franklin Commercial Code (FCC).

- Second, for each of the four defenses under FCC § 2-326(3), discuss how the facts we already know support the defense, identify additional facts that might be helpful to us, state why they would be helpful, and indicate from what sources we might be able to obtain them.

P-3

Artist's Exchange
West Keystone's Premier Gallery
9 Wharf Alley
West Keystone, Franklin 33322
(555) 942-5060

Inventory Receipt

Date: August 15, 1998
Artist: Steven Wallace
Agent: none
Address: 749 Galewood Circle
West Keystone, Franklin 33322
Phone: (555) 942-3342

Medium	Inventory Number	Size	Title	Artist's Net
Oil/Canvas	C 6076	2' x 3'	Hare Castle	Sale price minus 40% commission to Gallery

General Conditions:

The item(s) of artwork listed above is (are) being placed by the Artist or his/her agent, as consignor, on consignment with Artists' Exchange (Gallery), as consignee, to be sold by Gallery for the account of Artist. Artist retains title to the artwork until sold by Gallery. Gallery makes no representations regarding its ability to sell any or all of said artwork or the sales price thereof. Gallery may return artwork to Artist at any time if not sold. All offers shall be communicated to Artist by Gallery, and Artist shall have the right to accept or reject any offers. Artist shall have the right to determine price of sale, except that if an offer exceeds the appraised value of the artwork plus the amount of Gallery's commission, Artist shall be required to accept the offer. Risk of loss over and above amount of Gallery's liability and hazard insurance shall be borne by Artist. Artist's Net shall be paid to Artist upon payment in full of sale price by buyer.

Lottie Zelinka
Artists' Exchange
By: Lottie Zelinka

Steven Wallace
Artist or Agent

P-2

NOTES OF JULY 26, 1999 MEETING WITH STEVEN WALLACE

- Steven can't believe this letter he got (copy attached) two days ago—a bankruptcy attorney is demanding that Steven turn over one of his best paintings ("Hare Castle") to a Trustee.

- A friend of his, Lottie Zelinka, has an art gallery in West Keystone—the gallery is called Artists' Exchange. She operates it as a sole proprietorship.

- Lottie has a sizeable inventory of paintings and sculptures—Steven thinks (but isn't sure) that most of the art in the gallery is on consignment from artists and that Lottie doesn't really own it. That's how Steven and every other artist he knows deal with the galleries in town—i.e., by consignment. He's pretty sure that's how galleries work everywhere. Maybe Lottie owns some of the art, but, mainly, she shows the art, sells it for the artists, and makes her money on the sales commissions.

- Steven thinks (but is not sure) Lottie had placed a sign in the window at the front of the gallery that said something like, "All offers will be considered and forwarded to the artists."

- About a year ago, Lottie was at Steven's house for dinner with Steven and Ella, his wife. Lottie saw "Hare Castle" (oil on canvas—about 2' x 3') hanging on the dining room wall. She admired it and said she thought she could sell it for "a lot of money," maybe as much as $25,000 (some of Steven's recent paintings have been fetching pretty good prices, but he'd never thought about trying to sell "Hare Castle"—it was one of his favorite paintings and had been hanging in his dining room since he finished it a couple of years ago). Lottie told Steven, if he's interested, to bring it to her gallery and she'd put it up for sale.

- Steven and Ella talked it over and, although they had recently purchased a new rug for their dining room that coordinated with the colors in the painting, $25,000 sounded like a lot of money, so they decided to see if Lottie was right. Steven took "Hare Castle" to Lottie's gallery, they did some paperwork (copies attached), and Steven left the painting with Lottie. He had put a label (about 2" x 3") on the back of the painting that said: "Hare Castle—Property of Steven Wallace (+ his address and phone number)."

- From time to time, Lottie called Steven to tell him about offers for the canvas—three offers all told—the highest one for $6,000. Steven rejected them—not enough money.

- Maybe 10 days ago, Lottie called Steven at about 10 p.m.—told him she was going to come right over and leave "Hare Castle" at his house—she didn't think she could sell it and she needed the space in the gallery. He thought it was strange, but he didn't ask any questions and Lottie didn't let on that anything was unusual. Now he realizes she tried to do him a favor by returning the painting—apparently, she filed for bankruptcy.

- Steven is now into painting full time—retired from Univ. of Franklin at the end of the last school year. His paintings seem to have caught on, and he's been selling more and more of them (in fact, he has offered to buy back for $750 paintings he originally sold for $500—says he can probably sell them now for $2,500).

- He now has a studio in a loft on Parker St.—up until now, he's been working out of a spare room at home.

- Steven can't believe he jeopardizes his paintings every time he puts them up for sale in a gallery!

MPT Test Materials

Martin R. Feldner
Attorney at Law
2298 West Arden Boulevard
West Keystone, Franklin 33322
(555) 942-4324

July 23, 1999

Mr. Steven Wallace
749 Galewood Circle
West Keystone, Franklin 33322

Re: In the Matter of Lottie Zelinka dba
Artists' Exchange
Bkpcy No. 980-7 (99)

Dear Mr. Wallace:

I represent Charles A. Sims, Trustee in Bankruptcy in the Chapter 7 bankruptcy case of *Lottie Zelinka dba Artists' Exchange* ("Debtor"). The Debtor filed a petition for bankruptcy under Chapter 11 of the Bankruptcy Act on May 25, 1999. She converted the case to a liquidation under Chapter 7 on July 19, 1999, on which date Mr. Sims was appointed trustee.

The Debtor has recently provided us with an accounting and business records detailing certain actions taken by her after the filing of the petition. According to Ms. Zelinka, she transferred a piece of artwork titled "Hare Castle" to you on July 20, 1999. The transfer was improper under Franklin Commercial Code § 2-326 and § 544 of the Bankruptcy Act.

The Trustee has elected to exercise his power under § 549 of the Bankruptcy Act to avoid improper transfers made during the pendency of a bankruptcy case. Accordingly, demand is hereby made that you forthwith return to the Trustee the artwork titled "Hare Castle" or all proceeds from the sale thereof. If you fail to do so within 15 days of the date of this letter, the Trustee will commence legal action to recover the artwork or the proceeds.

Very truly yours,

Martin R. Feldner

Martin R. Feldner

Test Materials

APPRAISAL

APPRAISAL OF ARTWORK

Date: August 15, 1998

Title: "Hare Castle"

Artist: Steven Wallace

Medium: Original Oil on Canvas

Value: $25,000.00

Owner: Steven Wallace

THE ABOVE INFORMATION IS TRUE AND CORRECT TO THE BEST OF OUR KNOWLEDGE.

Signed: *Lottie Zelinka*
Lottie Zelinka

Title: Owner
ARTISTS' EXCHANGE

Franklin Commercial Code

* * *

§ 2-326. Sale on Approval and Sale or Return; Consignment Sales and Rights of Creditors.

(1) Unless otherwise agreed, if delivered goods may be returned by the buyer even though they conform to the contract, the transaction is

(a) a "sale on approval" if the goods are delivered primarily for use, and

(b) a "sale or return" if the goods are delivered primarily for resale.

(2) Except as provided in subsection (3), goods held on approval are not subject to claims of the buyer's creditors until acceptance; goods held on sale or return are subject to such claims while in the buyer's possession.

(3) Where goods are delivered to a person for sale and such person maintains a place of business at which he deals in goods of the kind involved, under a name other than the name of the person making the delivery, then, with respect to claims of creditors of the person conducting the business, the goods are deemed to be on sale or return. The provisions of this subsection are applicable even though an agreement purports to reserve title to the person making delivery until payment or resale or uses such words as "on consignment" or "on memorandum." However, this subsection is not applicable if the person making the delivery

(a) complies with an applicable law providing for a consignor's interest or the like to be evidenced by a sign, or

(b) establishes that the person conducting the business is generally known by his creditors to be substantially engaged in selling goods of others, or

(c) complies with the filing of provisions of the Article on Secured Transactions (Article 9), or

(d) delivers goods which the person making delivery used or bought for personal, family, or household purposes.

Franklin Civil Code

§ 3533 - Sign Law.

If a person transacts business and identifies his place of business by a sign and fails by another sign or signs in letters easy to read and posted conspicuously in his place of business to state that he is dealing in property in which others have an interest and identifying such property, then all the property, stock of goods, money, and choses in action used or acquired in such business shall, as to the creditors of such person, be liable for his debts and be in all respects treated in favor of his creditors as his property unless the provisions of Franklin Commercial Code § 2-326(3)(b) through (d) are applicable.

LIBRARY

Walker On Bankruptcy (3d. Ed. 1995)

A Short Course for the Non-Bankruptcy Lawyer

* * *

§ 4 - Definitions:

§ 4.07 - Chapter 11: A petition for a Chapter 11 "reorganization" commences a proceeding in which the insolvent debtor continues to operate as an ongoing business with certain restrictions. The business operates by the direction of the Bankruptcy Court under the management either of a court-appointed trustee or the debtor (debtor-in-possession). The Bankruptcy Act provides for an automatic stay of legal and self-help proceedings against the debtor pending the preparation and execution of a plan of arrangement" pursuant to which the debtor "works out" its obligations to its creditors over an extended period of time.

§ 4.08 - Chapter 7: Often, Chapter 11 proceedings that fail are converted to Chapter 7 cases. A petition for bankruptcy under Chapter 7 commences a proceeding for liquidation of the debtor's assets for the benefit of its creditors. A court-appointed trustee takes possession of the business, including all items in inventory, which thereafter come under the exclusive control of the trustee. The trustee is vested with all the rights possessed by the creditors of the bankrupt debtor prior to the filing of the petition. The trustee's principal function is to marshal and, subject to the rights of secured creditors, sell the assets and distribute the proceeds proportionately to the creditors in accordance with their interests. Under § 549 of the Bankruptcy Act, "the trustee may avoid a transfer of property of the estate...that occurs after commencement of the case..."

* * *

§ 4.27 - Schedules of Assets, Debts, and Creditors: It is incumbent on the debtor in any bankruptcy proceeding to file with the court schedules of its assets, debts and creditors. All property, including goods delivered on consignment and accounts receivable, in which the debtor has any interest must be described and its location shown on the schedule of assets. Likewise, the amount of each debt and the name and address of the creditor to whom each debt is owed are required to be listed on the schedules of debts and creditors, with designations in each case as to whether the particular creditor is secured or unsecured. The schedules of secured creditors must describe with particularity the property of the debtor in which the creditor has a security interest.

First National Bank v. Marigold Farms, Inc.

Franklin Court of Appeal

In this case, we determine the priority of the claims of First National Bank (the Bank) and Marigold Farms, Inc. (Marigold) to $139,000 in a bank account (the Fund) of Pacific Wholesalers (Pacific). The trial court held that the Bank was entitled to the Fund. Marigold appeals.

The Bank had loaned $600,000 to Pacific and Pacific, in turn, had executed a security agreement granting the Bank a security interest in certain assets of Pacific. The Bank had perfected its security interest by filing a financing statement with the Secretary of State. Pacific defaulted on the loan and the Bank sued. Pacific and the Bank negotiated a settlement pursuant to which cash received by Pacific in the conduct of its business would be delivered to the Bank and applied to the balance of the loan. Marigold asserted claims to the same cash and also asserted that its claims had priority over any claim of the Bank. The court approved the settlement subject to resolution of the competing claims of Marigold and the Bank and ordered $139,000 of Pacific's cash receipts held in a "blocked" account (i.e., the Fund).

The facts of the relationship between Marigold and Pacific are undisputed. Marigold was a grower of flowers. Pacific was a flower wholesaler. They had a longstanding relationship under which Marigold would deliver flowers to Pacific and obtain a delivery receipt. Pacific would mark the flowers with Marigold's name, package them, and attempt to sell them to retail florists at prices determined by Pacific. If the flowers were sold and Pacific received payment, Pacific would remit to Marigold 75% of the sale price, retaining 25% as its commission. If the flowers were not sold, Pacific would with Marigold's approval discard them, and Marigold would receive nothing for those flowers. It is also undisputed that the Bank had no actual knowledge of the nature of the commercial arrangement between Marigold and Pacific.

The Bank's financing statement and the security agreement between Pacific and the Bank describe the collateral as: "All inventory used in Pacific's business now owned or hereafter acquired; and all accounts and rights to payment of every kind now or hereafter arising in favor of Pacific out of Pacific's business, including all proceeds from the sale of inventory."

Under the Franklin Commercial Code, it is clear that, upon delivery of Marigold's flowers to Pacific, the flowers became part of Pacific's "inventory" because they were held by Pacific for sale. The Fund consists of "proceeds" of this inventory.

Marigold contends that its sale of flowers to Pacific was a "consignment sale," that Pacific never had title to the flowers and that, therefore, Pacific never owned the collateral (inventory) to which the Bank's security interest could attach. Marigold also asserts, *First National Bank v. Marigold Farms, Inc.,* Franklin Court of Appeal (1997), that Franklin Commercial Code § 2-326(3) is inapplicable in this case.

A consignment sale is one in which the merchant takes possession of goods and holds them for sale with the obligation to pay the owner of the goods from the proceeds of the sale. If the merchant does not sell the goods, the merchant may return them to the owner (or, as in this case of perishable flowers, discard them) without obligation. In a consignment sale transaction, title to the goods generally remains with the original owner. The arrangement between Marigold and Pacific was a consignment sale arrangement; Marigold was the consignor and Pacific was the consignee. Under FCC § 2-326(3), which clearly governs this transaction, the retention of title by Marigold is irrelevant to the ability of the Bank to obtain a security interest in the collateral.

Marigold does not contend that it complied with the filing requirement under the secured transactions division of the FCC as provided for in § 2-326(3)(c). Nor does Marigold claim that it complied with an applicable "sign law" under § 2-326(3)(a) or that it had delivered goods it had "used or bought for personal, family, or household purposes" as provided for in § 2-326(3)(d).[1] Rather, Marigold claims that, as provided for in § 2-326(3)(b), Pacific was generally known by its creditors "to be substantially engaged in selling goods of others."

At the evidentiary hearing, Bank officials testified unequivocally that the Bank was unaware that Pacific was selling the goods of others. Three flower growers who also consigned flowers to Pacific testified that Pacific was "well-known as a commission selling agent" and that other flower growers knew it as well. Although it is true that consignors, all of whom are necessarily also creditors, might know that Pacific deals in the goods of others, such knowledge cannot be extrapolated into a fact "generally known by its creditors." The purpose of § 2-326(3) is to protect general creditors of the consignee from claims of consignors who have undisclosed arrangements with the consignee. To impute as a matter of law the self-interested knowledge of the consignors/creditors to the general creditors does not give general creditors the opportunity to protect themselves from the undisclosed interests of the consignors.[2]

A consignor asserting that the consignee is "generally known by his creditors to be substantially engaged in selling the goods of others" must establish such general knowledge by proof other than that a few other consignors know that fact. He must establish that non-consignor creditors possess the requisite knowledge. Marigold failed to meet that burden of proof.

---

[1] The obvious reason for the exception for goods "used or bought for personal, family, or household purposes" is to avoid the situation where one who is not a merchant, and who should not therefore be deemed to know of the intricacies by which merchants protect their interests under the commercial code, unwittingly loses his right to property. If a householder occasionally delivers an item of property to a dealer to see if the dealer can sell it for him, the FCC protects that item from claims of the dealer's creditors. On the other hand, if the deliverer is one who deals in goods of the kind sold by the person to whom he delivers the goods, he should be held to the rules in the FCC that bind merchants. There are hybrid situations such as, for example, where one collects gemstones for his personal use and enjoyment but also regularly places the gems on consignment with jewelers to test the market and sell if the price is right. At some point the casual collector crosses over the line from being the householder, whom the personal goods exception is designed to protect, to being a merchant or dealer, who is bound by the filing or other protective provisions of § 2-326. In this case, Marigold is clearly at the extreme end of the merchant spectrum.

[2] The result might be different if all or most of Pacific's creditors were flower consignors but the fact does not appear from the evidence in this case. If all or most of the creditors were consignors, then one might be able to conclude that the creditors did have such "general knowledge."

P-10

In re Levy

Bankruptcy No. 29054
United States District Court, E.D. Pennsylvania (1993)

In December 1992, Bernard Levy, owner of a retail shoe store in Reading, Pennsylvania, filed a voluntary petition in bankruptcy. One of his suppliers, Acme Shoe Co. (Acme), had delivered a stock of shoes to Levy for resale in his store under the terms of a written agreement in which Levy, the bankrupt, acknowledged that the shoes were "on consignment" and could be returned to the consignor at any time.

Acme has filed a reclamation petition to recover the shoes it delivered to the bankrupt. The trustee resists the petition on the ground that the transaction was one of "sale or return," and, since there had been no compliance with § 2-326(3) of the Pennsylvania Uniform Commercial Code, the stock of shoes in Levy's possession was subject to the claims of Levy's creditors.

Acme concedes that it had not filed any financing statements in the public records offices. Acme did, however, produce evidence that small cards had been placed upon certain sections of shelving in Levy's store where Acme's shoes were stored and displayed, identifying the shoes placed on those sections of the shelving as shoes manufactured by Acme.

Under § 2-326 of the UCC, if goods are delivered to a consignor primarily for resale with the understanding that they may be returned by the consignor, the transaction is one of "sale or return" and such goods are subject to the claims of the buyer's creditors while in the buyer's possession even though the consignee has retained title. The consignee may avoid the consequences of having the goods subjected to the claims of the consignor's creditors by doing one or more of three things: (a) complying with "an applicable law" evidencing a consignor's interest or the like by a sign to that effect, or (b) establishing that the consignor is generally known by his creditors to be substantially engaged in selling the goods of others, or (c) complying with the provisions for filing financing statements and other

notice documents under UCC Article 9 having to do with secured transactions.

There was no filing under Article 9. There was an effort by Acme to protect its goods by posting signs on the sections of shelving where its shoes were kept, but Acme has failed to show that there is in Pennsylvania "an applicable [sign] law" as that term is used in § 2-326(3)(a). The phrase "an applicable law" means a statute, and there is no such statute in Pennsylvania. Absent such a statute or an Article 9 filing, Acme is left with the burden of proving that Levy was generally known by his creditors to be substantially engaged in selling the goods of others.

Acme argues that, although the absence of a sign law might mean that the cards Acme caused to be placed on the shelves did not invoke the "sign law" subsection of § 2-326, the cards nonetheless served to impart knowledge that Levy was selling the goods of others. That argument might have had some merit if Acme could have shown that the cards did in fact impart such knowledge to Levy's creditors to such an extent that it was "generally known" by the creditors and that the cards also suggested that Levy was "substantially engaged" in selling goods not owned by him. On the record before the United States District Court, E. D. Pennsylvania (1993) court, however, the most that can be said is that the cards were designed to impart to Levy's customers, not his creditors, the knowledge that the shoes were Acme's. Thus, Acme's proof fell short.

Under § 544 of the Bankruptcy Act, the trustee is vested with the rights that the creditors had prior to the filing of the petition in bankruptcy. Section 2-326(2) of the UCC expressly makes goods held on sale or return subject to the claims of the debtor's creditors. That is the situation in this case.

Acme's petition for reclamation is denied.

P-11

THE MPT

MULTISTATE PERFORMANCE TEST

In re Steven Wallace

POINT SHEET

The MPT point sheet, grading summary, and grading guidelines describe the factual and legal points encompassed within the lawyering task to be completed. They outline all the possible issues and points that might be addressed by an applicant. They are provided to the user jurisdictions for the sole purpose of assisting graders in grading the examination by identifying the issues and suggesting the resolution of the problem contemplated by the drafters. These are not official grading guides. Applicants can receive a range of passing grades, including excellent grades, without covering all the points discussed in these guides. The model answer is included as an illustration of a thorough and detailed response to the task, one that addresses all the legal and factual issues the drafters intended to raise in the problem. It is intended to serve only as an example. Applicants need not present their responses in the same way to receive good grades. User jurisdictions are free to modify these grading materials, including the suggested weights assigned to particular points. Grading the MPT is the exclusive responsibility of the jurisdiction using the MPT as part of its admissions process.

In Re Steven Wallace

DRAFTERS' POINT SHEET

In this performance test item, Steven Wallace, an artist, delivers a painting to Lottie Zelinka, an art dealer, on consignment. Lottie files bankruptcy under Chapter 11 and later converts it to a straight Chapter 7 case. Thereafter, she returns the painting to Steven, and the trustee demands that Steven return the painting to the bankrupt estate. Steven consults Eva Morales, the supervising attorney in this case.

The task for the applicant is to draft a two-part memo in which he/she: first, analyzes the facts and the law regarding the bankruptcy trustee's claim that the painting is an estate asset; second, identifies what UCC defenses are available to Steven, explains how the facts currently known support the defenses, and suggests what additional facts might be developed to support the defenses.

The File consists of the assignment memo from Ms. Morales to the applicant, notes of the interview with Steven, and some documents Steven left with Ms. Morales. The Library contains excerpts from a basic bankruptcy treatise, § 2-326 of the Franklin Commercial Code (FCC), a section of the Franklin Civil Code, and two cases. All of the materials the applicants will need to work their way through the problem are contained in the test item.

The following points that might be discussed by an applicant are suggested by the problem. Grades will be assigned depending on the degree of thoroughness, and an applicant can get an excellent grade without covering all of these points.

1. **Based on the facts as they appear in the file, does the bankruptcy trustee have a legitimate claim to the painting?**

   • The facts make it clear that the painting was redelivered to Steven by Lottie after the bankruptcy proceeding began. Thus, she made a "post-petition transfer" of property that was in the possession of the bankruptcy estate.

   • Drawing on the excerpts from Walker on Bankruptcy and *In re Levy*, the applicants should conclude that the trustee has the right to "avoid a transfer of property of the estate…that occurs after the commencement of the case." *Walker on Bankruptcy* § 4.08.

   • The real question then becomes whether the painting was "property of the estate." That calls for an in-depth analysis of the FCC provision on consignments—§ 2-326.

   • The interview notes and the Inventory Receipt show clearly that Steven (consignor) delivered the painting to Lottie (consignee) on a true consignment; i.e., he delivered it to her to see if she could sell it for him, he retained title, she would get a commission if she could sell it, and she could return it without obligation if she couldn't sell it. Thus, it was a "sale or return" transaction under FCC § 2-326.

   • Unless one or more of the exceptions provided for in § 2-326(3) applies, the FCC makes it clear that "goods held on sale or return are subject to [claims of the consignee's creditors] while in the [consignee's] possession," irrespective of whether the consignor (Steven) retained title. This point is fully discussed in the *First National Bank* and *Levy* cases, and the applicants should have no problem understanding the concept.

   • Thus, on the face of it, the trustee, standing as he does in the shoes of a lien creditor of Artists' Exchange, has a legitimate claim to the painting.

2. **The defenses and the current and additional facts that might support them.**

   • **Known facts:** The applicants should discuss each of the defenses under § 2-326(3) exceptions and whatever known facts there are to support them; and, if there are no supporting facts, simply say so and move on.

   • The "sign law" exception (§ 2-326(3)(a)) probably doesn't apply on the known facts. Although Steven put a 2" x 3" label on the back of the painting identifying himself as the owner, it is not likely that it was "posted conspicuously" within the meaning of Franklin Civil Code § 3533. See, also, the discussion in *Levy* as to whether the label was calculated to inform creditors or just possible customers. Whether there was a sign posted by Lottie in the front window (as Steven seems to "think" there was) is not known at this point.

   • There is no basis, on the facts currently known, to conclude that it was "generally known to [Lottie's] creditors" that she was "substantially engaged in selling goods of others." It is arguable that the very name of the art gallery, "Artists' Exchange," communicates such a notion and that the sign Steven "thinks" he saw in the window (i.e., "All offers will be considered and forwarded to the artists") does too, but there are not enough facts currently known. Thus, the § 2-326(3)(b) exception doesn't help at this stage.

   • There is no current information that Steven filed a UCC financing statement, so there is no basis for invoking the § 2-326(3)(c) exception.

   • The strongest defense based on the known facts is that the painting, before Steven delivered it to Lottie, was "used… for personal, family, or household purposes," and that the exception in § 2-326(3)(d) applies.[1] The interview notes are ambiguous on that point. On the one hand, they show that Steven had the painting hanging in his dining room and hadn't thought about selling it until Lottie suggested it. It is also helpful that Steven and his wife had purchased a new rug with colors that complemented the colors in the painting; this is evidence that they intended to keep the painting for personal use. On the other hand, it is clear enough that Steven did regularly sell his paintings. More facts are needed on what their intentions were.

   • **Additional facts, sources, and why the additional facts are important:** The notion in this part of the test item is to require the applicants to scour materials for facts that are hinted at in the File and Library, focusing on facts that would help invoke the protective exceptions listed in § 2-326(3).

   • **Whether Steven filed a UCC financing statement.**

     • **Why important:** Although it is not probable that he did file a financing statement, it does not appear affirmatively from the facts that Ms. Morales even asked the question. It would help if he had because it would invoke the protective exception of § 2-326(3)(c) and might get him home free.

     • **Sources:** Ask Steven himself or make a search with the Secretary of State's office or other public filing offices.

   • **Whether the painting can persuasively be characterized as "goods… used…for personal, family or household purposes."**

     • **Why important:** If that can be shown, it will, without more, invoke

[1] This exception, found in the library version of § 2-326, is not part of the official version of the UCC. It is part of the California UCC and is included here because it makes a good test issue.

Task F:

Organizing a Legal Memo Where the Work Product Requires Comparing Two Statutes or Regulations:

Franklin Asbestos Handling Regulations

FILE

INSTRUCTION FROM THE ATTORNEY GENERAL

Office of the Attorney General
State of Franklin
Environmental Protection Division

Candace G. Meyer, Attorney General

To: Applicant
From: Colin Dillard, Deputy Attorney General
Re: Regulations Implementing the Asbestos Handling Act
Date: July 27, 2000

Six months ago, the Franklin Legislature enacted the Asbestos Handling Act (AHA), which, among other things, requires the Franklin Department of Environmental Protection (DEP) to implement health and safety programs to train and certify workers who handle asbestos. DEP has asked us to review the proposed regulations it has drafted.

I anticipate the AHA statutory and regulatory scheme will be challenged on the ground that it is preempted by the federal Occupational Safety and Health Act (OSH Act) and the implementing federal regulations. Franklin has not adopted a State Plan under the OSH Act and has no intention of doing so.

Please prepare a memorandum for me that:

1) States the best case for why, in light of the absence of a State Plan, the statutory and regulatory scheme is not preempted in its entirety; and

2) Discusses whether each provision of Section 8 of the draft regulations can survive a preemption challenge.

ASBESTOS HANDLING ACT

Franklin Environmental Protection Code
Title 6 - Asbestos Control
Chapter 15. Asbestos Handling Act

Section 1. Findings and Purpose. The legislature of the State of Franklin finds that the predominant cause of asbestos becoming airborne is the performance of building renovation and demolition without adequate adherence to appropriate procedures for safeguarding the general public by persons who have not received adequate training in the handling of materials containing asbestos. The purposes of this subtitle are: 1) to safeguard the public health by requiring that renovation or demolition projects that disturb asbestos be conducted in accordance with procedures established pursuant to the provisions of this law; and 2) to ensure that workers who handle materials containing asbestos receive appropriate training designed to protect the public health.

* * *

Section 3. Unlawful Activities.

(a) It shall be unlawful for any person to perform a renovation or demolition project involving asbestos unless that person has received approval from the Franklin Department of Environmental Protection of a written plan specifying all steps that will be taken to protect the public, including monitoring air quality in the area surrounding the renovation or demolition site and restricting access to the site by anyone other than certified workers.

(b) It shall be unlawful to employ any person to handle asbestos material in the course of performing work for compensation on an asbestos project unless such person is a holder of a current, valid asbestos handling certificate.

* * *

Section 5. Fees and Assessments. The Franklin Department of Environmental Protection shall set reasonable fees and assessments to be used for the safe elimination of asbestos from buildings.

Section 6. Permits. No town or municipality shall issue a permit for a renovation or demolition project involving asbestos unless the applicant has established a plan pursuant to Section 3(a) and can show that each person working on the project holds a valid asbestos handling certificate pursuant to Section 3(b).

Section 7. Regulations to be Issued by the Secretary of the Franklin Department of Environmental Protection. In order to safeguard the health and safety of the public, including all persons who work at a renovation or demolition project involving asbestos, the Secretary of the Franklin Department of Environmental Protection shall establish criteria for: 1) certifying persons as eligible to receive an asbestos handling certificate; 2) certifying programs as approved safety and health programs; and 3) controlling asbestos during renovation or demolition projects. The Department shall implement an assessment procedure for funding the certification and training.

* * *

ASBESTOS HANDLING ACT

DRAFT

Department of Environmental Protection
Chapter 4 - Regulations Regarding Asbestos Control
Proposed Regulations Implementing Asbestos Handling Act
May 26, 2000

SUMMARY: These Proposed Regulations implement the Asbestos Handling Act, codified in Chapter 15 of Title 6 of the Franklin Environmental Protection Code. The Proposed Regulations govern procedures for conducting renovation and demolition projects that disturb asbestos and for training and certification of asbestos handlers, asbestos supervisors and asbestos investigators.

BACKGROUND: See attached Report of the Research and Investigation Unit of the Department of Environmental Protection (DEP) on The Dangers of Airborne Asbestos Created by Construction Work in the State of Franklin.

* * * *

Section 8. Training and Certification of Asbestos Handlers.

(a) Any employee seeking an asbestos handling certificate must complete a five-day, DEP-approved training course and pass a two-hour written examination.

(b) An approved DEP training course for asbestos handlers must cover the following specific topics:

(1) the physical characteristics, including hazards and effects, of asbestos
(2) worker protective equipment
(3) state-of-the-art practices for asbestos abatement and remediation
(4) procedures for collecting asbestos samples to minimize airborne fibers
(5) personal hygiene pertaining to asbestos handling

(c) Any employee having an asbestos handling certificate must complete a one-day, DEP-approved biennial review course to renew the handler certificate.

(d) Upon receiving proof of completion of a DEP-approved training or review course for asbestos handlers and payment of $100, DEP shall issue an asbestos handler's certificate.

(e) Each employer performing work on a project in which any employee must handle asbestos must provide to the DEP the names of all employees possessing an asbestos handler's certificate, along with an assessment of $600 per year for each such employee.

* * * *

RESEARCH PAPER

Department of Environmental Protection
State of Franklin

The Dangers of Airborne Asbestos Created by Construction Work
in the State of Franklin
John P. Ripka, Chief, Research and Investigation Unit

Asbestos, a family of inorganic fibrous mineral substances once thought to be "wonder materials," has been identified in recent years as a formidable health threat. Much attention has been given to workplace hazards created by asbestos, but only recently has the focus been broadened to encompass the public health hazards presented by the widespread presence of friable asbestos.

Asbestos is the name given to a group of minerals that occur naturally as masses of strong, flexible fibers that can be separated into thin threads and woven. Asbestos tends to break easily into a dust composed of tiny particles that can float in the air and stick to clothes. The fibers of this so-called "friable" asbestos may be easily inhaled or swallowed and can cause serious health problems.

Exposure to airborne asbestos fibers may induce several serious diseases: asbestosis, a nonmalignant scarring of the lungs that causes extreme shortness of breath and often death; lung cancer; gastrointestinal cancer; and mesothelioma, a cancer of the lung lining or abdomen lining that develops 30 years after the first exposure to asbestos and that, once developed, invariably and rapidly causes death.

Widespread public concern about the hazards of asbestos has resulted in a significant annual decline in U.S. use of asbestos. In 1972, Franklin completely banned asbestos spraying in construction. Before the deadly hazards of asbestos were understood, however, more than half of the high-rise commercial buildings built in the state between 1958 and 1972 used asbestos as fireproofing material and, moreover, virtually every boiler room used the material as a thermal insulator. Franklin buildings contain an estimated 3.5 million tons of asbestos.

Since the early 1940s, millions of American workers have been exposed to asbestos dust. Health effects have been recognized in workers exposed in many trades and occupations. Even workers who have not worked directly with asbestos but whose jobs were located near contaminated areas have developed diseases associated with asbestos exposure.

Family members of workers heavily exposed to asbestos face an increased risk of developing

asbestos-related diseases. This risk is thought to result from exposure to asbestos dust brought into the home on the shoes, clothing, skin, and hair of workers. Asbestos is so widely used that the entire population has been exposed to some degree. To protect all citizens, proper safety precautions should always be taken by people working with asbestos. Both the federal government and the state of Franklin have recognized that safety lies in speedy action, which each has taken. The federal Occupational Safety and Health Administration has promulgated regulations to minimize the threat to construction workers from asbestos exposure. To minimize the threat to the general public from asbestos removal, Franklin and its Department of Environmental Protection have established a program to ensure the safe elimination of asbestos from buildings for workers who handle asbestos.

LIBRARY

United States Code

OCCUPATIONAL SAFETY AND HEALTH ACT

29 U.S.C. § 652 Definitions

* * * *

(8) The term "occupational safety and health standard" means a standard which requires conditions, or the adoption or use of one or more practices, means, methods, operations, or processes reasonably necessary or appropriate to provide safe or healthful employment and places of employment.

* * * *

29 U.S.C. § 667 State jurisdiction and plans

(a) Assertion of State standards in absence of applicable Federal standards.
Nothing in this chapter shall prevent any State agency or court from asserting jurisdiction under State law over any occupational safety or health issue with respect to which no Federal standard is in effect.

(b) Submission of State plan for development and enforcement of State standards to preempt applicable Federal standards. Any State which, at any time, desires to assume responsibility for development and enforcement therein of occupational safety and health standards relating to any occupational safety or health issue with respect to which a Federal standard has been promulgated shall submit a State plan for the development of such standards and their enforcement.

OSHA STANDARDS

Code of Federal Regulations

CHAPTER XVII—OCCUPATIONAL SAFETY AND HEALTH ADMINISTRATION
U.S. DEPARTMENT OF LABOR
PXRT 1910—OCCUPATIONAL SAFETY AND HEALTH STANDARDS
SUBPART Z—TOXIC AND HAZARDOUS SUBSTANCES

29 C.F.R. § 1926 Asbestos.

* * * *

(f) Exposure limit. The employer shall ensure that no employee is exposed to an airborne concentration of asbestos in excess of 1.0 fiber per cubic centimeter of air (1 f/cc) as averaged over a sampling period of thirty (30) minutes.

(g) All employers of employees exposed to asbestos hazards shall comply with applicable protective provisions to protect their employees.

(h) Each employer who has a workplace or work operation where exposure monitoring is required shall perform monitoring to determine accurately the airborne concentrations of asbestos to which employees may be exposed.

(i) The employer shall notify affected employees of the monitoring results that represent that employee's exposure as soon as possible following receipt of monitoring results.

(j) When a building owner or employer identifies previously installed asbestos-containing material, labels or signs shall be affixed or posted so that employees will be notified of the presence of asbestos-containing materials.

(k) Where vacuuming methods are used, filtered vacuuming equipment must be used. The equipment shall be used and emptied in a manner that minimizes the reentry of asbestos into the workplace.

(l) All employees performing work covered by this paragraph shall be trained in a training program that meets the requirements of this section.

(m) Employee Information and Training.

(i) The employer shall, at no cost to the employee, institute a training program for all employees who are likely to be exposed to asbestos and ensure their participation in the program.

(ii) Training shall be provided prior to or at the time of initial assignment and at least annually thereafter.

(ii) Training shall be provided prior to or at the time of initial assignment and at least annually thereafter.

(iii) Training shall include "hands-on" training and shall take at least eight (8) hours.

(iv) The training program shall be conducted in a manner that the employee is able to understand. The employer shall ensure that each such employee is informed of the following:

(A) Methods of recognizing asbestos;

(B) The health effects associated with asbestos exposure;

(C) The relationship between smoking and asbestos in producing lung cancer;

(D) The nature of operations that could result in exposure to asbestos, the importance of necessary protective controls to minimize exposure, including, as applicable, engineering controls, work practices, respirators, housekeeping procedures, emergency procedures, protective clothing, decontamination procedures, and any necessaiy instruction in the use of these controls and procedures;

(E) The purpose, proper use, fitting instructions, and limitations of respirators;

(F) The appropriate work practices for performing the asbestos job;

* * * *

Gade v. National Solid Wastes Management Association

United States Supreme Court (1992)

In 1988, the Illinois General Assembly enacted the Hazardous Waste Crane Operators Licensing Act. The purpose of the act is both to promote job safety and to protect life, limb and property. We consider whether such a dual impact statute, which protects both workers and the general public, is preempted by the federal Occupational Safety and Health Act of 1970 (OSH Act) and the standards promulgated thereunder.

The OSH Act authorizes the Secretary of Labor to promulgate occupational safety and health regulations. In the Superfund Amendments and Reauthorization Act of 1986, Congress directed the Secretary of Labor to promulgate regulations for the health and safety protection of employees engaged in hazardous waste operations, including routine training.

The Occupational Safety and Health Administration (OSHA) promulgated the required regulations, including detailed regulations on worker training requirements. Those who have satisfied the eight-hour training requirement receive a written certification; uncertified workers are prohibited from engaging in hazardous waste operations.

The Illinois licensing act at issue here is designated as an act "in relation to environmental protection," and its stated aim is to protect both employees and the general public. The licensing act requires a license applicant to provide a certified record of at least 40 hours of training under an approved program conducted within Illinois, to pass a written examination, and to complete an annual refresher course. Employees who work without the proper license and employers who knowingly permit an unlicensed employee to work are subject to fines.

National Solid Wastes Management Association (Association) is a national trade association of businesses that dispose of waste material, including hazardous waste. The Association's members are subject to the OSH Act and OSHA regulations. For hazardous waste operations conducted in Illinois, certain of the workers employed by the Association's members are also required to obtain state licenses. Thus, for example, some of the Association's members must ensure that their employees receive not only the eight hours of field experience required for certification under the OSHA regulations, but also the 40 hours of training required for licensing under the state statutes.

The Association brought a declaratory judgment action against Mary Gade, the Director of the Illinois Environmental Protection Agency (IEPA), and sought to enjoin IEPA from enforcing the Illinois act, claiming that the act was preempted by the OSH Act and workplace safety and health while regulat-ing in other areas are not necessarily preempt-ed. The United States Court of Appeals for the Seventh Circuit affirmed in part and re-versed in part. We granted certiorari.

Before addressing the scope of the OSH Act's preemption of dual impact state regulations, we consider the threshold question of wheth-er the Act preempts nonconflicting state regula-tions at all. Whether a state action is pre-empted by federal law is a question of congressional intent. In the OSH Act, Con-gress endeavored "to assure so far as possible every working man and woman in the na-tion safe and healthful working conditions." Congress authorized the Secretary of Labor to set mandatory occupational safety and health standards applicable to all businesses affecting interstate commerce and thereby brought the federal government into a field that tradition-ally had been occupied by the states. Federal regulation of the workplace was not intended to be all encompassing, however. The Act does not prevent state regulation of any oc-cupational safety or health issue "with respect to which no Federal standard is in effect." 29 U.S.C. § 667(a). In addition to reserving areas for state regulation, the Act gave the states the option of entirely assuming regulation in an area. 29 U.S.C. § 667(b). Illinois has not sought or received the Secretary's approval for its own state plan. 29 U.S.C. § 667(b) pre-empts any state law or regulation that estab-lishes an occupational health and safety stan-dard on an issue for which OSHA has already promulgated a standard, unless the State has obtained approval for its own plan.

Absent explicit preemptive language, we have recognized at least two types of implied pre-emption: field preemption, where the scheme of federal regulation is so pervasive as to make reasonable the inference that Con-gress left no room for the states to supplement it, and conflict preemption, where compli-ance with both federal and state regulations is a physical impossibility or where state law stands as an obstacle to the accomplish-ment and execution of the full purposes and objec-tives of Congress.

We hold that nonapproved state regula-tion of occupational safety and health issues for which a federal standard is in effect is im-pliedly preempted as in conflict with the full purposes and objectives of the OSH Act. Congress intended to subject employers and employees to only one set of regulations, be it federal or state, and the only way a state may regulate an OSHA-regulated occupa-tional safety and health issue is through an approved state plan. The OSH Act as a whole evi-dences Congress' intent to avoid subject-ing workers and employers to duplicative regula-tion; a state may develop an occupa-tional safety and health program, but only if it dis-places applicable federal regulations with an approved state plan.

Also, 29 U.S.C. § 667(a), which saves from preemption any state law regulating an occu-pational safety and health issue with re-spect to which no federal standard is in effect, implies that state laws regulating the same is-sue as federal laws are not saved, even if they merely supplement federal law.

In determining whether state law stands as an obstacle to the full implementation of a fed-eral law, it is not enough to say that the ulti-mate goal of both federal and state law is the same. A state law is preempted if it inter-feres with the methods by which the federal statute was designed to reach that goal.

We now consider whether a state law that addresses public safety as well as occupa-tional safety, a dual impact law, can be an "occupa-tional safety and health standard" subject to preemption under the Act. The OSH Act does not lose its preemptive force merely because the state legislature articu-lates a purpose other than (or in addition to) workplace health and safety. In assessing the impact of a state law on the federal scheme, we have refused to rely solely on the legislature's professed purpose and have looked as well to the effects of the law. Any state legislation that frustrates the full effectiveness of federal law is rendered invalid by the Supremacy Clause.

The key question is at what point the state regulation sufficiently interferes with federal regulation that it should be deemed pre-empted. In the absence of an approved state plan, the OSH Act preempts all state law that constitutes, in a direct, clear and substantial way, regulation of worker health and safety. State laws of general applicability that do not conflict with OSHA standards and that regulate the conduct of workers and nonworkers alike would generally not be preempted. Although some laws of general applicability may have a direct and substantial effect on worker safety, they cannot fairly

be characterized as occupational standards because they regulate workers as members of the general public. A law directed at workplace safety, however, is not saved from preemption simply because it has effects outside of the workplace.

Because the provisions of Illinois law have a direct and substantial effect on the federal scheme for regulation of hazardous waste, they are preempted. Affirmed.

Chamber of Commerce v. Noter, Secretary of Franklin Department of Labor, et al.

United States Court of Appeals for the Fifteenth Circuit (1995)

This is an appeal from a summary judgment in consolidated actions challenging the con¬stitutionality of the Franklin Worker and Community Right-to-Know Act (Know Act), which requires the disclosure of substances that may pose workplace and environmental hazards. The district court held that some of the sections of the Know Act are preempted by the federal Occupational Safety and Health Act (OSH Act) and OSHA's Hazard Com¬munication Regulations. All parties appeal. We affirm in part and reverse in part.

The legislative findings and declaration of purpose, included in the Know Act, provide that

The proliferation of hazardous sub¬stances in the environment poses a threat to the public health. Individu¬als have a right to know the risks they face so that they can make informed decisions and take informed action concerning their employment and their living conditions. Local health, fire, police, safety and other govern¬ment officials require detailed informa¬tion about the identity of hazardous sub¬stances in order to adequately plan for, and respond to, emergencies. It is in the public interest to establish a com¬prehensive program for the disclosure of information about hazardous sub¬stances in the workplace and the com¬munity and to provide a proce¬dure for residents to gain access to this information.

The Know Act directs the Franklin Department of Environmental Protection (DEP) to develop an environmental hazardous substance list, which must contain substances used, manufactured, stored, packaged, repackaged, or disposed of or released into the environment of the state which, in the department's determination, may be linked to the incidence of cancer and other diseases.

Whether a state law or regulation is preempted by a federal statute is a question of congressional intent. Gade v. National Solid Wastes Management Association (U.S. Supreme Court, 1992).

The Chamber of Commerce contends that 29 U.S.C. § 667 (a) and (b) should be read ex¬pansively to preempt all state statutes that relate to a safety or health issue for which a standard has been promulgated. It further contends that, since all provisions of the Know Act relate to issues that are regulated by the OSHA Hazard Communication Regula¬tions, the Franklin statute is preempted in its entirety. We reject this broad reading.

The Supreme Court in Gade (supra) has acknowledged that a state law or regulation that has a "dual purpose" may escape complete preemption even though it might have an incidental effect upon the scheme of federal regulations. For example, a law or regulation the principal purpose of which is to train employees in safety-affecting measures aimed at protecting the public from dangers arising from processes or materials handled in the workplace1 may escape complete preemption even though it has incidental effects on work-place safety. Thus, it may be necessary to parse the components of the state regulation into its preempted and non-preempted provisions.

Consideration of whether a state provision violates the Supremacy Clause starts with the basic assumption that Congress did not intend to displace state law. A section is preempted only to the extent that congressional intent can be found expressly or by implication. The mere fact that a state law provision increases the regulatory burden on employers does not make the state law provision contrary to congressional intent. Portions of the Know Act, however, are preempted.

The first part of the Know Act directs the Franklin DEP and Department of Health to develop environmental and workplace hazard¬ous substance lists. In these provisions, Franklin has opted for a different hazard identification procedure than that adopted in the federal Hazard Communication Regula¬tions. The federal procedure depends primarily upon identification and communication of hazards by the original manufacturer or im¬porter of the substance.

Franklin's development of its own list of hazardous substances through governmental agencies in all sectors of the economy will in no way inhibit the implementation of the federal standard. The state lists are not an obstacle to the full implementation of the federal law because they do not "interfere with the methods" used in the Hazard Communica¬tion Regulations to achieve the goal of worker health and safety.

In addition, where, as here, a state statute has a dual purpose of promoting both the health and safety of the worker and the health and safety of the general population, the statute is preempted only if it has a "direct and substan¬tial" effect on the federal system of regulation. Therefore, the sections of the Know Act regarding the development of lists by the agencies of the Franklin government are not preempted.

The second part of the Know Act requires employers to complete both environmental and workplace hazard surveys and to furnish the workplace surveys to state agencies concerned with the protection of employees and to state and local agencies concerned with the protection of the public at large. The requirement that they be furnished to both kinds of agencies suggests that these sections of the Act may have a broader purpose than the federal Hazard Communication Regulations. However, any hazardous substance listed as a workplace hazard and not listed as an environmental hazard is deemed to be a specific threat to workers. The sections of the surveys about workplace hazards have a direct and substantial effect on the promotion of occupational health and safety through hazard communication. The federal Hazard Communication Regulations preempt these

THE MPT

MULTISTATE PERFORMANCE TEST

Franklin Asbestos Handling Regulations

POINT SHEET

The MPT point sheet, grading summary, and grading guidelines describe the factual and legal points encompassed within the lawyering task to be completed. They outline all the possible issues and points that might be addressed by an applicant. They are provided to the user jurisdictions for the sole purpose of assisting graders in grading the examination by identifying the issues and suggesting the resolution of the problem contemplated by the drafters. These are not official grading guides. Applicants can receive a range of passing grades, including excellent grades, without covering all the points discussed in these guides. The model answer is included as an illustration of a thorough and detailed response to the task, one that addresses all the legal and factual issues the drafters intended to raise in the problem. It is intended to serve only as an example. Applicants need not present their responses in the same way to receive good grades. User jurisdictions are free to modify these grading materials, including the suggested weights assigned to particular points. Grading the MPT is the exclusive responsibility of the jurisdiction using the MPT as part of its admissions process.

The judgment is affirmed in part, reversed in part, and the case remanded for proceedings consistent with this opinion.

sections because they are in conflict with the methods chosen by the federal government to promote hazard communication. Similarly, the obligation of employers to keep a central file of workplace surveys is also preempted.

However, since the sections requiring reporting of environmental hazards (as opposed to workplace hazards) to agencies concerned with public health and safety are not a matter governed by the OSH Act and OSHA regulations, they are not preempted. Neither are the sections requiring employers to keep and make available environmental surveys. OSHA regulations govern occupational safety and health issues; they do not preempt state laws that regulate other concerns. OSHA regulations cannot have a preemptive effect beyond that field.

The Know Act provides that the governmental activity will be funded by assessments against all Franklin employers. The Chamber of Commerce argues that since this financing mechanism indicates that the Act is aimed solely at occupational safety and health, rather than at community health and safety in general, all provisions of the Act should be preempted. That contention is without merit. The funding provision is a logical means for accomplishing a broad community health and safety purpose. It does not interfere with compliance with the OSH Act or impose obstacles to the accomplishment of the OSH Act's purposes. *John Saint, Secretary of the Franklin Department of Labor v. Port Orey Co.* (15th Cir. 1994)

Franklin Asbestos Handling Regulations

DRAFTERS' POINT SHEET

In this performance test item, the applicant is cast in the role of a lawyer in the Office of the Attorney General. The Franklin Department of Environmental Protection (DEP) has asked the Attorney General to opine whether the Franklin Asbestos Handling Act (AHA) and the proposed regulations implementing the AHA are preempted by the federal Occupational Safety and Health Act (OSH Act).

The File contains the relevant provisions of the AHA, a draft of the proposed regulations, and a recent report of the DEP on the dangers of airborne asbestos. The Library contains excerpts from the OSH Act and the federal OSHA regulations, and two cases dealing with the subject.

The task is for the applicant to prepare a two-part memorandum: 1) arguing that the AHA and the proposed DEP regulations as a whole are not preempted; and 2) discussing whether each of the particular provisions of the proposed regulations can survive a preemption challenge. The contending principles are whether the DEP regulations intrude upon the OSH Act's domain of workplace safety regulations or whether they can be justified in whole or in part as regulations aimed at non-workplace, public safety measures.

1. **Overview:** The applicants are not required to follow any particular format, except that the work product ought to end up looking like an office memorandum. It should consist of two separate parts, the first part dealing with the overall preemption issue and the second with the individual provisions of the proposed regulations, testing each provision against the preemption principles articulated in the cases. The following points are all the ones the drafters believe are raised in the test item. Applicants need not cover them all to receive "passing" or even very good scores.

2. **Overall Preemption:** Here, the applicants should set out the general grounds of federal preemption and examine the AHA and the proposed DEP regulations in light of the "dual impact" holding of the Gade case.

- In Gade, the Supreme Court states that, unless Congress has explicitly preempted state activity in a particular area of legislation, a state may act unless the two types of implied preemption preclude it: field preemption and conflict preemption.
  - Congress did not explicitly preempt all state activity in the area of safety and health regulation.
  - Congress did, however, intend to preempt *occupational* safety and health

regulation insofar as it pertains to employee workplace safety, unless:

- The state regulation purports to establish a protective measure as to which there is no federal "standard" and the state regulation does not burden commerce; or
- The state has chosen to retain jurisdiction by submitting and obtaining approval of its own "state plan."
  - It is clear from the facts that Franklin does not have or intend to submit a state plan.
- In matters relating to employee workplace safety and health, there is no "field" preemption but there will be "conflict" preemption when a state attempts to regulate employee workplace safety and health in a way that conflicts with or even purports to supplement an existing federal standard. *See Gade.*

However, it is possible to avoid total preemption if the state action under scrutiny has a "dual impact," e.g., is aimed both at workplace regulation and public safety.

- The preamble to the AHA states that, "The purposes of this subtitle are: 1) to safeguard the public health by requiring that renovation or demolition projects that disturb asbestos be conducted in accordance with procedures established pursuant to this law; and 2) to ensure that workers who handle materials containing asbestos receive appropriate training designed to protect the public health."
  - This section contains something of an ambiguity in that it says that one of the two purposes is 'to ensure that...*workers*...receive appropriate training," thus giving it a "dual impact" character.
- The "Background" section of the proposed regulations refers to the DEP's investigative report as the impetus for the regulations. The focus of that report is on the public health hazards associated with the handling of friable asbestos (i.e., asbestos-containing materials that, when dry, can be crumbled by hand) and the need for training of workers who handle the materials.
  - Again, the proposed regulations partake of a "dual impact" character because they involve both workers (the subject of the federal OSH Act regulations) and public health (not covered by the OSH Act).

- The Individual Provisions:
  - The DEP requirement for employee certification: The purpose of the DEP regulations is to implement the requirement of the AHA that persons employed to work in occupations involving the handling of friable asbestos in asbestos-containing renovation and demolition projects be certified in asbestos handling technology.
    - The OSHA regulations do not require certification of employees handling asbestos in the workplace. Arguably, therefore, because OSHA has established a "standard" that does not require certification, the OSHA regulations preempt the DEP regulations.
    - However, the threshold certification requirement under the AHA is designed basically to ensure public health and safety as opposed to employee workplace safety.
      - As such, it deals with an area not within the ambit of the OSH Act.
    - Resolution: Because of the disparate purpose of the AHA certification requirement, it is not preempted by the OSH Act. As the court said in *Gade*, even though this dual impact law might have a direct effect on worker safety, it is not preempted as an occupational standard because it regulates workers as members of the general public.
  - DEP Reg. § 8(a)—Five-day training course and two-hour exam: Both the proposed DEP regulations and the existing OSHA regulations require employees to undergo asbestos training. Under the OSHA regulations, it is the employer's responsibility to "institute a training program....and ensure [employee] participation." Under the DEP regulations, it is the employee's obligation to "complete a five-day, DEP-approved training course."
    - Both sets of regulations are aimed at *employees* who handle asbestos in their occupations and places of employment.
    - It is a distinction without a difference. That, under the OSHA regulations, the employer must initiate the program while, under the DEP regulations, it is the employee's responsibility to take the course.

- In the final analysis, the AHA probably avoids complete preemption because of its dual impact character.
  - As the *Gade* court says, the key question is at what point the state regulation sufficiently interferes with the federal regulation that it should be preempted.
    - Merely labeling a statute as having a dual impact will not avoid preemption.
      - The AHA and the proposed regulations are arguably preempted because they deal with an area where the federal OSH Act and the OSHA regulations have established a "standard," i.e., asbestos handling in the workplace.
      - But, according to *Gade*, a statute of general application will not be preempted, even though it has a direct effect on worker safety, if the focus is on workers as members of the general public rather than as employees working in a regulated workplace.
  - The conclusion the applicants should reach is that the AHA and the proposed regulations are not completely preempted because they are not aimed principally at protecting workers but, rather, at training and certifying them in work methods designed to protect the public.

3. **Whether each of the particular provisions of the proposed regulations can survive a preemption challenge:** Having concluded that the proposed regulations are not completely preempted, the applicants must turn to the teaching of the *Noter* case: that certain parts might be preempted if they have a "direct and substantial effect on the federal system of regulation."
  - The task here is to test each of the provisions of the proposed regulations against the guidelines articulated in *Noter*, i.e.:
    - Whether the particular provision is preempted because it interferes with the federal regulations or the methods chosen by the federal regulations to implement the OSH Act;
    - Whether any particular provision relates so much to a workplace safety standard that it *per se* falls within the ambit of the OSHA regulations and is therefore preempted; or
    - Whether it is not at all a workplace safety measure within the ambit of the OSH Act and is, for that reason, not preempted.

The DEP regulations require each employee to take a five-day training course and to pass a two-hour written exam.

- By way of contrast, the OSHA regulations provide for a course of "at least eight (8) hours" and do not require passage of an exam.

- Resolution: It is probable that this part of the DEP regulation is preempted to the extent that it requires a five-day course and a two-hour test, i.e.:

- Although its ultimate aim is to train employees in methods of protecting the public, it is nonetheless a workplace regulation in an area where the federal OSHA regulations have an existing standard and the two are in conflict. It can be argued that DEP's five-day requirement is not in conflict because the OSHA regulations say "at least" eight hours, but the disparity is so great that the two cannot be reconciled.

- See *Gade*, which holds that a state regulation is preempted if it tries to regulate the same "issue" as the federal regulation, even if it purports only to supplement the federal issue.

    - Thus, this requirement is preempted either because it is inextricably related to a workplace regulation and is therefore in the sole domain of federal OSHA or because it interferes with the method chosen by the federal regulation to implement the OSH Act.

- DEP Reg. § 8 (b)—Required content of the training course: Both sets of regulations specify the areas in which the employees shall be trained. The corresponding provisions regarding *worker* protection, as to which federal OSHA has exclusive jurisdiction (e.g., respiratory protection, personal protective equipment, hazards and effects of asbestos), are largely identical. There appears to be no conflict and no reason to assert preemption.

    To the extent that the DEP regulations impose additional requirements, those additional requirements appear to be aimed at protection of the *public* (e.g., asbestos abatement and remediation, collection of samples) and are not within the ambit of the OSH Act.

    However, it can be argued that if the five-day training course is

preempted (as argued *supra*), then all components of it, including the course content, are also preempted.

- Resolution: On balance, however, this part of the DEP regulations would probably not be preempted.

    - See *Note*, where it holds that preemption only occurs in a dual purpose statute where there is a direct and substantial effect on the federal system of regulation.

- DEP Reg. § 8 (c)—Periodic review course: Both sets of regulations require that employees undergo a periodic review course. The DEP regulations require a one-day *biennial* review course in each of the specified subjects. The OSHA regulations require it annually and, by implication, for eight hours (the equivalent of one day).

- Although there is no apparent conflict, the OSHA regulation prevails because it has established a standard relating to a workplace activity, over which the OSH Act has exclusive jurisdiction.

    - It can be argued, however, that as to the additional, non-workplace training requirements (*supra*), federal OSHA has no jurisdiction and, therefore, the DEP biennial review requirement is not preempted.

- Resolution: This part of the DEP regulations is probably preempted as to the mutually required training topics because they are workplace issues and federal OSHA regulations have established a standard. As to the training topics related to public safety issues, however, the biennial review requirements are not preempted.

- DEP Reg. 6 8(d)—The requirement for payment of $100 upon completion of the training course: Here, there is a direct conflict. The DEP regulations require payment of $100 for issuance of an asbestos handler's certificate. The OSHA regulations require that the training be at no cost to the employee.

- It is unclear from the DEP regulations whether the employer or the employee must pay the $100, but it is fair to assume that, because having a certificate is a condition of employment in an asbestos handling occupation, the burden falls on the employee.

- <u>Resolution</u>: This provision of the DEP regulations is almost certainly preempted because it is in direct conflict with the OSHA regulation and interferes with the method chosen by federal OSHA to implement the OSH Act.

- <u>DEP Reg. § 8 (e)—The employer's reporting requirement and the $600 assessment</u>: The OSHA regulations are silent on this subject. Because the DEP requirements for employee certification are designed to implement a public safety measure and not to advance workplace safety, the annual assessment does not intrude upon an area where federal OSHA has jurisdiction. As the court observed in *Noter*, "The funding requirement is a logical means for accomplishing a broad community health and safety purpose. It does not interfere with compliance with the OSH Act or impose obstacles to the accomplishment of the OSH Act's purposes."

  - <u>Resolution</u>: This part of the DEP regulation is probably not preempted.

Perform Your Best™ Materials
For Task A:
In re Lisa Peel

MPT-Matrix™ *In re Lisa Peel*, MPT, February 2008, *cont'd*

FRSA	A. Lisa Peel Interview	B. Blog Post	C. America Today	D. Dictionary	E. In re Bellows (Franklin Ct. App. 2005)	F. Lane v. Tichenor (Franklin Sup. Ct. 2003)
	Against Peel: "writer" and "editor" refer to traditional media. Against Peel: **P-2.** She includes pet photos and family news.					
"**For publication through a news medium**" "**Any newspaper,…**"		Lisa Peel's blog post reads like a news story. Posting is like printing. Against Peel: Blog nor a newspaper or magazine.	**P-6.** Some bloggers have press credentials. Blogs are alternative media.	**P-8.** "Publication" is communication of information to the public.		**P-11.** Burden is on the party claiming the reporter's privilege, so court may look to external aids. **P-11.** To determine whether hayriding is included in "other similar activities," the court must give effect to the intent of the legislature. **P-11.** General words after particular words mean things of the same kind.

MPT-Matrix™ *In re Lisa Peel*, MPT, February 2008, *cont'd*

FRSA	A. Lisa Peel Interview	B. Blog Post	C. America Today	D. Dictionary	E. In re Bellows (Franklin Ct. App. 2005)	F. Lane v. Tichenor (Franklin Sup. Ct. 2003)
"issued at regular intervals"	**P-2.** Lisa Peel blogs every weekend, normally but not always on Friday. Against Peel: less regular than newspaper.				**P-9.** In *Haush*, defamatory posts were neither "news" nor posted at regular intervals.	
"Having a general circulation"	**P-2.** Ms. Peel's blog has 3500 registrants in town of 38,000 people, plus numerous non-registered viewers.			**P-8.** "Circulation."		
This act "is intended to promote the free flow of information to the public by prohibiting courts from compelling reporters to disclose unpublished news sources or information received from such sources." "Source" is the person from whom or the means through which the information was obtained.	**P-3.** Peel talks to people on the inside, promises confidentiality. **P-3.** Peel says that because of the limits on subject matter in the local newspaper, her blog is the "only avenue for real news" in the county.				**P-10.** Principal rule of statutory construction is to ascertain and give effect to the legislature's intent. Court must give legislative language "its plain and ordinary meaning and construe the statute as a whole . . . ." **P-9.** The burden is on the party claiming the reporter's privilege under the Act. **P-10.** Extending FRSA to photographers "consistent with the purposes of the act."	

MPT-Matrix™ *In re Lisa Peel*, MPT, February 2008, *cont'd*

FRSA	A. Lisa Peel Interview	B. Blog Post	C. America Today	D. Dictionary	E. In re Bellows (Franklin Ct. App. 2005)	F. Lane v. Tichenor (Franklin Sup. Ct. 2003)
	Against Peel: "writer" and "editor" refer to traditional media. Against Peel: **P-2.** She includes pet photos and family news.					
"For publication through a news medium" "Any newspaper,…"		Lisa Peel's blog post reads like a news story. Posting is like printing. Against Peel: Blog not a newspaper or magazine.	**P-6.** Some bloggers have press credentials. Blogs are alternative media.	**P-8.** "Publication" is communication of information to the public.		**P-11.** Burden is on the party claiming the reporter's privilege, so court may look to external aids. **P-11.** To determine whether hayriding is included in "other similar activities," the court must give effect to the intent of the legislature. **P-11.** General words after particular words mean things of the same kind.

MPT-Matrix™ *In re Lisa Peel*, MPT, February 2008, *cont'd*

FRSA	A. Lisa Peel Interview	B. Blog Post	C. America Today	D. Dictionary	E. In re Bellows (Franklin Ct. App. 2005)	F. Lane v. Tichenor (Franklin Sup. Ct. 2003)
"issued at regular intervals"	**P-2.** Lisa Peel blogs every weekend, normally but not always on Friday. Against Peel: less regular than newspaper.				**P-9.** In *Haush*, defamatory posts were neither "news" nor posted at regular intervals.	
"Having a general circulation"	**P-2.** Ms. Peel's blog has 3500 registrants in town of 38,000 people, plus numerous non-registered viewers.			**P-8.** "Circulation."		
This act "is intended to promote the free flow of information to the public by prohibiting courts from compelling reporters to disclose unpublished news sources or information received from such sources."	**P-3.** Peel talks to people on the inside, promises confidentiality. **P-3.** Peel says that because of the limits on subject matter in the local newspaper, her blog is the "only avenue for real news" in the county.				**P-10.** Principal rule of statutory construction is to ascertain and give effect to the legislature's intent. Court must give legislative language "its plain and ordinary meaning and construe the statute as a whole . . . ." **P-9.** The burden is on the party claiming the reporter's privilege under the Act. **P-10.** Extending FRSA to photographers "consistent with the purposes of the act."	
"Source" is the person from whom or the means through which the information was obtained.						

Perform Your Best™ Sample Answer for *In re Lisa Peel*

Black, Fernandez & Hanson LLP

Attorneys at Law
Suite 215
396 West Main Street
Greenville, Franklin 33755

MEMORANDUM

To: Henry Black

From: Bar Candidate

Re: Peel subpoena

Date: _____

INTRODUCTION

You have asked me to prepare an objective memorandum examining both sides of the question whether our client Lisa Peel qualifies under the Franklin Reporter Shield Act (FRSA) to resist a subpoena ordering her to appear before a grand jury and produce notes regarding persons she interviewed for a post on her blog. I conclude that Lisa Peel is a "reporter" under the FRSA, and that she qualifies for its protection. The court will probably grant her motion to quash the subpoena.

DISCUSSION

I. Lisa Peel qualifies as a "reporter" under the Franklin Reporter Shield Act (FRSA), if her blog is a "news medium."

The Franklin Reporter Shield Act (FRSA) gives reporters a privilege not to "disclose the source of any information or any unpublished material" except as the Act provides. FRSA sec. 902. For the Franklin Reporter Shield Act to apply to blogger Lisa Peel she must be a "reporter." The burden is on Peel to show that she qualifies. *In re Bellows* (Franklin Sup. Ct. 2002).

The principal rule of statutory construction is to ascertain and give effect to the legislature's intent. *In re Bellows*. The primary purpose of the FRSA is to "safeguard the media's ability to gather news," promoting the free flow of information by prohibiting courts from "compelling reporters to disclose unpublished news sources or information received from such sources."

Section 901(a) of the FRSA defines "reporter" as follows:

"[R]eporter" means any person regularly engaged in collecting, writing, or editing news for publication through a news medium.

In *Bellow*s, where the court held that a photographer is a reporter under the FRSA, the court said that the key is the person's intent at the inception of news-gathering. Here, like the photographer in *Bellows*, Lisa Peel does all her news-gathering with the intent of publishing it.

Peel is also like a freelance writer and like the author of a medical journal article, both of them held to be reporters in cases cited in *Bellows*. Peel's blog is arguably distinguishable from the venues where the court found that writers were not reporters: paid ads or defamatory messages on sports bulletin boards.

On the other hand, Peel may appear not to qualify as a reporter because she has no training as a reporter, she does not get paid, and she includes pet pictures, family news, and other matter lacking newsworthiness on her blog. In light of her performing the work of a reporter, however, these arguments are not compelling.

Collecting news. Lisa Peel does the work of a reporter collecting news. She attends meetings and collects and posts agendas and minutes of local government agencies, and she makes calls and does interviews. Peel Interview. Writing news. Ms. Peel writes news and commentary about the news. Peel Interview. Editing news. Ms. Peel edits what goes into the blog. She decides which stories to pursue and what to post.

II. Posts on Lisa Peel's blog are "publication" through a "news medium" within the meaning of the Franklin Reporter Shield Act, and her source for information about Assistant Superintendent Frank Peterson's retaining equipment belonging to the Greenville School District qualifies as a "source" within the meaning of the FRSA.

Publication through a news medium. The FRSA protects work done "for publication through a news medium," but it does not define "publication." Thus, the court may look to external aids. *Lane*. According to the *American Heritage Dictionary* (4th ed., 2000), "publication" is "communication of information to the public." Lisa Peel's blog is definitely communication of information to the public.

News medium. "News medium" under Section 901(b) of the Franklin Reporter Shield Act (FRSA) means any "newspaper, magazine, or other similar medium issued at regular intervals and having a general circulation: a radio station; a television station; a community antenna television service . . . ."

For the following reasons, I conclude that Lisa Peel's blog is likely to be held a "news medium" within the meaning of the FRSA. While the blog is neither a newspaper nor a magazine, the blog post in issue here ("$10,000 in School Equipment Diverted from Schools to Home of Assistant Superintendent") reads like a news story in a newspaper. And Ms. Peel's posting on the internet is arguably like a newspaper's printing and distributing its stories. In addition, blogs are replacing newspapers. According to *America Today*, some 30 per cent of Americans "read one or more blogs regularly." *America Today* says that blogs are even replacing news web sites. They provide "more means of sharing news." Even traditional newspapers are now publishing blogs. *America Today*, July 5, 2007.

Other similar medium. Although the blog is not a newspaper or magazine, the FRSA also includes the language "other similar medium," and it gives a list: "a radio station; a television station; a community antenna television service . . . ." The court in *Lane v. Tichenor*, says that where the legislature provides a list and says "other similar activities," the court must inquire into legislative intent. Where the intent is not clear and enumeration is neither exclusive nor exhaustive, courts may use external aids, e.g., a dictionary. *Lane*.

According to *America Today*, today some 30 per cent of Americans "read one or more blogs regularly." *America Today*, July 5, 2007. While blogs did not exist when the FRSA was enacted in 1948, the fact that the legislature included examples of media that were relatively new in 1948, arguably indicates legislative intent to include new media.

"Issued at regular intervals." Ms. Peel blogs every week-end, normally on Friday. Thus, on the one hand, her schedule is regular, unlike the internet bulletin board in *Haush*. On the other hand, her blog does not always appear on the same day of the week, so it is not totally regular.

"Having a general circulation." *The American Heritage Dictionary* defines "circulation" as "the passing of something, such as money or news, from place to place or person to person . . . distribution . . . ." Ms. Peel can argue that her blog has a general circulation. It has 3,500 registrants in a town of 38,000 people, or almost 10 per cent of the population, and there have been more than 15,000 visitors. Peel Interview.

Source. The final question is whether the person whose identity Lisa Peel wishes to keep confidential is a "source" within the meaning of the FRSA. The statute says that a "source" is "the person from whom or the means through which the information was obtained." Ms. Peel's source is the person from whom she obtained the information in her blog post.

III. Lisa Peel meets her burden under the Franklin Reporter Shield Act of showing that protecting her against the subpoena compelling her to reveal the source of her story about Frank Peterson fulfills the intent of the statute.

The intent of the FRSA is "to safeguard the media's ability to gather news." It serves the purpose of "promoting the free flow of information to the public." FRSA sec. 900.

If, as Lisa Peel says, the publisher of the only newspaper in Montgomery County discourages reporters from doing stories and investigations that might portray the communities in a bad light, then her blog is necessary to provide the public in Montgomery County with information. Peel Interview. To afford the protections of the FRSA to her blog is to promote the "free flow of information to the public."

Examination of the plain and ordinary meaning of the FRSA and construction of the statute as a whole, above, yields the conclusion that Peel is a "reporter" within the meaning of the FRSA, and that she is entitled to its protections.

CONCLUSION

Having examined both sides of the question, I conclude that our client Lisa Peel can meet her burden of showing that she is a "reporter" within the meaning of the Franklin Reporter Shield Act (FRSA), and that protecting Peel's sources is consistent with the purposes of the FRSA. If so, the court cannot compel Peel to reveal the identity of the source for her blog post about Frank Peterson, and the court is likely to grant her motion to quash the subpoena.

Perform Your Best™ Note on Analyzing *In re Lisa Peel*

Objective Memorandum
Context: Litigation
Structure: Statutory Analysis

The Partner Memo for *In re Lisa Peel* tells the bar candidate to write a memorandum analyzing whether the firm can use the Franklin Reporter Shield Act (FRSA) to quash a subpoena against client Lisa Peel, compelling her to divulge the source for one of her blog posts. Since this entails looking at both sides of the question, your memorandum will be an objective memorandum. Your memorandum will state explicitly that it is an objective memorandum. The sample memo in this book begins:

> You have asked me to prepare an objective memorandum examining both sides of the question whether our client Lisa Peel qualifies under the Franklin Reporter Shield Act (FRSA) to resist a subpoena ordering her to appear before a grand jury and produce notes regarding persons she interviewed for a post on her blog.

How to Read the Partner Memo to Make Your Outline in the MPT-Matrix™. Following the instructions in the Partner Memo is always the key to success on the MPT. With the *Perform Your Best™* MPT System, the instructions in the Partner Memo, also called the task memorandum, are the starting point for the outline in the MPT-Matrix™. The Partner Memo for *In re Lisa Peel* asks the bar candidate to write an objective memorandum, that is, a memorandum that argues both sides of the assigned question.

You must normally divide each instruction in the Partner Memo into its smallest parts. But the instruction in the Partner Memo for *In re Lisa Peel* asks a simple Yes-No question, whether the firm's client Lisa Peel can use the Franklin Reporter Shield Act (FRSA) to quash a subpoena demanding her sources for a post she published on her blog. Thus, that statute is what you will divide into its smallest parts. The Partner Memo says:

> Please draft an objective memorandum for me analyzing whether we can use the FRSA to move to quash Peel's subpoena.

The first line of your outline in the MPT-Matrix™ cannot be just the Yes-No question "Does the FRSA apply to Lisa Peel?" Nor can it be just "Is Lisa Peel a reporter under the FRSA?" Bar candidates who do not read the instructions in the Partner Memo carefully enough will run into trouble.

Second Document to Use in the Outline in the MPT-Matrix™: The Statute. To do a lawyerlike job on *Lisa Peel*, you must pull apart Section 901 of the FRSA, which defines "reporter" as any person regularly engaged in *collecting, writing*, or *editing* news for publication through a *news medium*." (Italics added.)

Under Section 901, as used in the FRSA:

(a) "reporter" means any person regularly engaged in collecting, writing, or editing news for publication through a news medium.

(b) "news medium" means any newspaper, magazine, or other similar medium issued at regular intervals and having a general circulation; a radio station; a television station; a community antenna television service; or any person or corporation engaged in the making of newsreels or other motion picture news for public showing.

(c) "source" means the person from whom or the means through which the information was obtained.

Your outline on the <u>MPT-Matrix</u>™ will have a separate row for each applicable key term in the FRSA. The assignment is to write an objective memorandum, so in each row, you will put the page numbers from the File and Library where you find material that cuts either for or against Lisa Peel. Does Peel *collect* news? Does she *write* news? Does she *edit* news? And so on. Since she must be a reporter for a *news medium* to be covered by the FRSA, analyzing whether Peel can quash the subpoena also requires analyzing whether her blog qualifies as a *news medium* under the FRSA. That means pulling *news medium* apart. Is her blog a *newspaper* or one of the other types of publications enumerated in the statute? Or do the cases suggest that the statute may cover kinds of media that are not enumerated? Is the blog *issued at regular intervals*? Does it have a *general circulation*? And so on.

The sample answer in this book provides the following analysis of the application of the statutory terms *issued at regular intervals* and *having a general circulation*. This is typical of statutory analysis.

"<u>Issued at regular intervals.</u>" Ms. Peel blogs every week-end, normally on Friday. Thus, on the one hand, her schedule is regular, unlike the internet bulletin board in *Haush*. On the other hand, her blog does not always appear on the same day of the week, so it is not totally regular.

"<u>Having a general circulation.</u>" The *American Heritage Dictionary* defines "circulation" as "the passing of something, such as money or news, from place to place or person to person . . . distribution . . . ." Ms. Peel can argue that her blog has a general circulation. It has 3,500 registrants in a town of 38,000 people, or almost 10 per cent of the population, and there have been more than 15,000 visitors. Interview.

Since the Partner Memo calls for an objective memorandum, you must point out that some facts cut against Lisa Peel's qualifying as a "reporter," for example, the fact that she posts not only news but pictures of animals. The weight of the facts, however, is in her favor.

Finally, under *Bellows*, the burden is on Peel to show that to bring her blog under the FRSA fulfills the intent of the legislature. According to the Preamble of the Franklin Reporter Shield Act:

The primary purpose of this Act is to safeguard the media's ability to gather news. It is intended to promote the free flow of information to the public by prohibiting courts from compelling reporters to disclose unpublished news sources or information received from such sources.

Again, in the third row of your MPT-Matrix™ you will put down the page numbers in the File and the Library where you find material that cuts either for or against Peel.

<u>How to Apply the Rule of Three.</u> You may choose to divide the Discussion part of the memorandum for *In re Lisa Peel* into either two or three sections. The sample answer in this book applies the Rule of Three and divides the memo into three sections. The section headings

in the sample answer conform to the strong, persuasive, style the National Conference of Bar Examiners prefers. Note that each section heading in the sample memorandum argues both law and facts:

   I. Lisa Peel qualifies as a "reporter" under the Franklin Reporter Shield Act (FRSA), if her blog is a "news medium."
  II. Posts on Lisa Peel's blog are "publication" through a "news medium" within the meaning of the Franklin Reporter Shield Act, and her source for information about Assistant Superintendent Frank Peterson's retaining equipment belonging to the Greenville School District qualifies as a "source" within the meaning of the FRSA.
 III. Lisa Peel meets her burden under the FRSA of showing that protecting her against the subpoena compelling her to reveal the source of her story about Frank Peterson will fulfill the intent of the legislature.

The primary question, since the FRSA protects only reporters, is whether Lisa Peel is a "reporter" under the FRSA. If analysis of the facts in the light of the statute and the case law reveals that a court is more likely to decide that Lisa Peel is a "reporter," then the statute will protect her, and the court will probably grant her motion to quash the subpoena.

The final issue is, what are the purposes of the FRSA, and is protecting Lisa Peel consistent with those purposes? The intent of the legislature is discussed in *Bellows*, which states that the burden is on the party seeking protection under the FRSA. According to the Preamble of the Franklin Reporter Shield Act:

> The primary purpose of this Act is to safeguard the media's ability to gather news. It is intended to promote the free flow of information to the public by prohibiting courts from compelling reporters to disclose unpublished news sources or information received from such sources.

Franklin Reporter Shield Act, Section 900. The purpose of the Franklin Reporter Shield Act is to promote the "free flow of information."

Lisa Peel's blog arguably fills an important gap in providing news in her community. If the FRSA keeps courts from compelling her to disclose her sources, this promotes the "free flow of information."

Thus, a bar candidate might write a Conclusion like the following for *In re Lisa Peel*:

CONCLUSION

Having examined both sides of the question, I conclude that our client Lisa Peel can meet her burden of showing that she is a "reporter" within the meaning of the Franklin Reporter Shield Act (FRSA), and that protecting Peel's sources is consistent with the purposes of the FRSA. If so, the court cannot compel Peel to reveal the identity of the source for her blog post about Frank Peterson, and the court is likely to grant her motion to quash the subpoena.

Perform Your Best™ Materials
For Task B:
In re Velocity Park

Perform Your Best on the Multistate Performance Test

Note to the Reader: Your MPT-Matrix™ will have only page numbers, not words. The words in this MPT Matrix™ simply show you the information you will be indexing and cross-referencing. Do not attempt to write words in your own MPT-Matrix™.

MPT-Matrix™ *In re Velocity Park*, MPT, February 2008

	A. Interview with client Zeke Oliver	B. *The Banford Courier*, Newspaper Article 2/2/08	C. Franklin Civil Code sec. 41	D. *Lund v. Swim World* (Franklin Sup. Ct. 2005)	E. *Holum v. Bruges Soccer Club, Inc.* (Columbia Sup. Ct. 1999)
1. Whether proposed waiver will protect Velocity Park from liability for injuries.	**P-2.** Usual injuries are scrapes, bruises, and occasional sprained wrist. **P-2.** Signs will state that skateboarders must wear helmets. **P-3.** Usefulness of Velocity Park to Branford. Better to have kids skateboarding in park than on streets, which city council doesn't like. Eventually client would like to "partner with the city of Branford to operate the park and make it free."	**P-6.** Injuries to skateboarders often result from flaws in the surface. **P-6.** The most common injuries are wrist sprains and fractures; possibility of serious head injuries or even death. **P-6.** Injuries can result from carelessness of other skaters.		**P-9.** Three factors for an enforceable exculpatory clause: (i) whether the language is overly broad and ambiguous as to types of injuries contemplated and types of actions covered. The language cannot be overbroad, including even reckless or intentional conduct, or failing to make clear what types of acts the words encompass. Exculpatory agreements "will bar only those claims that the parties contemplated . . . ."	
	P-2. "suppose some kids may not read it closely, especially if they're anxious to get in and skateboard . . . ."				

MPT-Matrix™ *In re Velocity Park*, MPT, February 2008, *cont'd*

	A. Interview with client Zeke Oliver	B. *The Banford Courier*, Newspaper Article 2/2/08	C. Franklin Civil Code sec. 41	D. *Lund v. Swim World* (Franklin Sup. Ct. 2005)	E. *Holam v. Bruges Soccer Club, Inc.* (Columbia Sup. Ct. 1999)
2. Design and layout of waiver.				**P-10.** (ii) whether the waiver is conspicuous. The liability waiver must "alert the signer to the nature and significance of what is being signed." Lund was not alerted to the waiver, had too little time to read it, had no opportunity for clarification or negotiation.	
				P-10. (iii) [nor dispositive] whether there is a substantial disparity in bargaining power between the parties.	
3. Enforceability of waiver signed only by a minor.			**P-7.** Except as to contracts for necessaries, contract signed only by a minor is voidable by the minor.		**P-11.** An adult's waiver of liability for negligent acts during recreational activities on his own behalf is enforceable. **P-12.** There is a public policy basis for finding waiver enforceable where signed by parent on behalf of minor where activity is volunteer-staffed non-profit.

Perform Your Best™ Sample Answer
for *In re Velocity Park*

Hall & Gray, LLP
Attorneys at Law
730 Amsterdam Avenue
Banford, Franklin 33701

DRAFT

MEMORANDUM

To: Deanna Hall

From: Bar Candidate

Re: Liability Waiver for Velocity Park

Date: _____

INTRODUCTION

Our client Zeke Oliver will soon open an outdoor skateboarding park ("skate park") called Velocity Park. You have asked me to analyze whether the waiver form that he proposes using will protect Velocity Park from liability for injuries; to suggest specific revisions to the waiver, including replacement language and changes to design and layout; and to discuss whether any waiver will be enforceable if signed only by a minor. I conclude that Velocity Park must revise the language and the layout of the waiver. Velocity Park must require an adult to sign the form. There is no law in Franklin as yet, however, on whether this will relieve Velocity Park of liability.

DISCUSSION

I. A waiver may protect Velocity Park from liability for injuries, but Velocity Park must modify the form and require a parent to sign it.

In *Lund v. Swim World, Inc.* (2005), relying on *Schmidt v. Tyrol Mountain* (Franklin Sup. Ct. 1996), the Franklin Supreme Court stated the requirements for an enforceable waiver of liability. First, the language of the waiver cannot be overbroad, but "must clearly, unambiguously, and unmistakably inform the signer of what is being waived." In *Lund*, the waiver aimed to absolve the defendant of fault, but it did not make clear "what type of acts the word 'fault' encompassed." Indeed, the word "fault" was broad enough to cover a reckless or an intentional act. A waiver of liability for an intentional act, however, would clearly violate public policy.

A well-drafted waiver, by contrast, will not be overbroad but will bar "only those claims that the parties contemplated when they executed the contract." Exculpatory clauses will be strictly construed against "serious injury and/or death."

Velocity Park must therefore substitute new language for this overbroad language:

> any and all legal liability, including but not limited to all causes of action, claims, damages in law, or remedies in equity of whatever kind I have or which hereafter accrue to me, whether such injuries and/or claims arise from equipment failure, conditions in the park, or any actions of Velocity Park, its employees, third parties, or other skateboarders.

Velocity Park must specify the most frequent types of injuries suffered by skateboarders and clearly inform the user of the types of risks he is assuming. According to our client and according to the *Banford Courier*, wrist injuries are the most common, either sprains or fractures. The form must say so.

Velocity Park should also use the word "negligence," to remove doubt about the type of conduct as to which users will waive claims. Because of the risk of injury caused by the aggressive behavior of other users, the waiver should clearly absolve Velocity Park of liability for negligent supervision.

Accordingly, I suggest the following language:

> I hereby release Velocity Park from all liability for negligent injury, including injuries resulting from the negligence of Velocity Park or its employees or of third parties, including other users of the Park. I understand that the most frequent injuries are wrist injuries, whether sprains or fractures.

Although waivers of liability may sometimes be vulnerable where there is a "substantial disparity in bargaining power" between the parties, the *Lund* court stated emphatically that a disparity in bargaining power, by itself, would not automatically render an exculpatory clause void under public policy.

Here, as in *Lund*, there might be pressure on young people waiting in line to sign the form quickly so as not to hold up the other patrons waiting to get in. The waiver portion might not be pointed out to patrons, nor might the terms be explained to them.

Accordingly, Velocity Park may wish to institute procedures for explaining the form to all skateboarders and for making sure that everyone entering the Park has ample time to read and understand the form.

Under *Lund*, in addition, the effort to extend the waiver of liability to third parties may be unenforceable. Finally, our client should be aware that new or unexpected types of injuries may occur, and even the best waiver form will not protect them.

II. Velocity Park must revise the waiver's design and layout so as to "alert the signer to the nature and significance of what is being signed."

The form itself must "alert the signer to the nature and significance of what is being signed." The waiver in *Lund* was invalidated in part because "the exculpatory language appeared to be part of, or a requirement for, a larger registration form." It was all on one page, and there was only one place to sign the form.

Velocity Park must, therefore, change the format of the form, which currently places the waiver on the same page with general information about the Park, including hours of operation and admission fees. If everything is in the same font and the same size, it will leave users confused about whether being admitted to Velocity Park is the same as or different from waiving liability.

Accordingly, I suggest that the waiver be placed on a separate form with a label reading "Waiver of Liability" conspicuously at the top and a place for a signature conspicuously at the bottom. Above the signature should be a line saying: "I have read and understood this waiver, and I understand what rights I am waiving."

III. Velocity Park must require a parent to sign on behalf of every minor who uses the Park, since in Franklin, no waiver signed only by a minor will be enforceable. Indeed, the Franklin courts have not yet decided whether a waiver signed by the parent is enforceable.

Under Franklin law, an adult's release from liability for injuries he suffers owing to negligent acts during recreational activities is enforceable. *Lund v. Swim World, Inc.* A recent Columbia case concludes that parents may release their own claims arising out of injury to their minor children. *Holum v. Bruges Soccer Club, Inc.* Under Franklin Law of Civil Actions, Section 41(b)(1), however, except for contracts for necessaries, in Franklin, contracts of minors are voidable by the minor. While *Holum* presents persuasive public policy arguments for permitting parents to sign waivers on behalf of their minor children when they participate in sports activities of nonprofit associations staffed by volunteers, Franklin courts appear not to have decided whether an adult parent may waive liability, especially against a for-profit business, on behalf of a minor child.

Accordingly, Velocity Park must require a parent to sign the waiver of liability on behalf of every minor who uses the Club and on his own behalf. The waiver will be effective as to the adult's causes of action. The Franklin courts have not decided whether the releases will be effective against a for-profit business like Velocity Park with regard to minors' injuries. As to the adults' causes of action, however, the waiver will be effective.

Should the issue arise, Velocity Park has plausible public policy arguments, along the lines of those in *Holum*, for recognizing the right of parents to waive liability on behalf of their children, and for acknowledging the fact that Velocity Park provides a type of recreational facility that is much needed but not available elsewhere in Franklin. Velocity Park can argue that it is performing a public service and should be treated as though it were a non-profit.

Note, incidentally, that, even where the Club does not believe a waiver will in fact be enforceable, there is a good reason for requiring one, since signing may make it less likely that lawsuits will be brought.

CONCLUSION

I have examined the waiver form our client Zeke Oliver proposes for Velocity Park. I conclude that to protect Velocity Park from liability, Velocity Park must include language specifying the types of injuries anticipated and the kind of conduct referred to. Velocity Park must change the design and layout to distinguish the waiver from other printed material. We must also emphasize to the client that although a parent may waive his own rights growing out of his child's injuries, the courts of Franklin have not decided whether a parent may waive the rights of a minor taking part in recreational activities sponsored by a for-profit business.

Perform Your Best™ Note on Analyzing *In re Velocity Park*

Objective Memorandum
Document Analysis
Purpose: Advice to Client

The Partner Memorandum for *In re Velocity Park* states that the firm's client, Zeke Olive is about to open an outdoor skateboarding park, to be called "Velocity Park." He has brought t the partner a sample form that he would like to use to ask patrons to waive liability for injuries To help him advise the client, the partner asks the bar candidate to write an objectiv memorandum. An objective memorandum argues both sides of the question. This is a commo type of MPT task.

How to Outline the Instructions in the Partner Memorandum. The first question for th assigned memorandum is "whether the proposed waiver will protect Velocity Park from liabilit for injuries occurring at the skate park." That question, which does not contain parts that mus be pulled apart, must occupy the first row in the outline down the leftmost column of the MPT Matrix™. When you find material in the File or the Library that is relevant to this question, yo will put the page numbers into that first row. One of the cases in the Library, *Lund v. Swi World*, turns out to set out the standard in Franklin for enforceable exculpatory clauses. You wi look at the interview with the client in the File for the information about typical injuries that th waiver form must specify and supplement that information with a report in the Library from th *Banford Courier* on injuries to skateboarders.

The second task is to suggest "specific revisions to the proposed waiver, includin replacement language as well as any changes in the waiver's design and layout," but withou redrafting the whole thing. You will reserve the second row of the MPT-Matrix™ for you analysis of the proposed waiver. This requires document analysis. Document analysis is commo on the MPT. It is normally straightforward, even where, as here, analyzing a document sectior by-section is coupled with making suggestions for re-drafting. In document analysis, you tak the key sections of the document one at a time and examine available facts and case law and, a necessary, other sources, to decide whether each section of the document in turn is satisfactory a it reads, or whether it needs to be eliminated or re-drafted. Finally, you will consider the desig of the waiver in the light of *Lund*.

The third task is to discuss whether any waiver will be enforceable if signed only by minor. That is the third row of the MPT-Matrix™. Phrased another way, the question is whethe a parent can waive liability on behalf of a child. It turns out that since Velocity Park is a for profit business, albeit one serving a civic purpose, rather than a non-profit, there is no case la answering that question in Franklin. You must be careful to note that the case in the Librar called *Holum v. Bruges Soccer Club, Inc.*, is not a Franklin case, but a Columbia case. It provide public policy arguments for finding a waiver enforceable where it is signed by a parent on beha of a minor, but only where the activity is volunteer-staffed and non-profit. Not only is the cas not controlling, it does not apply on the facts.

How to Use the Rule of Three. *In re Velocity Park* makes it easy to use the Rule of Three The Partner Memo gives the bar candidate three instructions. The Discussion section of you memorandum will have three sections.

The sample memorandum in this book reaches the following conclusion:

CONCLUSION

I have examined the waiver form our client Zeke Oliver proposes for Velocity Park. I conclude that to protect Velocity Park from liability, Velocity Park must include language specifying the types of injuries anticipated and the kind of conduct referred to. Velocity Park must also change the design and layout to distinguish the waiver from other printed material. We must also caution the client that the courts of Franklin have not decided whether parents can waive the rights of minors taking part in recreational activities sponsored by a for-profit business.

Perform Your Best™ Materials
For Task C:
In re Phoenix Corporation
v.
Biogenesis, Inc.

Note to the Reader: Your MPT-Matrix™ will have only page numbers, not words. The words in this MPT Matrix™ simply show you the information you will be indexing and cross-referencing. Do not attempt to write words in your own MPT-Matrix™.

MPT-Matrix™ *Phoenix Corporation v. Biogenesis, Inc.,* MPT, February 2009

	A. Interview with Carol Ravel 2/23/09	B. Schetina Letter 1/2/98	C. Rule 4.4 Franklin Rules of Professional Conduct 7/1/02	D. *Indigo v. Luna Motors* (Franklin Ct. App. 1998)	E. *Mead v. Conley Machinery* (Franklin Ct. App. 1999)
Phoenix Brief for Disqualification February 9, 2009					
1. Document on its face is confidential Lawyer-Client communication. Argument. Amberg has violated ethical obligations in a case of inadvertent disclosure and threatens Phoenix with incurable prejudice.	**P-2.** Amberg concedes document is privileged	**P-4.** Document marked "confidential," sent by president of corporation to attorney for plaintiff corporation. Asks: "Can't we interpret the agreement to require Biogenesis to pay royalties on other categories, not only the specified ones?"			

MPT-Matrix™ *Phoenix Corporation v. Biogenesis, Inc.* (MPT February 2009), *cont'd*

Phoenix Brief for Disqualification February 9, 2009	B. Interview with Carol Ravel February 23, 2009	C. Schetina Letter January 2, 1998	D. Rule 4.4 Franklin Rules of Professional Conduct July 1, 2002	E. *Indigo v. Luna Motors* (Franklin Ct. App. 1998)	F. *Mead v. Conley Machinery* (Franklin Ct. App. 1999)
Argument. Rule 4.4 requires prompt notification. Says attorney must not just notify sender, but must refrain from examining document and must await sender's instructions. I.e., *Indigo v. Luna* rule.			**P-8.** Where document "relevant to representation" is inadvertently sent, receiving attorney must promptly notify sender. Comment: Rule 4.4 expressly supersedes *Indigo v. Luna*, attorney receiving document inadvertently sent may examine it, need not follow instructions of sender. Comment: Rule 4.4 does not treat unauthorized disclosure.	**P-9.** If document is Attorney-Client privileged and received inadvertently, attorney must promptly notify adversary's attorney, must not examine; must await instructions from sender.	
Argument. In violation of their ethical obligation, the attorneys did not notify the sender, examined the document, and refused to return it.	**P-3.** Amberg wants to use the letter. **P-3.** Amberg did not notify sender. Did examine, refused to return.				

MPT-Matrix™ *Phoenix Corporation v. Biogenesis, Inc.* (MPT February 2009), *cont'd*

Phoenix Brief for Disqualification February 9, 2009	A. Interview with Carol Ravel 2/23/09	B. Schetina Letter 1/2/98	C. Rule 4.4 Franklin Rules of Professional Conduct 7/1/02	D. *Indigo v. Luna Motors* (Franklin Ct. App. 1998)	E. *Mead v. Conley Machinery* (Franklin Ct. App. 1999)
2. **Argument. The same rule would apply if the letter had been sent without authorization.**				**P-9.** In *Indigo*, disclosure is inadvertent.	**P-11.** Held. Trial court abused its discretion by disqualifying plaintiff's attorney. **P-11.** If document is Attorney-Client privileged and disclosed without authorization, receiving attorney must notify adversary's attorney; refrain from examining; either await instructions or submit to the court for instructions. Violation is only one of the facts the court must consider.
3. **Argument. Failure to disqualify Amberg will cause "incurable prejudice."**		**P-4.** Letter asks: "Can't we interpret the agreement to require Biogenesis to pay royalties on other categories, not only the specified ones?"		**P-10.** Disqualify where threat of incurable prejudice.	**P-11, P-12.** Counter-indications to disqualification: information did not significantly prejudice other side; can exclude documents from evidence; whether disqualification causes hardship.

Perform Your Best™ Sample Answer for *Phoenix Corporation v. Biogenesis, Inc.*

Forbes, Burdick & Washington, LLP
777 Fifth Avenue
Lakewood City, Franklin 33905

MEMORANDUM

To: Ann Buckner
From: Bar Candidate
Re: Phoenix Corporation v. Biogenesis, Inc.
Date: _____

INTRODUCTION

Amberg & Lewis ("Amberg") represents the defendant Biogenesis, Inc., in a breach of contract action brought by Phoenix Corporation. Amberg has sought our advice because Phoenix, which is represented by the Collins Law Firm, has moved to disqualify Amberg, alleging inadvertent receipt and possible prejudicial use of a confidential attorney-client document. You have asked me to evaluate the merits of Phoenix's arguments for disqualification. I conclude that Amberg has not violated any ethical rule and that Amberg has strong arguments why the court should in any event not disqualify it.

DISCUSSION

I. Amberg has not violated Rule 4.4 of the Franklin Rules of Professional Conduct, which appears to be the only applicable rule.

The Franklin Court of Appeal has affirmed the power of the courts to disqualify counsel for improper use of privileged documents. The leading case, *Indigo v. Luna Motors*, decided in 1998, made that clear. It concerned inadvertent, not unauthorized, disclosure. *Luna* required the attorney who received a privileged document inadvertently (i) to notify the sender, (ii) to resist the temptation to examine the document, and (iii) to await the sender's instructions about what to do.

Phoenix argues that *Indigo v. Luna* applies here, and that Amberg has violated the applicable ethical rules by not acting in conformity with the *Indigo* requirements. I conclude, on the contrary, that *Indigo* does not apply. Even if it did, Amberg should not be disqualified.

Amberg concedes that the letter at issue here, the Schetina letter, is subject to the attorney-client privilege. It is labeled "Confidential," and it is from the president of Phoenix, Gordon Schetina, to one of the corporation's attorneys, Peter Horvitz. Amberg has nonetheless not violated any ethical rule.

When Amberg received the document on February 2, 2009, receipt was not inadvertent. The document came without authorization from some undisclosed person in the Collins Law Firm. Amberg did not, contrary to the first *Indigo v. Luna* requirement, promptly notify the Collins Law Firm. Rather, although the Collins Law Firm almost immediately found out, it was only because a member of the Collins firm accidentally overheard two Amberg associates talking about the letter that same day. Amberg can argue that it simply did not have enough time to notify Collins. Amberg plainly failed to follow the second and third *Indigo v. Luna* requirements, however, since it examined the document and did not await the sender's instructions. Indeed, when Collins asked Amberg to return the letter, Amberg refused. Further, Amberg wishes to use the letter at trial.

The conclusion does not follow, however, that *Indigo v. Luna* applies and disqualifies Amberg. Rule 4.4 of the Franklin Rules of Professional Conduct was adopted by the Franklin Supreme Court in 2002. According to the Comment, Rule 4.4 expressly supersedes *Indigo v. Luna*. Rule 4.4 requires the attorney who inadvertently receives a privileged document only to notify the sender promptly. He or she need do no more.

Rule 4.4 states in its entirety:

> An attorney who receives a document relating to the representation of the attorney's client and knows or reasonably should know that the document was inadvertently sent shall promptly notify the sender.

The Comment to Rule 4.4 says that Rule 4.4 applies only to inadvertent disclosure and that neither Rule 4.4 nor any other rule applies to unauthorized disclosure. Therefore, since the document Amberg received was an unauthorized disclosure, Phoenix misapplies it, and Amberg has not violated the plain language of Rule 4.4.

The open question is whether *Mead v. Conley Machinery Co.,* dealing with unauthorized disclosure, and requiring the receiving law firm to await the court's instructions, remains good law in light of Rule 4.4. Dating from 1999, *Mead* predates Rule 4.4, and it states much the same three requirements as *Indigo v. Luna*. Under *Mead*, moreover, a firm in Amberg's position need not await the sender's instructions but may wait for the court to decide what it should do. Violation of this standard, however, is only one of the facts that *Mead* says the court should consider.

II. The court should in any event not disqualify Amberg, since Amberg's use of the Schetina letter does not threaten Phoenix with incurable prejudice, while disqualification of Amberg would cause serious hardship to Biogenesis.

While the court may disqualify Amberg even if Amberg has not violated any explicit ethical rule, *Mead v. Conley Machinery Co.,* it should not do so here. Phoenix suggests that failure to disqualify Amberg will result in incurable prejudice. *Mead*, however, said that the court must balance a number of factors in deciding whether or not to disqualify counsel who have received a privileged document:

(1) the attorney's actual or constructive knowledge of the material's attorney-client privileged status;

(2) the promptness with which the attorney notified the opposing side that he or she had received such material;

(3) the extent to which the attorney reviewed the material;

(4) the significance of the material, i.e., the extent to which its disclosure may prejudice the party moving for disqualification, and the extent to which its return or other measure may prevent or cure that prejudice;

(5) the extent to which the party moving for disqualification may be at fault for the unauthorized disclosure; and

(6) the extent to which the party opposing disqualification would suffer prejudice from the disqualification of his or her attorney.

As the length of this list of factors suggests, *Mead* does not consider disqualification of counsel an open-and-shut question. Indeed, the footnote to *Mead* says that even the threat of "incurable prejudice," as in *Indigo*, "is neither a necessary nor a sufficient condition for disqualification."

Amberg can argue, moreover, that the Schetina letter will not create incurable prejudice because it is not conclusive evidence on any point in issue in the case. While it is arguably an admission by Phoenix that it did not have a contractual right to the damages it seeks, it is not dispositive on that point. The fact that Phoenix had not sought the licensing fees earlier does not mean that a closer and entirely proper reading of the Phoenix-Biogenesis contract would not have disclosed such an entitlement.

An additional important consideration weighing against disqualification is that Biogenesis would suffer serious hardship were Amberg to be disqualified. The case has been going on for six years, and now it is finally only a month away from trial. To require Biogenesis to start over with new counsel would not serve the interests of justice.

CONCLUSION

Amberg has not violated any ethical rule, since Rule 4.4 supersedes *Indigo v. Luna* and in any event does not apply to use of documents obtained in unauthorized ways rather than inadvertently. Unless *Mead v. Conley Machinery Co.*, despite Rule 4.4, has continuing vitality as to unauthorized disclosures, no other ethical constraints apply. The court should not, in any event, disqualify Amberg, since the Schetina letter does not have conclusive evidentiary weight on any point in issue, and requiring Biogenesis to start over with new counsel would impose a serious hardship.

Perform Your Best™ Note on Analyzing *Phoenix Corporation v. Biogenesis, Inc.*

Type of Task: Objective memorandum
Context: Litigation
Structure: Statutory and case law analysis and application

The Partner Memorandum in *Phoenix Corporation v. Biogenesis, Inc.*, asks the associate to write a memorandum "evaluating the merits of Phoenix's argument for Amberg & Lewis's disqualification." The firm's client is Amberg & Lewis ("Amberg"), the law firm that represents the defendant Biogenesis in the litigation. Amberg has received a damaging attorney-client document without authorization, a letter from the president of plaintiff Phoenix to the company's attorney. Perhaps a disgruntled employee of Phoenix's law firm sent it to Amberg. Since the partner asks for an objective memorandum, the associate must examine both sides of the question, whether Phoenix is justified in demanding Amberg's disqualification. Other MPT tasks may raise points of attorney ethics in an incidental way. This MPT task is entirely about attorney ethics.

How to Read and Outline the Instructions in the MPT-Matrix™ Using a Second Document, Phoenix's Brief. The Partner Memo's instruction to the bar candidate is to "evaluate the merits of Phoenix's argument." You cannot tear this simple instruction apart to make your outline. Accordingly, the starting point for the outline in the MPT-Matrix™ must be the document the instruction refers to, Phoenix's brief in support of its motion to disqualify Amberg. Each of the three parts of the Phoenix brief will be a line in the outline in the MPT-Matrix™. In each of those three lines you will note the page numbers in the File and the Library of materials that cut for and against each of Phoenix's points.

How to Apply the Rule of Three. Following the instructions in the Partner Memo, the bar candidate's work product may simply present arguments for and against each of the three points in the Phoenix brief.

The Phoenix brief has three parts:

1. Phoenix's Document is Protected by the Attorney-Client Privilege;
2. Amberg & Lewis Has Violated an Ethical Obligation;
3. Amberg & Lewis Has Threatened Phoenix with Incurable Prejudice.

The bar candidate's work product may therefore have the following parts:

1. Amberg & Lewis concedes that Phoenix's document is protected by the attorney-client privilege;
2. Amberg & Lewis has not violated its ethical obligations;.
3. Amberg & Lewis does not threaten Phoenix with incurable prejudice, but disqualification on the eve of trial would result in severe prejudice to Biogenesis.

The Partner Memo instructs the bar candidate to "bring to bear" both the applicable legal authorities and the relevant facts as described by Ms. Ravel, a partner in the Amberg firm. As so often on the MPT, the Partner Memo tells the bar candidate not to draft a separate statement of facts.

Amberg's argument is clear, but to see it you must first distinguish between *inadvertent* and *unauthorized* receipt of a privileged document. The fact that Amberg's receipt of the document in issue here was unauthorized, not inadvertent, is key. You must also note the dates of the two cases and one rule in the File. Phoenix relies on *Indigo v. Luna Motors* (1998), which deals with inadvertent receipt of a privileged document. The *Indigo* rule required the attorney who receives a privileged document inadvertently not to examine it and to await instructions from the sender. Rule 4.4 of the Franklin Rules of Professional Conduct, however, superseded *Indigo* in 2002. In contravention of *Indigo*, the Comment to Rule 4.4 expressly states that the attorney may examine a privileged document he receives inadvertently, and need not await or follow instructions from the sender. The same analysis would arguably apply where, as here, the receipt of the privileged document is unauthorized rather than inadvertent. The Comment tells us, however, that Rule 4.4. does not include unauthorized transmission. *Mead v. Conley Machinery,* another decision of the Franklin Court of Appeals, dates from 1999, after *Indigo*, and it fulfills two functions in this MPT task. First, although, unlike *Indigo v. Luna Motors*, it applies to unauthorized receipt of a privileged document, it states much the same strict rules as *Indigo* for the attorney who receives the document. *Mead* concluded that the receiving attorney should review the document—there, an attorney-client privileged document—only to the extent necessary to determine how to proceed, notify the opposing attorney, and either abide by the opposing attorney's instructions or refrain from using the document until a court disposed of the matter. These are rules Amberg has not followed. Thus, as of the date of researching the issue here, the question is open whether *Mead* applies to this case of unauthorized transmission.

But *Mead* has a second function. It provides an escape route for Amberg. *Mead* says that even an attorney's violation of the rules is not dispositive as to disqualification. *Mead* lists counterindications to disqualification. These include the information's not significantly prejudicing the other side; the possibility of excluding the documents from evidence; and disqualification's causing hardship. Thus, even if *Mead* applies much the same strict requirements as *Indigo*, despite its having violated those rules, Amberg can argue that all three of *Mead's* counterindications cut against the court's disqualifying it.

In particular, the bar candidate can point out that to disqualify Amberg on the eve of trial would result in severe hardship to Amberg's client Biogenesis.

The sample brief in this book concludes as follows:

CONCLUSION

Amberg has not violated any ethical rule, since Rule 4.4 supersedes *Indigo v. Luna* and in any event does not apply to use of documents obtained in unauthorized ways rather than inadvertently. Unless *Mead v. Conley Machinery Co.,* despite Rule 4.4, has continuing vitality as to unauthorized disclosures, no other ethical constraints apply. The court should not, in any event, disqualify Amberg, since the Schetina letter does not have conclusive evidentiary weight on any point in issue, and requiring Biogenesis to start over with new counsel would impose a serious hardship.

Perform Your Best™ Materials
For Task D:
In re Gardenton Board of Education

Note to the Reader: Your MPT-Matrix™ will have page numbers and many fewer words. The words in this MPT-Matrix™ simply show you the information you will be indexing and cross-referencing.

MPT-Matrix™ *In re Gardenton Board of Education*, MPT, February 1998						
Proposed Code	A. U.S. Constitution	B. Franklin Constitution	C. Sec. 48 Franklin Education Act	D. *Hazelwood* (U.S. 1988)	E. *Lopez v. Union* *High School* *District* (Franklin Sup. Ct. 1994)	F. *Leeb v. DeLong* (Franklin Ct. App. 1995)
Preamble	**P-5.** Congress shall make no law "abridging the freedom of speech, or of the press . . . ."	**P-5.** "A law may not restrain or abridge liberty of speech or press . . . except [obscenity, libel, slander]	**P-5.** Students have editorial control. Except for obscenity, libel and slander, or speech that incites students to create a clear and present danger of unlawful acts, students have right of free speech. Responsibility of advisors to maintain "professional standards of English and journalism."	**P-6.** "Educational mission outweighs [free] speech." Censorship Ok for valid educational purpose.	**P-8.** Film subject to same standards/ rights as newspaper. **P-9.** Student publications are "limited public forum": State must show compelling state interest to censor.	**P-10.** Under sec. 48 students' rights are broader than under U.S. Constitution.
1. "Professional Standards"			**P-5.** It is the duty of school advisers to maintain "professional standards."	**P-7.** School may "disassociate itself" from certain speech.	**P-8.** Profanity violates "professional standards" under sec. 48.	
2. "Good taste"			Query. Included under "professional standards" in sec. 48? If so, permissible. But probably not.		**P-9.** Film/ newspaper is "limited public forum." Compelling state interest required for restrictions.	

MPT-Matrix™ *In re Gardenton Board of Education*, MPT, February 1998, *cont'd*						
Proposed Code	A. U.S. Constitution	B. Franklin Constitution	C. Sec. 48 Franklin Education Act	D. *Hazelwood* (U.S. 1988)	E. *Lopez v. Union High School District* (Franklin Sup. Ct. 1994)	F. *Leeb v. DeLong* (Franklin Ct. App. 1995)
3. "Accuracy"			Q. Students have editorial control. However, probably Ok. Use "Professional standards."			
4. Quotes/ permissions			**P-5.** Probably Ok: "Obscene, libelous," . . . and also under "Professional standards."			
5. No materials: a. Libel, etc.			**P-5.** Ditto.		**P-8.** Prior restraint Ok where material "violation" of sec. 48. Prior restraint Ok to forestall actions against school in defamation.	**P-10.** Prior restraint by school Ok to forestall actions in defamation. **P-10.** Must limit deletion to the offending material.
b. Profanity			**P-5.** Ok if profanity violates "professional standards"? Definitely Ok to prohibit it if it is "obscenity."	**P-7.** School may "disassociate" itself from profanity.	**P-8.** Sec. 48 permits prior restraint of profanity. **P-8.** Profanity violates "professional standards" under sec. 48. **P-8.** School also has interest in protecting students.	

Proposed Code	A. U.S. Constitution	B. Franklin Constitution	C. Sec. 48 Franklin Education Act	D. *Hazelwood* (U.S. 1988)	E. *Lopez v. Union High School District* (Franklin Sup. Ct. 1994)	F. *Leeb v. DeLong* (Franklin Ct. App. 1995)

MPT-Matrix™ *In re Gardenton Board of Education*, MPT, February 1998, *cont'd*						
Proposed Code	A. U.S. Constitution	B. Franklin Constitution	C. Sec. 48 Franklin Education Act	D. *Hazelwood* (U.S. 1988)	E. *Lopez v. Union High School District* (Franklin Sup. Ct. 1994)	F. *Leeb v. DeLong* (Franklin Ct. App. 1995)
c. Criticize public officials				**P-7.** School may refuse to associate itself with political positions.		**P-10.** *New York Times v. Sullivan* standard applies to public figures. So section not Ok.
d. "Not in school's best interest."			Ok under "professional standards"? But if provision is too broad, strike it.	**P-7.** School may "disassociate itself" from certain speech. However, this provision of the Code is probably too broad as written.		
6. Need prior approval of principal			Ok under "professional standards"?	**P-7.** Arguably permissible [?] because school may "disassociate itself."	**P-8.** Prior restraint Ok where material "violation" of sec. 48. Or to protect the students. **P-9.** Or where it is a limited public forum and there is a compelling state interest.	**P-10.** Prior restraint by school Ok to forestall actions in defamation. **P-10.** Must limit deletion to the offending material.

Perform Your Best™ Sample Answer for *In re Gardenton Board of Education*

MEMORANDUM

To: Frank Eisner
From: Applicant
Subject: Gardenton Board of Education—Proposed Communications Code
        for Gardenton High School
Date: _____

INTRODUCTION

For the Board's guidance as they prepare for a public meeting, the Gardenton Board of Education have asked us how to edit the proposed Gardenton High School Student Communications Code ("the Code") so that the school has the greatest possible latitude to censor objectionable material in student publications and productions. I conclude that the School Board should have little difficulty. Sec. 48 of the Franklin Education Act gives school boards authority to enforce "professional standards" of journalism, so most sections of the proposed code are unexceptionable. Most sections, furthermore, are also unexceptionable under constitutional, statutory, and case law. I provide a section-by-section analysis below, with suggestions for revision where necessary.

DISCUSSION

PREAMBLE OF THE CODE. The Preamble suggests that under the Communications Code the school can impose prior restraint on all official and extracurricular student publications and presentations, in all media, whether on campus or off. Legal issues: (1.) whether the Preamble is impermissibly broad; (2.) whether student films are subject to the same standards as student newspapers; (3.) whether off-campus activities are subject to the same standards as on-campus activities.

Is the Preamble permissible? Yes. Reasons: (1.) Sec. 48 of the Franklin Education Act does give students broader free speech rights than does the United States Constitution and limits prior restraint of speech. But sec. 48 also gives the school power to require "professional standards" of English and journalism. That means it may sometimes impose prior restraint.

(2.) The *Lopez* court says that student films are subject to the same standards as student newspapers.

(3.) If students' off-campus activities are what the *Lopez* court calls a "public forum," then critics might argue that the school cannot regulate them. If, on the other hand, they are a "limited public forum," then the school can regulate them, but only if it demonstrates (i) a compelling state interest and (ii) that the regulations are both narrowly drawn to achieve that compelling interest and sufficiently precise to withstand a challenge as void for vagueness.

Suggestions: If the School Board strikes the words "off campus," in specific cases the Board can support censoring off-campus productions using the "disassociate itself" language of *Hazelwood* ("a school may . . . disassociate itself . . . from speech that is . . . vulgar or profane, or unsuitable for immature audiences"), perhaps together with the "professional standards" language of sec. 48.

Sec. 1. Is the requirement of professional standards of English language and journalistic style permissible? Legal issues. Whether this standard is clear, definite, and not too broad. Permissible? Yes. Reasons: Courts have upheld sec. 48 of the Education Act, allowing schools to require "professional standards."

Sec. 2. Is the requirement of good taste, having regard to the "age, experience and maturity" of the students permissible? Legal issues. Is the term "good taste" unconstitutionally void for vagueness? Is "age, experience," etc.?

Permissible? Yes. But term "good taste" should nonetheless be changed. Reasons: Critics will argue that "good taste" is too vague. Suggestion: To avoid fruitless controversy, this section should read: "avoid language and depictions that violate professional standards of taste . . . ."

Sec. 3. Is the requirement that accuracy of facts and quotations be verified permissible? Legal issues: whether this requirement violates the students' right to editorial control under sec. 48; whether it is an impermissible prior restraint. Permissible? Yes. Reasons: Sec. 48 requires, again, application of "professional standards." Responsible newspapers of general circulation do require accuracy of facts and quotations. The School Board can require accuracy of facts, and probably also that quotations be verified by the supervising teacher.

Sec. 4. Is the requirement permissible that no quotes or photos be used without prior permission of that person or of a parent or guardian of a minor? Legal issues: whether this Code section imposes an impermissible prior restraint. Permissible? Yes. Reasons: Sec. 48 makes "professional standards" the touchstone, and prior permission is consistent with professional standards. In the *Leeb* case, where a group photograph was used for a purpose for which the subjects had not given permission, the court upheld censorship.

Sec. 5a. Is the requirement to avoid libel permissible? Legal issues: whether this Code section imposes an impermissible prior restraint. Permissible? Yes. Reasons: Sec. 48 by its terms proscribes obscenity, libel, and slander. *Lopez* permits prior restraint to prevent a "violation" of sec. 48. The cases also permit prior restraint to forestall an action in defamation against the school. Note that the *Leeb* court stipulated that the school must limit the deletion to the offending material. Suggestion: The school may prefer to avoid controversy about what is libelous by using the "professional standards" language here instead.

Sec. 5b. Profanity. Legal issues: whether this Code section imposes an impermissible prior restraint. Permissible? Yes. Reasons: Sec. 48 does not by its terms proscribe profanity. The School Board can argue, however, that profanity in student publications violates "professional standards." The Supreme Court of the United States has said that a school may "disassociate itself" from profanity. *Hazelwood*. In *Lopez*, the Franklin Supreme Court held that sec. 48 permits prior restraint of profanity. The school may also cite Lopez to argue that it exerts its interest in protecting students when it censors profanity.

Sec. 5c. No criticism or demeaning of public officials. Legal issues: whether this Code section impermissibly limits freedom of the press under the First Amendment. Permissible? No. Reasons. The Franklin Court of Appeal in *Leeb* made it clear that when students criticize public figures the applicable standard is *New York Times v. Sullivan*. Accordingly, this provision must be stricken.

Sec. 5d. May the school suppress material deemed not in school's best interest? Legal issues: whether this Code section impermissibly limits freedom of the press under the First

Amendment. Permissible? Probably not. Reasons: Under *Hazelwood*, a school may "disassociate itself" from certain speech. "Not in the school's best interest," however, is a very broad standard. It may also be void for vagueness under the United States Constitution. Conclusion: The School Board should strike this section.

Sec. 6. Is the requirement of prior approval of the principal permissible? Legal issues: whether this Code section impermissibly limits freedom of the press under the First Amendment by imposing prior restraint. Permissible? Yes. Reasons: The Education Act and the cases all assume that student publications require prior approval of the school. Sec. 48 of the Education Act affirms the authority of the school to teach and enforce professional standards. The Franklin Supreme Court in *Lopez* held that the school may censor official school publications to protect the students. Both *Lopez* and *Leeb* asserted that prior restraint by the school is permissible to forestall an action in defamation.

CONCLUSION

I have examined the proposed Code and concluded that most parts of the Preamble and most sections of the Code are unexceptionable under constitutional, statutory, and case law. I have made suggestions for deleting, modifying, or adding items in the few instances where it is necessary to help the Board achieve its goal. The School Board should have little difficulty responding to critics.

Perform Your Best™ Note on Analyzing *In re Gardenton Board of Education*

Objective Memorandum
Code Analysis and Drafting
Analysis for partner: to use for advising client
Statutory interpretation, with suggestions for deleting, adding or re-drafting sections

In the MPT task called *In re Gardenton Board of Education,* the client, the Gardenton Board of Education, has asked how to draft the Gardenton High School Student Communications Code ("the Code") so that the school has the greatest possible latitude to censor objectionable material in student publications and productions. This task may appear especially challenging because it requires bar candidates to apply constitutional principles in assessing the proposed Code.

In fact, this task is straightforward, and both the legal format and the analytic pattern are familiar. The task calls for writing an objective memorandum to the partner, so the format is one of the familiar basic legal formats. In addition, this task is yet another instance of the familiar MPT pattern in which the student must analyze a code or a proposed code, one section at a time. And as always where the MPT asks the bar candidate to examine a code one section at a time, the File or Library contains a document that provides the standard for judging the sections. Here, sec. 48 of the Franklin Education Act is that useful document. Sec. 48 allows school boards the authority to enforce "professional standards" of journalism. When you test the code sections against the "professional standards" clause of sec. 48, almost every section of the proposed Code turns out to be permissible.

The main challenge of completing *In re Gardenton Board of Education* is finding your framework within the partner's instructions in the task memo and then using that framework efficiently to keep the material under control. As always, you must finish the whole task within 90 minutes, and the work product you hand in must be not only intellectually compelling but also visually clear and simple.

As always, again, the key to success on this MPT task is reading the partner memo with exquisite care. Having first stated the scope of the task in general terms, the partner memo then gives you your analytic framework. Read the partner memo with exquisite care and you will see what the parts of your analysis of each code section must be. I have underlined the key terms in the partner's framework below:

> Please prepare a memorandum in which you evaluate the preamble and each of the guideline provisions in the draft of the communications code that Dr. Kantor left with me. Identify the <u>legal issues</u> that can give rise to constitutional challenges to each of the provisions and analyze whether each such provision is likely to be found legally <u>permissible</u>. Make <u>suggestions for deleting, modifying, or adding</u> any items in order to help the Board achieve its goal. Be sure to state your <u>reasons</u> for concluding that each guideline provision is legally permissible or impermissible, as well as the <u>reasons for any suggestions</u> you make. Support your reasons with <u>appropriate discussion of the facts and law</u>.

The sample answer uses these key terms as a framework. For example:

> <u>Sec. 4. Is the requirement permissible that no quotes or photos be used without prior permission of that person or of a parent or guardian of a minor?</u> <u>Legal issues:</u> whether this Code section imposes an impermissible prior restraint. <u>Permissible?</u> Yes. <u>Reasons:</u> Sec. 48 makes "professional standards" the touchstone, and prior permission is consistent with professional standards. In the *Leeb* case, where a group photograph was used for a purpose for which the subjects had not given permission, the court upheld censorship.

If you handle every section of the proposed code this way, you will submit a work product that will merit a good grade.

This MPT task does present one significant challenge of legal analysis. You must use exactly the same framework to handle it that you use for all of your other treatments of code sections. The problem here is chiefly one of exam-taking tactics. Managing time while completing the work product is always a primary consideration, and here, unfortunately, it is the Preamble of the proposed code, the opening section, that presents the challenge. Don't let yourself get bogged down, and don't let yourself be intimidated. I suggest that if you run into a challenging issue that concerns only one section of the code you are analyzing, as here, you should leave space in your bluebook, complete the rest of your work product, and return to the challenging issue at the end of your 90 minutes.

Here is the way the sample answer handles the potentially challenging legal issue in *In re Gardenton Board of Education*:

> PREAMBLE OF THE CODE. The Preamble suggests that under the Communications Code the school can impose prior restraint on all official and extracurricular student publications and presentations, in all media, whether on campus or off. <u>Legal issues:</u> (1.) whether the Preamble is impermissibly broad; (2.) whether student films are subject to the same standards as student newspapers; (3.) whether off-campus activities are subject to the same standards as on-campus activities.
>
> <u>Is the Preamble permissible?</u> Yes. <u>Reasons:</u> (1.) Sec. 48 of the Franklin Education Act does give students broader free speech rights than does the United States Constitution and limits prior restraint of speech. But sec. 48 also gives the school power to require "professional standards" of English and journalism. That means it may sometimes impose prior restraint.
>
> (2.) The *Lopez* court says that student films are subject to the same standards as student newspapers.
>
> (3.) If students' off-campus activities are what the *Lopez* court calls a "public forum," then critics might argue that the school cannot regulate them. If, on the other hand, they are a "limited public forum," then the school can regulate them, but only if it demonstrates (i) a compelling state interest and (ii) that the regulations are both narrowly drawn to achieve that compelling interest and sufficiently precise to withstand a challenge as void for vagueness.
>
> <u>Suggestions:</u> If the School Board strikes the words "off campus," in specific cases the Board can support censoring off-campus productions using the "disassociate itself" language of *Hazelwood* ("a school may . . . disassociate itself . . . from speech that is . . . vulgar or profane, or unsuitable for immature audiences"), perhaps together with the "professional standards" language of sec. 48.

As always, in the Conclusion of the memorandum you will restate the partner's assignment, state that you have completed it and say what general conclusions you have reached:

> I have examined the proposed Code and concluded that most parts of the Preamble and most sections of the Code are unexceptionable under constitutional, statutory, and case law. I have made suggestions for deleting, modifying, or adding items in the few instances where it is necessary to help the Board achieve its goal. The School Board should have little difficulty responding to critics.

Perform Your Best™ Materials
For Task E:
In re Steven Wallace

Note to the Reader: Your MPT-Matrix™ will have only page numbers, not words. The words in this MPT Matrix™ simply show you the information you will be indexing and cross-referencing. Do not attempt to write words in your own MPT-Matrix™.

MPT-Matrix™ *In re Steven Wallace*, MPT, July 1999						
	A. Meeting 2/26/99	B. Receipt 8/15/98	C. *Walker on Bankruptcy*	D. Franklin Commercial Code sec. 2-326, Franklin Civil Code sec. 3533	E. *First Natl. Bank v. Marigold Farms* (Franklin Ct. App. Undated)	F. *In re Levy* (E.D. Pa. 1993)
1. Asset of bkrpty estate 1. Bkrpy. Act b. Legal Basis			**P-6.** Trustee can avoid transfer of property after case begins; Assets include consignments.			
2. ii. Factual Basis	**P-2.** Painting was on consignment; Lottie attempted to transfer it after case began.	**P-3.** Receipt indicates painting on consignment.				
3. Franklin CC i. Legal Basis				**P-7.** FCC § 2-326. Goods on consignment are subject to creditors' claims.	**P-8.** Goods held on sale or return are subject to claims of creditors regardless of consignor's retaining title.	
4. ii. Factual Basis	**P-2.** Painting was on consignment.	**P-3.** Receipt indicates painting on consignment.				
5. Defense: Sign Law (i) How supports	**P-2.** (a) SW's label on back; (b) Sign in window?			**P-7.** Franklin Civil Code sec. 3533.	**P-9.** Must be generally known to all creditors, not just consignors.	**P-10.** Signs must impart knowledge to creditors, not just customers.
6. (ii) Add'l. Helpful Facts	Regarding other artists' signs: Would be evidence of notice. Regarding whether Lottie had a sign in the window: What do the neighbors of the shop say? What have the other creditors seen? Ask them.					

	A. Meeting 2/26/99	B. Receipt 8/15/98	C. *Walker on Bankruptcy*	D. Franklin Commercial Code sec. 2-326, Franklin Civil Code sec. 3533	E. *First Natl. Bank v. Marigold Farms* (Franklin Ct. App. Undated)	F. *In re Levy* (E.D. Pa. 1993)
MPT-Matrix™ *In re Steven Wallace*, MPT, July 1999, *cont'd*						
7. (iii) Why Helpful	Artists' signs would show general notice, if intended to give notice to non-customers. Lottie's sign would show that owner complied with the sign law.					
8. (iv) Possible Sources	The other consignors are the best source regarding artists' signs. Go to the shop: is the sign still there? Ask other shop owners on the same street. Ask person from whom Lottie bought the sign, or seller, if any, from whom she bought the shop. Beat cop. Letter carrier. Caterers who worked at gallery openings. Other creditors. Photographs.					
9. Creditors Know Selling Goods of Others	Name of shop, Artists' Excg.				**P-9.** Other creditors, not just the artists/consignors.	**P-10.** Must be creditors, not just customers.
10. (ii) Add'l. Helpful Facts	Are most of the creditors in fact consignors? (If so, perhaps can distinguish *First National Bank*.) Is there evidence from Lottie's correspondence with creditors that Artists' Exchange was primarily engaged in selling the goods of others? Ask other creditors. Include bank, newspaper advertising department, advertising agency. Was there a sign in the window?					
11. (iii) Why helpful.	If we can find other non-artist creditors and customers who know that Lottie was selling the goods of others, this will satisfy the defense that she is "generally known" to be in the business of selling the goods of others.					
12. (iv) Possible Sources	Ask Lottie. Look at the property schedules filed with the court, which will contain the names and addresses of the creditors. Ask the banker, the cleaning service, the printers who do announcements of shows, the newspaper advertising department, the advertising agency. Question whether most art galleries deal on a consignment basis may call for expert testimony.					
13. Compliance With filing Provisions of UCC Art.	Would be complete defense under FCC sec. 2-326(3)(c). No evidence now. No record that Ms. Morales asked the question. Ask Steven Wallace. Look in Sec'y of State files, etc. Ask whether any other consignors complied with Art. 9. Would be constructive notice.					
14. Consignor used for personal/ family/ household.	If this can be shown, it will be a complete defense under the FCC. However, SW did sell his paintings. See footnote in *First National Bank*.					
15. (ii) Add'l. Helpful Facts	Has Steven Wallace kept other paintings for personal use? Has he ever refused to sell a painting in his personal collection? Make sure to check SW's personal files and records. What discussions did the Wallaces have at the time they bought the rug?					
16. (iii) Why helpful.	It would show that these paintings are for household use, not commercial stock in trade.					
17. (iv) Possible Sources	Steven Wallace's friends and acquaintances who might have tried to buy a painting. SW's own records: does he maintain separate records for the inventory of paintings he holds for sale and the ones he keeps for his family's use?					

Perform Your Best™ Sample Answer for *In re Steven Wallace*

MEMORANDUM

To: Eva Morales
From: Applicant
Date: _____
Subject: Steven Wallace—Painting Titled "Hare Castle"

INTRODUCTION

You have asked me to analyze the legal and factual bases for the trustee's claim that under the Bankruptcy Act and under the Franklin Commercial Code, our client Steven Wallace's painting "Hare Castle" is an asset of art dealer Lottie Zelinka's bankruptcy estate. You have also asked me to assess possible defenses under FCC sec. 2-326(3).

DISCUSSION

IA. Since Lottie Zelinka held the painting "Hare Castle" on consignment, and since she returned the painting to Steven Wallace only after she filed for bankruptcy, the Bankruptcy Act provides legal bases for the trustee to avoid returning the painting to Steven Wallace.

Under the Bankruptcy Act, the assets of the bankruptcy estate include goods left with the bankrupt on consignment. In addition, the trustee can avoid any transfer of property made after the case begins. *Walker on Bankruptcy,* sec. 4.08.

Here, Steven Wallace reports, and the receipt indicates, that he placed the painting with Lottie Zelinka on consignment. Wallace Interview; Receipt; Appraisal. In addition, the facts show that Lottie did attempt to transfer the property, i.e., the painting "Hare Castle," back to Wallace after she filed for bankruptcy. Ms. Zelinka came to Wallace's house with the painting, 10 days or so before he spoke with Ms. Morales, saying that she wished to return the painting to him. Wallace reports learning that Ms. Zelinka had already filed for bankruptcy protection on the date when she tried to return the painting to him. Wallace Interview.

Therefore, if the painting was an asset of the bankruptcy estate, then the trustee has legal and factual bases for his claim. If, that is, Steven Wallace has no effective defense, the trustee can avoid Lottie Zelinka's transfer of the property back to Steven Wallace after the bankruptcy filing.

IB. Since Lottie Zelinka held the painting "Hare Castle" on consignment, the Franklin Commercial Code provides legal bases for the trustee's claim that Steven Wallace's painting is part of the bankruptcy estate.

Under the Franklin Commercial Code, goods on consignment are subject to creditors' claims. FCC sec. 2-326. Under *First National Bank* and *In re Levy*, it does not matter that the consignor retained title.

Here, the interview notes and the receipt Lottie Zelinka gave Steven Wallace show that the painting "Hare Castle" was delivered on consignment. Wallace Interview; Receipt.

Therefore, again, unless Steven Wallace can assert an effective defense, the trustee has legal and factual bases under the Franklin Commercial Code for his claim.

<u>II. Depending on how our factual investigations turn out, Steven Wallace may possibly assert one or more of the defenses available under FCC 2-326, and oppose the trustee's claim.</u>

Depending on the facts, Steven Wallace may be able to assert an effective defense under FCC 2-326(a). The best defense may be the defense of use for "personal, family, or household purposes."

(a) <u>Defense of compliance with the sign law.</u> Under FCC 2-326(a), goods delivered to another person for sale are not subject to the claims of the latter's creditors where the person making the delivery "complies with all applicable law providing for a consignor's interest or the like to be evidenced by a sign."

(i) <u>How the facts we already know support this defense.</u> First, Steven Wallace had a label on the back of his painting, saying that it was the property of Steven Wallace. Wallace Interview. Other artists may have done the same. Second, Lottie Zelinka's sign in the window of the shop—if there was one, as Steven Wallace thinks—may have indicated the consignors' interests in their art work. Note that these two supports are entirely different from one another.

(ii) Additional helpful facts.

(ii)(a) Artists' signs would show notice to customers.

(ii)(b) Lottie Zelinka's sign, if any, would show that the owner complied with the sign law, if it stated that she was dealing in property in which others had an interest. FCC 3533.

(iii) Why helpful:

(iii)(a) If most artists had signs on the backs of their paintings, that might arguably constitute adequate notice to customers, even if it would not notify non-customers.

(iii)(b) If Lottie Zelinka had a sign in the window, it would show that she complied with the sign law.

(iv) <u>Possible sources.</u> The other consignors are the best source of information about their own signs. As to the possibility of a sign in the window, we can send an investigator to the shop. Ask other shop owners on the same street whether they ever noticed a sign. Ask the person from whom Lottie Zelinka bought the shop, if any. Ask the beat cop. Ask the letter carrier. Ask the caterers who work at gallery openings. Ask other creditors. Find out if there are reliably dated photographs of the front of the shop, perhaps in municipal archives.

(b) <u>Defense of creditors' knowledge that the gallery sold on consignment.</u> Under FCC 2-326(b), the person making the delivery has a defense if he establishes that "the person conducting the business is generally known by his creditors to be substantially engaged in selling goods of others." Under *First National Bank*, these creditors must persons other than consignors. Under *In re Levy*, these creditors must not be just customers of the bankrupt.

(i) <u>How the facts we already know support this defense.</u> We can argue that the name of the shop, "Artists' Exchange," Inventory Receipt, indicates that the gallery was selling the goods of others. And if galleries everywhere work on consignment, as Steven Wallace believes, then creditors probably know it.

(ii) <u>Additional helpful facts.</u> Find out whether creditors such as newspaper advertising departments know that Lottie Zelinka was operating on consignment.

(iii) <u>Why helpful.</u> All we need is evidence that Lottie Zelinka was "generally known" to be selling goods on consignment.

(iv) <u>Possible sources.</u> Ask Lottie Zelinka. Look for a list of creditors with the petition in bankruptcy. Ask the banker, the cleaning service, the printers who do announcements of openings, the newspaper advertising department, the ad agency. Send an investigator to talk to them.

    (c) <u>Defense of compliance with Article 9 of the UCC.</u> Check the Article 9 filings in the Secretary of State's files. If artists filed, this would be constructive notice.

    (d) <u>Defense of use for "personal, family, or household purposes."</u> If this can be shown, it will be a complete defense under the FCC. However, note that Steven Wallace did sell other paintings. See footnote in *First National Bank.*

(i) <u>How the facts we already know support this defense.</u> First, at the meeting of July 26, 1999, Steven Wallace reported that he had never thought about trying to sell "Hare Castle." Second, it was "one of his favorite paintings and had been hanging in his dining room since he finished it a couple of years ago." Third, Steven Wallace and his wife "had recently purchased a new rug for their dining room that coordinated with the colors in the painting." Fourth, up until now, Steven Wallace has been working out of a spare room at home. Wallace Interview.

(ii) Additional helpful facts. Does Steven Wallace keep separate inventories of paintings for sale and paintings for personal use? Has he ever refused to sell a painting because for family use?

(iii) Why helpful. Such facts might prove that "Hare Castle" was for family use only.

(iv) Possible sources. Look at Steven Wallace's personal and business records. Arrange for interviews with friends who might have tried unsuccessfully to buy his paintings.

CONCLUSION

My research indicates that the trustee has sound legal and factual bases, both under the Bankruptcy Act and under the Franklin Commercial Code, for claiming that our client Steven Wallace's painting "Hare Castle" is an asset of Lottie Zelinka's bankruptcy estate. Depending on the results of our factual investigations, however, our client may be able to assert one or more defenses under FCC sec. 2-326(3). If the facts turn out to support it, the best defense may be that Steven Wallace used the painting for family and household purposes.

Perform Your Best™ Note on Analyzing *In re Steven Wallace*

Objective memorandum
Possible litigation
Advise client on best response to a demand from trustee in bankruptcy
Structure of work product: Statutory and case law analysis and application,
with suggestions for factual investigation

In this case, the firm represents Steven Wallace, a professor recently retired from the University of Franklin who now intends to turn being a painter from an avocation into a full-time career. A year ago he consigned one of his paintings, called Hare Castle, to a local art gallery owned by his friend Lottie Zelinka. She returned the painting to him, but only after she had filed for bankruptcy. Now the trustee of Ms. Zelinka's estate in bankruptcy seeks to claim the painting as part of her bankruptcy estate. The Partner Memorandum asks the associate to write a memorandum evaluating the trustee's claims under both the Bankruptcy Act and the Franklin Commercial Code. The associate is also to analyze the client's factual defenses under the statute and to propose additional factual research. Both evaluating the trustee's claim and analyzing the client's defenses are objective tasks. You will examine both sides of the issues.

How to Read and Outline the Instructions in the Partner Memo. Nothing is more important on the MPT than understanding the main issues in the case and meticulously following the instructions in the Partner Memo, painstakingly outlining the instructions by dividing and sub-dividing the topics. Here, the instructions say,

> Please draft for me a two-part memorandum:
> * First, analyze the legal and factual bases of the trustee's claim that the painting is an asset of the bankruptcy estate under the Bankruptcy Act and the Franklin Commercial Code (FCC).
> * Second, for each of the four defenses under FCC § 2-326(3), discuss how the facts we already know support the defense, identify additional facts that might be helpful to us, state why they would be helpful, and indicate from what sources we might be able to obtain them.

Outlining the instructions for Part I, which ask for analysis of legal and factual bases for the trustee's claim under the Bankruptcy Act and the Franklin Commercial Code, is straightforward. As usual, you must tear each instruction apart into the smallest possible elements. Clearly, you will have separate lines in your MPT-Matrix™ in which you will note the page numbers of items in the File and the Library that are useful for analyzing the Bankruptcy Act and the Franklin Commercial Code. But note that the Partner Memo says, "analyze the legal and factual bases of the trustee's claim." For each code, that is, under both the Bankruptcy Act and the Franklin Commercial Code, you must assign one line in the MPT-Matrix™ to "legal" bases and one line to "factual." For Part II, in addition, careful reading is required to note that the Partner Memo asks four questions as to each of the four possible defenses. That is sixteen questions in all.

So far as practical, you will use the same four-part analysis to look for facts that would support each of the four defenses the statute provides. You cannot simply skip anything the Partner Memo asks you to do, although in this case, some of the partner's questions about possible defenses will lead in more promising directions than others. Accordingly, you will try to answer the same four questions in the Partner Memo for each of the four defenses:

     (i)   How the facts we already know support this defense.

     (ii)   Additional helpful facts.

     (iii) Why helpful:

     (iv) Possible sources.

The four defenses are as follows. You will apply all four questions from the Partner Memo to each of the four defenses, in some cases more successfully than others. You have a practical option. You can either assign 16 separate lines to this analysis in the MPT-Matrix™ or you can note these four topics on a separate sheet of paper to one side, and consider each one in relation to the four questions the Partner Memo poses.

     (a)   Defense of compliance with the sign law.

     (b)   Defense of creditors' knowledge that the gallery sold on consignment.

     (c)   Defense of compliance with Article 9 of the UCC.

     (d)   Defense of use for "personal, family, or household purposes."

For step-by-step, treatment of how to outline the instructions for *In re Steven Wallace* in your MPT-Matrix™, consult Part 3 of this book, above. It treats *In re Steven Wallace* in detail.

How to Apply the Rule of Three. The instructions in the Partner Memorandum for *In re Steven Wallace* tell the applicant to draft a two-part memorandum. Where the Partner Memo tells you to write a two-part memorandum, you have no choice. You must write a two-part memorandum. Here, you will nonetheless apply the Rule of Three, since you will sub-divide the first part of your memorandum, applying two different statutes, into two parts.

In the first main part, the partner has asked you to apply both the Bankruptcy Act and the Franklin Commercial Code and to analyze the legal and factual bases for the claim of the trustee in bankruptcy that your client Steven Wallace's painting "Hare Castle" is an asset of art dealer Lottie Zelinka's bankruptcy estate. In the second main part of your Discussion you will assess the possible defenses under FCC sec. 2-326(3).

Your strong persuasive headings, which you will underline in your work product, might read as follows:

     IA. Since Lottie Zelinka held the painting "Hare Castle" on consignment, and since she returned the painting to Steven Wallace only after she filed for bankruptcy, the Bankruptcy Act provides legal and factual bases for the trustee to avoid returning the painting to Steven Wallace.

     IB. Since Lottie Zelinka held the painting "Hare Castle" on consignment, the Franklin Commercial Code provides legal and factual bases for the trustee's claim that Steven Wallace's painting is part of the bankruptcy estate.

     II. Depending on the results of our factual investigations, Steven Wallace may assert one or more of the defenses available under FCC 2-326, and oppose the trustee's claim.

The second part of this memorandum often causes bar candidates trouble. It requires responding to four factual questions as to each of four code sections. Thus, on the one hand, it is like the other tasks in this book in which the MPT requires analyzing code sections, one after the other. In this instance, however, applying the code sections requires suggesting avenues for factual investigation, rather than applying a rule of law. To do this task, you must apply your street smarts to the bar exam. You must think about the facts, and then think about how to obtain more facts. Students who try to substitute book-learning for factual proof will do an unsatisfactory job on this part of the task. See Part 3 of this book for further discussion of the use of facts for *In re Steven Wallace*.

Observe that in the MPT-Matrix™ for *In re Steven Wallace*, this book has included some notes about where one might look for the needed facts.

As usual, the Conclusion of your objective memorandum will summarize the partner's instructions and briefly summarize your conclusions. Here is the Conclusion from the sample memorandum for *In re Steven Wallace* in this book.

CONCLUSION

My research indicates that the trustee has sound legal and factual bases, both under the Bankruptcy Act and under the Franklin Commercial Code, for claiming that our client Steven Wallace's painting "Hare Castle" is an asset of Lottie Zelinka's bankruptcy estate. Depending on the results of our factual investigations, however, our client may be able to assert one or more defenses under FCC sec. 2-326(3). If the facts turn out to support it, the best defense may be that Steven Wallace used the painting for family and household purposes.

Perform Your Best™ Materials
For Task F:
In re Franklin Asbestos Handling Regulations

Note to the Reader: Your MPT-Matrix™ will have only page numbers, not words. The words in this MPT Matrix™ simply show you the information you will be indexing and cross-referencing. Do not attempt to write words in your own MPT-Matrix™.

	A. Franklin Environmental Protection Code, Title 6, Chapter 13	B. 29 C.F.R. sec. 1926 Asbestos	C. *Gade v. National Solid Wastes Management Association,* (U.S. 1992)	D.	E.	F. *Chamber of Commerce v. Noter* (15th Cir. 1995)
Perform Your Best™ MPT-Matrix™ *Franklin Asbestos Handling Regulations*, MPT, July 2000						
1. Best case for why statutory and regulatory scheme not preempted in its entirety.	**P-2.** State law purpose (1) to safeguard public health; (2) to ensure that workers handling asbestos receive training to protect public health.		**P-10.** Congressional intent determines preemption. No preemption if there is (i) no federal standard, or (ii) approved state plan. *Implied preemption.* (a) *Field preemption.* Congress has left no room in the field for states to supplement. (b) *Conflict preemption.* Impossible to comply with both, or else state law interferes. **P-11.** *Dual impact law.* Absent approved state plan, OSH Act preempts state law that in a *direct, clear and substantial way*, is regulation of worker health and safety. But state law may regulate workers as members of general public.			**P-13.** Where dual purpose, state law preempted only if it has a "direct and substantial" effect on the federal system of regulation. **P-13, P-14.** Sections of surveys re workplace hazards—not environmental hazards—are in conflict with methods of federal government to promote hazard communication.

	A. Franklin Environmental Protection Code, Title 6, Chapter 13	B. 29 C.F.R. sec. 1926 Asbestos	C. *Gade v. National Solid Wastes Management Association,* (U.S. 1992)	D.	E.	F. *Chamber of Commerce v. Noter* (15th Cir. 1995)

Perform Your Best™ MPT-Matrix™ *Franklin Asbestos Handling Regulations*, MPT, July 2000, *cont'd*

	A. Franklin Environmental Protection Code, Title 6, Chapter 13	B. 29 C.F.R. sec. 1926 Asbestos	C. *Gade v. National Solid Wastes Management Association,* (U.S. 1992)	D.	E.	F. *Chamber of Commerce v. Noter* (15th Cir. 1995)
2. Discussion re whether each provision of Section 8 of Franklin regulations can survive preemption challenge. Section 8(a): Employees must complete 5-day course and 2-hour exam.		Sec. (m) (iii). Training program takes at least 8 hours. No exam. State can argue dual purpose: objective to protect public.				
(b) Course must cover (1) Physical characteristics of asbestos		Sec. (iv)(A) Methods of recognizing asbestos. **Same: no conflict.**				
(2) Worker protective equipment		Sec. (iv)(D) Respirators. Clothing. Sec. (iv)(E). Purpose, use, fitting, limits/ respirators. **Same: no conflict.**				
(3) State-of-art practices for abatement and remediation.		Sec. (iv)(F). Appropriate work practices for performing asbestos job. **Same: no conflict.**				

Perform Your Best™ MPT-Matrix™ *Franklin Asbestos Handling Regulations*, MPT, July 2000, *cont'd*						
	A. Franklin Environmental Protection Code, Title 6, Chapter 13	B. 29 C.F.R. sec. 1926 Asbestos	C. *Gade v. National Solid Wastes Management Association,* (U.S. 1992)	D.	E.	F. *Chamber of Commerce v. Noter* (15th Cir. 1995)
(4) Procedures for collecting samples to minimize airborne fibers.		Sec. (iv)(D), (F). Work practices. Same: no conflict.				
(5) Personal hygiene pertaining to asbestos handling.		Sec. (iv)(D). Housekeeping. Hygiene. Same: no conflict.				
(c) Required one-day biennial review course to renew certificate.	Sec. 3(b). Workers handling asbestos material need valid asbestos handling certificate.	Training to be provided prior to or at the time of initial assignment and at least annually thereafter. Possible conflict.				
(d) Certificate on completion of course/fee of $100.		No cost to employee. Direct conflict.				
(e) Employer provides to DEP names of all employees with certificate, plus $600 each per year.		[Silent.] No conflict.				P-14 Funding system that does not interfere with compliance with federal law is permitted. Funding provision a logical means to accomplish community health and safety purpose.

Perform Your Best™ Sample Answer for *Franklin Asbestos Handling Regulations*

Office of the Attorney General
State of Franklin
Environmental Protection Division

MEMORANDUM

To: Colin Dillard, Deputy Attorney General
From: Applicant
Date: _____

INTRODUCTION

You have asked me for the best arguments that the statutory and regulatory scheme of the Franklin Asbestos Handling Act (AHA) is not preempted in its entirety by the federal Occupational Safety and Health Act (OSH Act) and the implementing federal regulations. The best argument why the AHA is not preempted in its entirety is that it is a dual impact law, affecting both workplace safety and public health. In addition, most aspects of the Franklin regulatory scheme should survive challenge, as either complementary to federal law or concerned with public health. The DEP training-and-certification requirement under section 8(a) and the $100 training-and-review course fee under section 8(e), however, are in conflict with the federal regulations and will probably be preempted.

DISCUSSION

1. The best argument that the Franklin Asbestos Handling Act is not preempted in its entirety is that it is a dual impact law, addressing both workplace safety and public health.

In *Gade v. National Solid Wastes Management Association* (1992), the Supreme Court stated that whether a state act is preempted by federal law is a question of congressional intent. Congress intended the OSH Act to preempt regulations related to workplace safety, but it did not intend the OSH Act to prevent state regulation of any occupational safety or health issue "with respect to which no Federal standard is in effect." 29 U.S.C. 667(a)

In the absence of an approved state plan, a state dual impact law may be permissible. A dual impact law addresses workplace safety and some other field. Where such a law is not in a direct, clear and substantial way a regulation of worker health and safety, and where it does not burden commerce, such a law is not preempted. One part of a statutory and regulatory scheme may be permissible, while another part is not. *Chamber of Commerce v. Noter.* Nonetheless, "conflict" preemption may occur where a section of a state code conflicts with or occupies the same field as a federal regulation. *Gade.*

The Franklin Environmental Protection Code is a state dual impact law. Its purposes are (1) to safeguard public health; and (2) to ensure that workers handling asbestos receive training. Therefore, portions of the Franklin law that are intended to safeguard public health, and that are not regulation of worker health and safety, may be permissible.

2. Some provisions of the Franklin Asbestos Handling Regulations will stand, either because they are intended to protect public health rather than workplace safety, or else because they are similar to the federal requirements. Other provisions are in conflict with the federal regulations and will be preempted.

Logically, there are four possibilities:

(i)   A state regulation is not a workplace safety measure, but has some other objective: it is not preempted;

(ii) The effect of the state regulation is similar to that of the federal regulation: it is not preempted;

(iii) A regulation conflicts with the federal regulation: it is preempted;

(iv) A regulation is a workplace safety measure: it is preempted.

Comparison of the Franklin AHA and regulations with the federal OSH Act and regulations yields the following results:

(a) The Franklin employee certification requirement will probably not be preempted, because the purpose is not to regulate workplace safety. The Franklin statute is a dual-purpose statute, protecting both workers and the general public. The State of Franklin may argue that the purpose of the certification requirement in Section 3(b) of the Franklin statute and Section 8 of the regulations is not to regulate workplace safety, but to protect the general public.

Section 8(a) of the Franklin regulations, however, requiring a 5-day course and an examination, will probably be preempted. The federal regulations require an 8-hour training program and do not require an examination, 29 C.F.R. 1926 sec. (m) (iii), while Section 8(a) of the Franklin regulations requires a 5-day DEP-approved course and a 2-hour examination for certification. While the State of Franklin can argue that the longer course and the examination are not in conflict with the federal regulations because they support public health, not worker safety, these regulations do not clearly on their face concern public health. They will probably be found to be both workplace regulations and in conflict with the methods specified by the federal regulations.

Section 8(b). There is no preemption of the required topics for the course. Where the topics regard worker safety, the Franklin requirements and the federal requirements are similar if not identical. There is therefore no preemption. As to the training requirements related to public safety issues, the DEP requirements do not fall within the ambit of the OSH Act and are not preempted.

Section 8(c). As to the biennial review course, there is preemption of the topics dealing with worker safety, but no preemption of the topics dealing with public health.

Section 8(d). The Franklin requirement of a $100 certificate fee is preempted. The federal regulations state that there must be no cost, while the AHA regulations are in direct conflict, requiring that the handler's certificate have a fee of $100.

Section 8(e). The Franklin requirement that the employer must provide DEP with names of all employees, and must pay $600 per year for each employee, is not preempted. Neither reporting names of employees nor paying a fee for each one is required under the OSHA regulations, and the State may argue that the DEP requirement is intended to safeguard the general public, not to assure workplace safety. In addition, a funding requirement is permissible under *Noter* where it is a "logical means for accomplishing a broad community health and safety purpose," without conflicting or interfering with the OSH Act.

CONCLUSION

The best argument that the Franklin Scheme as a whole should survive a preemption challenge from OSHA is that the scheme has a dual effect: it protects public health in addition to worker safety. Some aspects of the scheme as touching workplace safety should also survive challenge, either as complementary to federal law or as also concerned with public health. The DEP training-and-certification requirement under section 8(a) of the regulations and the $100 training-and-review course fee under section 8(e), however, are likely to be preempted.

Perform Your Best™ Note on Analyzing *Franklin Asbestos Handling Regulations*

Type of Task: Persuasive *and* objective memorandum
Context: Litigation
Purpose: Frame best arguments *and* evaluate regulations section-by-section
Structure of Work Product: Statutory interpretation and case law analysis and application

The author of the task memo for *Franklin Asbestos Handling Regulations* is a Deputy Attorney General. He tells the applicant that he anticipates a challenge to the recently-enacted Asbestos Handling Act (AHA), which requires the Franklin Department of Environmental Protection (DEP) to implement health and safety programs to train and certify workers who handle asbestos. The DEP has asked his office to review the proposed regulations it has drafted. He anticipates that the AHA statutory and regulatory scheme will be challenged as preempted by the Federal Occupational Safety and Healthy Act (OSH Act) and the implementing federal regulations. The instructions ask you to draft a memorandum that answers two questions. Most MPT tasks are either persuasive or objective. This MPT task is unusual in that the memorandum must be both persuasive and objective. The part of your memorandum in which you respond to the first instruction will be persuasive, while the part in which you respond to the second will be objective.

How to Outline the Instructions in the Partner Memo. The task memo provides the following instructions:

Please prepare a memorandum for me that:

States the best case for why, in light of the absence of a State Plan, the statutory and regulatory scheme is not preempted in its entirety; and
Discusses whether each provision of Section 8 of the draft regulations can survive a preemption challenge.

The first instruction is straightforward. To take it apart into its component parts, you will first note that it says "in the absence of a State Plan." The main point, however, is that the statutory and regulatory scheme is not preempted in its entirety. So you must figure out the relevance of the fact that Franklin has no State plan. The first row in your MPT-Matrix™, will be devoted mainly to noting page numbers of materials in the File or Library that bear on whether the AHA is preempted in its entirety. It will include the page number for the Supreme Court case *Gade v. National Solid Wastes Management. Gade* stated that where there is an approved State Plan, there is no preemption. Constructing the MPT-Matrix™ for the first instruction thus requires both tearing apart the instruction and teasing apart the cases.

The second instruction, asking for section-by-section assessment of draft regulations, introduces a standard MPT task. As usual, to respond to that instruction, you will analyze each section of the draft regulations one at a time. Your MPT-Matrix™ will list each section of the Franklin regulations separately down the lefthand column. Your job is to discuss whether each provision of Section 8 of the draft Franklin regulations is preempted or not. You will compare each section of the Franklin regulations with the corresponding section of the federal regulations, one after the other.

How to Use the Rule of Three. Where the task memo contains two clear-cut instructions, but they ask for two such different types of writing, you may wish to divide the Discussion section of your memorandum into two main parts. Whether the Discussion section of your memo has two or three parts, however, the first part of your Discussion must be persuasive, arguing only one side of the case and answering this question:

What are the best arguments that the statutory and regulatory scheme of the Franklin Asbestos Handling Act (AHA) should not be preempted in its entirety by the federal Occupational Safety and Health Act (OSH Act) and the implementing federal regulations?

Your answer the second question must be objective, analyzing both sides:

Will each provision of Section 8 of the Franklin draft regulations survive a preemption challenge?

Answering the second question requires using the classic MPT structure where you examine the sections of a code one at a time. Your starting point must always be the MPT File and Library, where you will find, somewhere, the standard against which you can test the proposed code sections one-by-one. Here, the standard for testing each section of the proposed Franklin regulations is found in the Code of Federal Regulations, 29 C.F.R. sec. 1926. As always with such MPT tasks, as a matter of test-taking tactics, you must first calculate the amount of time available for critiquing each of the code sections, then take care not to exceed the time available for each section. Note that for convenience, the sample MPT-Matrix™ in this book includes a note about the conclusion as to each comparison, e.g., "No conflict" or "Probably preempted."

Logically, there are four possibilities:

(i) A state regulation is not a workplace safety measure, but has some other objective: it is not preempted;

(ii) The effect of the state regulation is similar to that of the federal regulation: it is not preempted;

(iii) A regulation conflicts with the federal regulation: it is preempted;

(iv) A regulation is a workplace safety measure: it is preempted.

How to Apply the Rule of Three. The Partner Memo clearly divides the task into two parts. Using the Rule of Three is entirely optional. You may wish to divide your memorandum into the two parts suggested by the partner's two questions, without further sub-division. The sample answer in this book illustrates a Discussion divided into two parts. Alternatively, you may wish to employ the Rule of Three and divide your memorandum into three parts as follows:

1. The best argument that the Franklin Asbestos Handling Act is not preempted in its entirety by the Federal Occupational Safety and Health Act (OSH Act) is that it is a dual impact law, intended to address not only workplace safety but also public health.

2A. Some provisions of the Franklin Asbestos Handling Regulations will survive challenge, either because they are intended to protect public health rather than workplace safety, or else because they are similar to the federal requirements.

a. There is probably no preemption of the Franklin employee certification requirement. The federal regulations do not require employee certification. But the Franklin statute is a dual purpose statute. The State's best argument that there is no preemption is that the purpose of the Franklin certification requirement is not to protect the workers as a matter of workplace safety, but rather to protect public health.

b. There is no preemption of the required topics for the course. Where the topics regard worker safety, the Franklin requirements and the federal requirements are similar if not identical. There is therefore no preemption of those requirements.

   As to the training requirements related to public safety issues, moreover, the DEP requirements do not fall within the ambit of the OSH Act and are therefore not preempted.

c. As to the biennial review, again, the Franklin statute is a dual-purpose statute. There is no preemption of the topics dealing with protection of the public.

d. The Franklin requirement that the employer must provide DEP with names of all employees, and must pay $600 per year for each employee, is not preempted.

2B. Other provisions are in conflict with the federal regulations and will be preempted.

a. The requirement of a 5-day course and an examination in Section 8(a) of the Franklin regulations will probably be preempted. The federal regulations require an 8-hour training program and do not require an examination. 29 C.F.R. 1926 sec. (m) (iii). Section 8(a) of the Franklin regulations requires a 5-day DEP-approved course and a 2-hour examination for certification. The Franklin regulation will probably be found to be both a workplace regulation and in conflict with the methods specified by the federal regulation.

b. As to the biennial review, there will be preemption of the topics dealing with worker safety.

c. The Franklin requirement of a $100 certificate fee will be preempted, as directly in conflict with the federal regulations. The federal regulations require that there be no cost, while the AHA requires a $100 fee for the handler's certificate. This is a direct conflict, and the Franklin requirement will be preempted.

   The sample answer in this book proposes the following Conclusion:

> The best argument that the Franklin Scheme as a whole should survive a preemption challenge from OSHA is that the scheme has a dual effect: it protects public health in addition to worker safety. Some sections of the code as touching workplace safety should also survive challenge, either as complementary to federal law or as concerned with public health. The DEP training-and-certification requirement under section 8(a) and the $100 training-and-review course fee under section 8(e), however, are likely to be preempted.

Displaying the structure of your work product visually is an important aid to the grader. Notice how in the analyses above, this book has indented the parts of the analysis and numbered and lettered them. Visual presentation counts on the MPT. "it's all in there" is an unsatisfactory defense of not presenting your logic in a way the grader can see on the page.

Conclusion

The aim of this book has been to help junior lawyers develop both lawyerlike skills and strong habits for writing efficient, well-organized, legal memos. I hope it helps you to become a more confident and comfortable writer.

What is the assignment? That is always the first question. *What am I supposed to do? How can I organize the work product to achieve that objective?*

Thinking clearly about every assignment and organizing your work product to achieve the objectives of the assignment efficiently will help make you a better lawyer. It will make life easier for you and for those who supervise your work. In the end, clear and efficient legal writing will benefit us all, lawyers and judges and clients and the public.

About the Author

Mary Campbell Gallagher, J.D., Ph.D.

Dr. Mary Campbell Gallagher is a nationally-recognized authority on the bar examination, lawyer practice-readiness, and efficient writing in law and business. Trained as a lawyer at Harvard and holder of the Ph.D. in linguistic theory from the University of Illinois, she is the author of the book and CDs, *Scoring High on Bar Exam Essays* and of the book *Perform Your Best on the Bar Exam Performance Test (MPT): Train to Finish the MPT in 90 Minutes "Like a sport™."* She is president of BarWrite® and BarWrite Press, which offer courses and coaching for lawyers and business people on efficient writing, as well as courses and coaching for the bar examination. She lectures nationwide.

Dr. Gallagher is a widely-published professional writer and an active professional member of the National Speakers Association New York City Chapter, on whose board she served for nine years, and which awarded her its highest honor. She is a member of the Committee on Legal Education and Admission to the Bar of the New York State Bar Association.

To inquire about Dr. Gallagher's availability for speaking or consulting, write to: Info@BarWrite.com

Write Fast Legal Memos "Like a Sport"™
CLE Workshops

If you are the managing partner or the director of associate development or a supervising attorney in a law firm. a corporation, or a non-profit, and if your junior lawyers would benefit from learning to write legal memos efficiently, your firm can invite Dr. Mary Campbell Gallagher to offer her Write Fast Legal Memos™ Workshop at your office.

Or if you enjoyed this book and you would like more intensive practice writing fast legal memos, you can enroll in one of Dr. Mary Campbell Gallagher's public Write Fast Legal Memos™ Workshops in New York City.

Participants in the Workshops receive abundant support and feedback as they do the exercises in this book. They enjoy supervised and timed practice in a collegial atmosphere. They learn to write more quickly and efficiently than they had dreamed possible.

Workshops are planned frequently in New York City and elsewhere by arrangement.

You can email us for more information, at Info@BarWrite.com, or you can register for Dr. Gallagher's next public CLE Workshop in New York City at http://www.BarWrite.com.

To see the brochure and the agenda for the Write Fast Legal Memos™ Workshop, visit: http://www.BarWrite.com/Brochure.